peedster

Cabrio

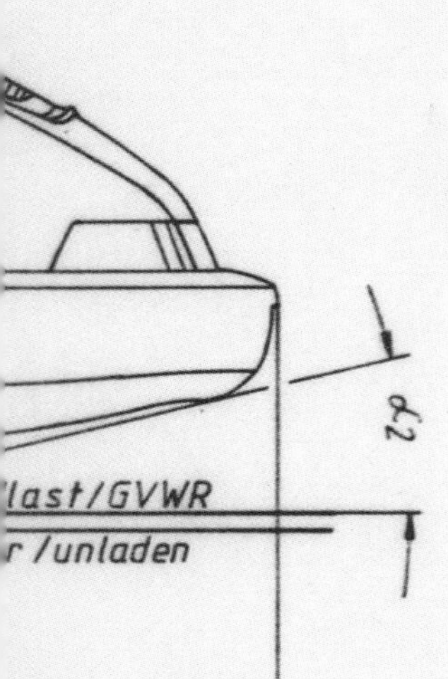

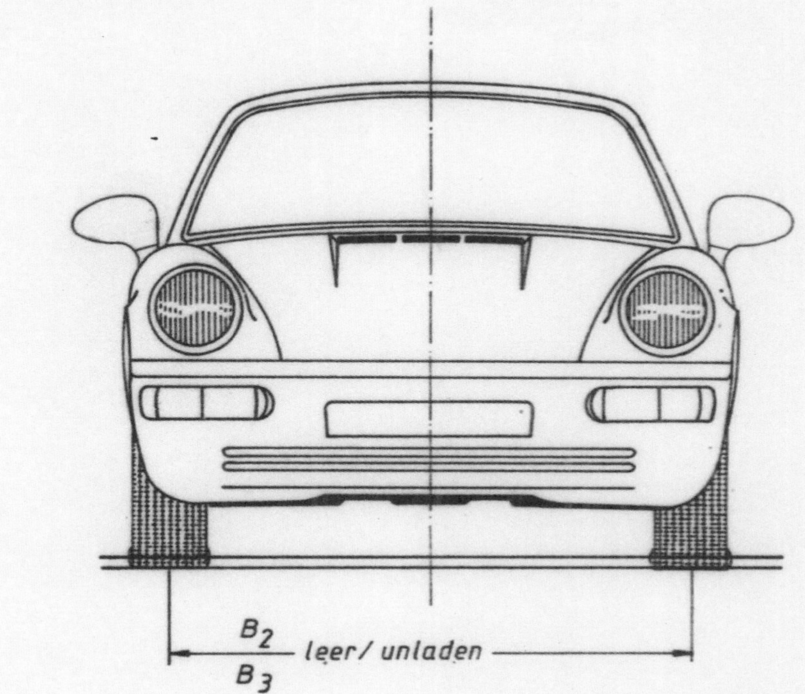

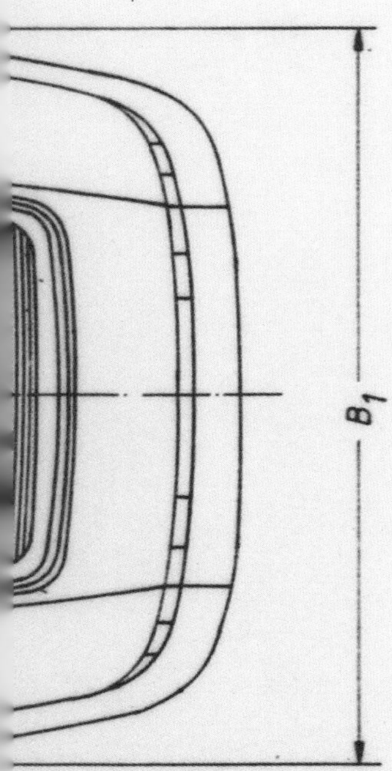

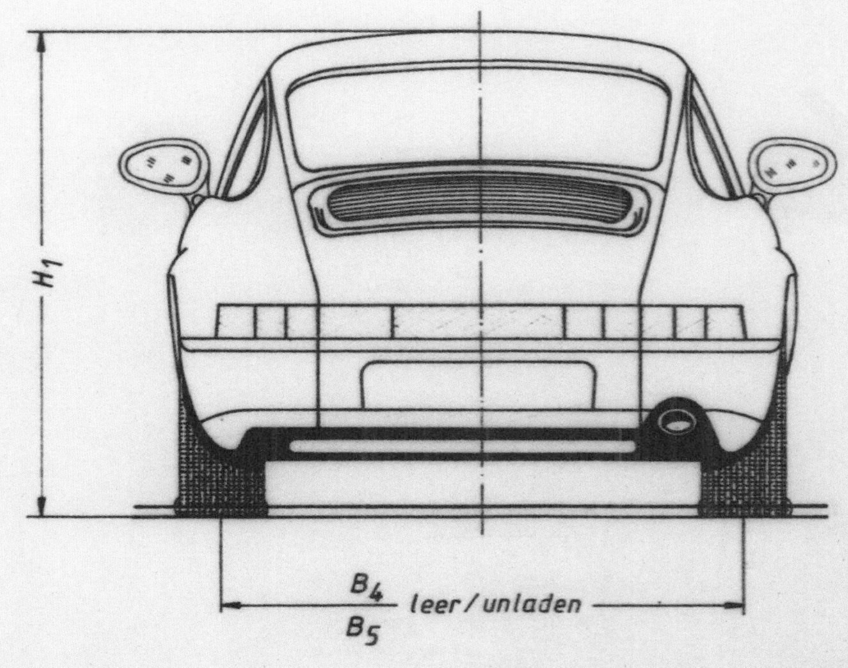

nsions

964.003.503.03

PORSCHE 75TH ANNIVERSARY

Expect the Unexpected

Randy Leffingwell

Foreword by Hurley Haywood

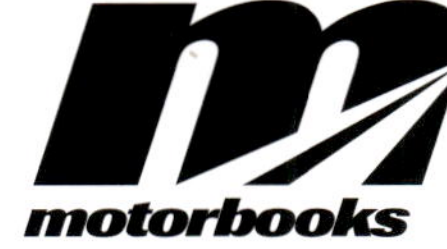

Contents

Foreword

by Hurley Haywood

I was honored to be asked by the esteemed author Randy Leffingwell to write this piece for his latest book, *Porsche 75th Anniversary*. In it, he addresses several revolutionary developments Porsche has introduced to the automotive world since its founding in 1948. As a Porsche racer and brand ambassador for over fifty years, I can speak to many of them personally.

Reflecting on the history of Porsche isn't hard for me, since my life has intersected with the prestigious German brand almost from my birth. I was born on May 4th, 1948, a birthday I shared with my mentor Peter Gregg. Porsche No. 1 was introduced a month later, on June 8. When I was four, one of my relatives brought his then-new Porsche 356 to my grandmother's farm home in Wheaton to show off during one of our family gatherings. I still remember the distinct sound it made, so different from the American Fords, Cadillacs, and Packards that usually parked in our driveway. I remember very distinctly running my hands over its smooth curves and marveling over its futuristic shape. As a young child, I could never have predicted the lifelong professional relationship I would have with Porsche as both a racer and a brand ambassador. In many ways, my own career was an unexpected part of Porsche history.

Porsche's racing cars throughout the 1950s and much of the 1960s were regarded as "giant killers"—small, lightweight cars that almost always won their class and often beat the larger, more powerful cars for overall victories. At the beginning of my career, the 911s and 914s frequently beat the Mustangs, Camaros, and Corvettes with lighter weight, responsive handling, and strong, reliable braking. That was also true of Porsche's prototype cars, like the 907, the 910, and the 908, which raced against Ford GTs and Ferraris.

One of the most unexpected racing cars in history, the Porsche 917, was introduced to the world in 1969. Rough and ill handling at first, it dominated the FIA endurance championship in 1969 and 1970, then the Can-Am series in 1972 and 1973. The turbocharged 917/10 I raced in 1973 was certainly an unexpected adventure for me as I had mostly been driving cars with about 900 less horsepower.

When the FIA dramatically changed the formula for its World Championship category for 1972, rather than following Ferrari and Matra, Porsche turned its attention toward the GT category, giving the 911 more power, a wider stance, and better brakes. The world was shocked when Peter and I won the opening round of the FIA

Haywood rounds Turn Four at Road Atlanta in July 1973 in the Brumos Porsche 917/10. *Bill Warner © 2022*

Hurley Haywood celebrates his first Le Mans victory in June 1977 alongside four-time winner Jacky Ickx while third-driver Jürgen Barth (hidden) drives the car to the winner's circle.

season at Daytona in 1973 with the 911-based Carrera RS, then repeated that feat just a few weeks later at Sebring. Road-racing history buffs will recall that Porsche 911-based racing cars dominated road racing for the rest of the 1970s and into the first couple of years of the 1980s.

When the FIA again changed the rules in 1982 to create a class of fuel-limited prototype racers, Porsche engineers introduced computer-controlled injection to maximize power. Soon after, computer-designed systems influenced both handling and gear shifting on the 956 and 962 racing cars to make them some of the fastest and most sophisticated cars in racing history. All this technology eventually made its way into the road-car line with the supercar 959 and then on the 964 variant of the 911. Supercars like the GT1, the Carrera GT, and the 918 continued to display Porsche's commitment to cutting-edge technology.

Perhaps Porsche's most unexpected move was its introduction of the water-cooled engines in the 996 and Boxster lines of the late 1990s and its groundbreaking move into the world of SUVs and luxury sedans shortly after. While air-cooled traditionalists rankled, the water-cooled engines were able to make greater amounts of power far more efficiently and dramatically less expensively. The Cayenne and Panamera dramatically increased customer base in the Porsche camp. The follow-up Panamera sedan only enhanced the line, making the company one of the most profitable businesses in the world.

The most evidential case for unexpected advances at Porsche can be seen in its flagship model, the 911. Looking at its introduction in September 1964 through its various stages of evolution in each decade since, we see a car that continues to draw upon its original shape and concept but has increased its performance dramatically, all while maintaining the fun and enjoyment of a true sports coupe. Much as it was during the year of its introduction, owning a 911 is every automotive enthusiast's dream.

More recent developments in hybrid and electric vehicle technology have kept Porsche on the cutting edge of technology as we head into the mid-twenty-first century. Much as Peter Gregg never expected some kid from Illinois to beat him at that parking-lot autocross in 1968, no one working at Porsche in its early years could have expected or predicted the trajectory Porsche has taken in its line of racing and road cars through the decades. I'm honored, privileged, and humbled to have been part of it.

Introduction

1900 Lohner-Porsche Voiturette Ferdinand Porsche's Voiturette relied on an electric motor in each front wheel hub for power. Each developed between 2.5 and 3.5 horsepower and controls were as simple as on-off with the addition of a speed selector offering up to 20 miles per hour (32 kilometers per hour). It weighs 2,160 pounds (980 kg).

Porsche's ongoing shift to partial and full electric power brings the company full circle to Ferdinand Porsche's first efforts with electric and battery power in the late 1890s. Some historians have suggested that Ferdinand was born with electricity on his mind and electric current in his blood. But technology in the early twentieth century was a hundred-plus years away from its accomplishments in the twenty-first century. Batteries in the early 1900s were heavier and had much shorter lives than today. Reality forced Ferdinand to abandon pure electric power in his earliest automobiles for the internal combustion engine. These at first powered onboard generators to run the motors and recharge the batteries. When it became clear that this system was redundant—why run a gas engine to charge batteries to run an electric motor?—Ferdinand moved on and never looked back.. For nearly ninety years, the cars he and later his son, Ferry, designed and produced ran reliably, and ever more powerfully and economically, on gasoline.

From the start, Ferdinand saw benefits to racing his cars. Working toward a race date on a calendar motivated him and his staff: competing against others established essential benchmarks to meet and exceed, and running successfully against a clock for a prize garnered public attention. This was not egomania. He understood from his father's work as a tinsmith that customers sought products and services at a fair price and companies needed that revenue, or "turnover," to pay employees and fund future development. Successful racing for a carmaker was, in many ways, the desirable win-win situation. There was even a bonus in this equation: racing provided an accelerated testing program for future series-production, road-going cars and equipment. Disc brakes and safety belts were among the most fundamental improvements that migrated from racing to the public road.

It was inevitable that from Ferdinand's earliest efforts through his son's establishing a car-production firm in 1948, racing sat with equal weight on the balance scales of Porsche's business. Readers will notice that fifteen of this book's thirty chapters concern racing. Because with Porsche, racing has for seventy-five years directly affected the cars the company offers its customers on road *and* on track.

2017 Typ 919-Hybrid LMP1 Coupe Porsche's 919-Hybrid also relied on two power sources. One was an internal-combustion 2.0-liter, 90-degree single-turbo V4 that developed 500 horsepower and the other was battery packs converting "recovered" energy into kinetic energy powering an electric motor, which delivered as much as 400 additional horsepower to the front wheels through a differential. At Le Mans, it completed 3,108 miles (5,001 km). an average speed of 129.4 miles per hour (208.2 kilometers per hour). It weighed 1,929 pounds (875 kg).

PORSCHE
T 222

1938–1940

1

We're Racing to Rome in a Beetle?

Typ 60 and 64

From his earliest days with the Lohner carriage and automobile manufacturing firm in Vienna starting in 1899, young Ferdinand Porsche had ambition. Not only did he imagine constructing automobiles for wealthy and royal clients, but he intended to make a small, affordable automobile for everyone, a vision few shared with him. (Whether he or Henry Ford developed the idea first is hard to establish; in 1899 Porsche was twenty-four and Henry was thirty-six. By this time, Ford's first "automobile" was seven years old.) By the time his ideas met receptive ears, he'd been fired five times, gone through five prototypes for five firms, and decided to go into business working only for those he selected.

He and his staff opened their doors in Stuttgart, Germany, in January 1931, and they soon had work. To differentiate one project from another, they established a numbering system and started at "Typ 7," so clients would assume the team had done other work. Clients came, and Porsche continued his campaign for a small car. But it took the changing politics in Germany to deliver a receptive client.

In between the Typ 12 (a "people's car" for Zündapp in 1932) and the Typ 32 (a similar car for NSU), Porsche initiated projects to keep his engineers busy. The Typ 22 was a

1939 Porsche Typ 64 Coupe: Porsche designed and assembled three of these for a proposed open-road race from Berlin to Rome in September 1939. That race never happened and after World War II, Austrian Otto Mathé acquired this car, the third one, and raced it in the early 1950s.

race car designed to the newest regulations, which earned him several audiences with Germany's new chancellor, Adolf Hitler. But in January 1934, he wrote the "*Exposé*," a kind of personal mission statement for local newspapers in which he exposed to the public his ideas for a future German "people's car": a Volkswagen. By then, this mostly self-taught automotive engineer had directed engineering for automakers Lohner, Austro-Daimler, Daimler-Benz, and Steyr. His Volkswagen resonated with Hitler, who had his own ideas, namely a car to sell for roughly US $250 (1,000 reichsmarks) at the time. Porsche knew that price was impossible for a reliable auto with four seats and the power to drive a steady 62 miles per hour (100 kilometers per hour) on Hitler's new Autobahn. The car also needed to climb any of Europe's steepest mountain passes. He figured its price at about $375 (RM 1,500).

Endless discussions and countless designs ensued. Porsche argued for an opposed four-cylinder air-cooled engine since, unlike water coolant, air did not freeze. Placing it at the rear ensured best traction for the rear-engined car in winter snow. Porsche technical design engineer Karl Fröhlich designed a simple chassis and a body that became lastingly identifiable, designated the Porsche Typ 60.

The design firm was a small operation. Porsche provided the garage of his family home, a spacious house he had commissioned during his lucrative contract with Daimler-Benz. The first prototype, designated V1, emerged from the garage in July 1935. The pressure on Porsche was immense. Hitler expected to introduce the car to Germany at the Berlin Motor Show on February 15, 1936. Teething and reliability problems intensified the race to this deadline.

This was Porsche's second Typ 64, completed in 1939. With no race, it became a development vehicle and by 1941 engineers had fitted "black-out" covers for the headlights and a radio. It underwent countless changes and modifications; unfortunately, few records survive of these experiments.

Unexpectedly, others introduced ideas as well. Daimler put forward designs; Henry Ford got his Cologne, Germany factory involved in designing a Model T for Europe; and Opel announced plans for a small car for RM 1,400. These generated a political battle all their own.

Through this time, Porsche's new body engineer, Erwin Komenda, drew a series of slightly smaller bodies, designated Typ 60 K, 60 K3, 60 K4, and so on. (The *K* represented the German word for small, *klein*). Engineers and fabricators started work on the second prototype, the K2, as a cabriolet, V2. Ferdinand's son, Ferry, began testing this in November 1935. The 60 K5 became the prototype V3.

The manufacturers' rivalry intensified after Porsche ran V1 to Munich in December 1935 to show it to Hitler. Porsche didn't bother to notify the German motor industry association, the RDA, which accused Porsche of failing to meet *its* requirements and having "dreams of becoming the technical director of a large factory specially built for the construction of the Volkswagen," as according to VW historian Chris Barber.

The Porsches drove V1 and V2 to Berlin for the RDA members to inspect. Germany's largest automakers found the interiors surprisingly spacious, but they questioned the somewhat radical "aerodynamic" body design; they had expected something in the German tradition. In their final slam, they expressed doubt anyone could manufacture such an automobile in sufficient numbers to reduce the costs to meet the expected price.

Ferdinand Porsche, an engineer known for verbally lacerating fools—whether fellow engineers or board members—underwent an all-new education in diplomacy, debate, and promotion. For nine months, he explained his decisions and fended off both valid

Racer Otto Mathé's Typ 64, racer, assembled in 1939, sits at the start line of the 1952 Krems-Autostrassen Rundrennen. It presents an unexpected contrast between it and the 1939 BMW Typ 328 beside it. The "T" in Mathé's license tag represents Tyrol, the district in Austria in which he lived.

criticisms and periodic petty jealousies. Meanwhile, his staff continued on V3 while V1 and V2 continued testing. As often as not, it was Ferry in one car or the other.

The V3-series cars underwent longer tests, including a drive to Monza, Italy, where Porsche's racing project Typ 22 was racing as the Auto Union car in the Grand Prix. The V3s regularly drove a route that took them into Austria and back. Often their destinations were political, to show the cars to one influential decision-maker or another. On one visit, military officials asked the mechanics to completely remove the car body so they could determine whether they might fit some kind of utility body instead. The cars each completed 31,070 miles (50,000 km), the longest test taking seventy-three days, and they averaged 425.64 miles (685 km) per day. Ferdinand earned approval for the next tests: thirty prototypes designated W30 were to cover a combined 1,242,742 miles (2,000,000 km).

By late 1937, Porsche had sent his W30s off on their extended tests. His Auto Union racing team was finishing its fourth season; it had started in 1934 with the Typ A (called the P-Wagen), run a Typ B in 1935, and run

Mathé crouches near the rear of the car during one of the few repair opportunities during the grueling 1950 Austrian Alpenfahrt, the legendary Austrian Alpine Rallye. Mathé, who lost his right arm in a motorcycle crash before the war, went on to win his class in this car in the Rallye.

triumphant seasons in 1936 and 1937 in the Typ C. He let his mind wander. His destination? A car of his own, for his own purposes: high speed.

Hitler had turned automobile racing into a kind of weapon, relying on the richly supported Auto Union "Silver Fish" versus Mercedes-Benz's "Silver Arrows" to captivate the citizenry and dominate competitors from every other nation. Each team's annual calendar contained dates to advance national, European, and world speed records; this they did with clockwork reliability. In Porsche's wandering mind, he envisioned a car "based very loosely on the Volkswagen concept," as VW historian Chris Barber wrote in his book *Birth of the Beetle*.

Erwin Komenda's protégé, Franz Xaver Reimspiess—and his assistant Karl Fröhlich—had designed some futuristic representations of the Beetle, the Typ 114 and 116, each slightly longer than the standard coupe. These looked as if one of his wooden scale models had melted in the sun. His staff quickly nicknamed it the F-Wagen. Porsche's engineers had dreamed up a water-cooled V-10 aluminum-block engine with double overhead camshafts to operate intake and exhaust valves; it displaced 91.5 cubic inches (1.5 liters) and was derived from his Auto Union creations. Not surprisingly, Ferdinand Porsche again ran into politics.

Neither he nor his company could afford to develop and assemble this "land speed record Volkswagen." Porsche needed government assistance. But the national labor organization, which was paying for materials and providing workers to assemble all the Volkswagens

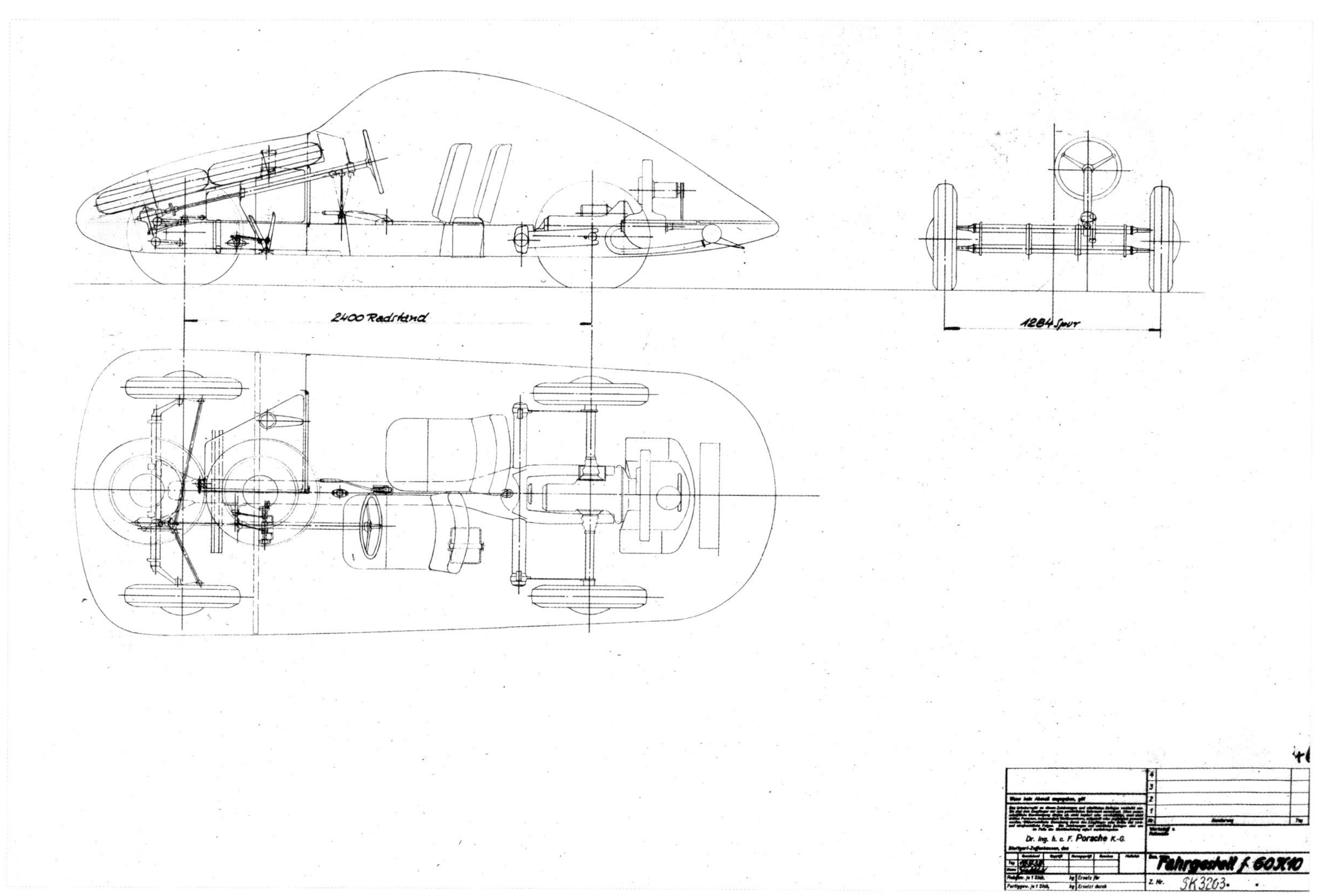

This was the first drawing made for the "Typ 60 K10 Rekordwagen," as Porsche's engineers designated the car. It became the Typ 64. The 94.5-inch (2,400-mm) wheelbase dimension was the same as prototype VW Beetles. Porsche engineer Karl Frölich designed the car with staggered seating to fit two adults inside.

possible, could not justify development of a limited-production sports car. Then Porsche learned he could not purchase from the government the hundreds of parts his employees had designed for the Volkswagen. That was selling government property for private use. Not possible.

The labor organization bosses who had refused Porsche still saw benefits to developing another showpiece automobile. Unexpectedly, the Volkswagenwerk AG, the newly created management company created to build a massive factory to assemble tens of thousands of cars and manage that production near the city of Fallersleben (renamed Wolfsburg in 1945), issued just such a request to Porsche! He had his funds.

Early in 1938, Porsche approached Major Adolf Hühnlein, who was Hitler's director of all automobile activities. They knew each other well from numerous Grand Prix events, and according to Barber, it seems likely the two discussed "the latest Volkswagen developments, and the lack of national interest in promoting the vehicles' sporting potential." Within months, Hühnlein announced a race from Berlin to Rome, some 930 miles (1,500 km), scheduled for early September 1939. This gave anyone interested a year to prepare. Hühnlein envisioned using Germany's new Autobahn system from Berlin to Munich, crossing into Austria and racing through the Alps via the Brenner Pass. The last leg ran south on Italy's old "consular roads" connecting Florence to Rome.

With theoretical engineering completed on the soon-to-be-production Volkswagens, Porsche's engineers set to work on the racer. The standard VW engine developed 23.5 brake horsepower out of the air-cooled 985cc flat four. By enlarging valves and increasing the compression ratio, they achieved 32 brake horsepower at 3,500 rpm, which, by calculation, gave them a theoretical top speed of 94.5 miles per hour (152 kilometers per hour). Mechanics began assembling three cars during the summer of 1939. Working nearly around the clock, Reutter Karosserie, a Stuttgart coachworks, completed the bodies using thin-gauge aluminum; the car was now designated Typ 60 K10 and ran on the standard VW wheelbase. The first one, the Typ 60 K10, renamed

The first of the three Typ 64s sat in the shade of the Porsche Villa garden. Porsche's original concept used a newly designed alloy V-10 with water cooling and three carburetors. With the race cancelled, engineers installed a modified VW engine developing 33hp. Car One weighs 615 kilograms, 1,365 pounds.

Typ 64 by this time, emerged from the shops on August 19, 1939, fourteen days before race start.

Then politics intervened again.Before dawn on Friday, September 1, 1939, the German Luftwaffe bombed Wieluń, a city in Poland, at the same moment a German destroyer on a "courtesy visit" to Danzig (modern-day Gdańsk) shelled a garrison there. An hour later, Hitler addressed all his armed forces. He announced that Poland had "refused the peaceful settlement of relations which I desired . . . In order to put an end to this lunacy I have no other choice than to meet force with force from now on."

The real lunacy had just begun. At 9:00 p.m., Britain demanded Germany withdraw from Poland. With no response from Germany, British prime minister Neville Chamberlain told BBC audiences that Britain and Germany were at war as of 11:15 a.m. on Sunday, September 3. It was Ferdinand Porsche's sixty-fourth birthday.

In a postscript, Porsche completed two other Typ 64s. The company provided one to a labor official, who soon wrecked it in a bout of enthusiastic driving. The other two stayed with the family. Ferdinand used one as his personal car; his driver chauffeured him far and wide as other German government agencies found other projects for Porsche's engineering.

1946–1960

2

Wait! Dusio Pays the Ransom?

Typ 360 Cisitalia Grand Prix Car

Like Ferdinand Porsche, Piero Dusio was a man with big ambitions. Before World War II, he had been a successful fabric salesman. Born in 1899, he owned Italy's first oil-cloth manufacturer by age twenty-seven. Then he caught the automobile bug, and at thirty-six, he made a racing debut at Monte Carlo driving his own Maserati. When World War II came and racing stopped, his biggest financial success arrived with the contract to produce all the uniforms for Italy's troops. But his interest in cars never left, and by early 1946, rumors spread that Dusio planned to go racing in an open-wheel car of his own design, the D46 (Dusio 1946). He and friends had designed it in his kitchen during the winter of 1944 and made it their dream. When the Italian Coppa Brezzi race resumed in Turin on September 3, 1946, Dusio had a team of seven D46s in the 1,100 and 1,500cc classes (the 1,100cc cars were run in both classes), driven by most of his country's greatest drivers. He called his cars Cisitalia, an abbreviation of his company name, Compagnia Industriale Sportiva Italia.

Tazio Nuvolari made racing history in one of the cars in that race. The D46 incorporated a tilt-up steering wheel to ease entry, hinged on a crossbar attached to the steering column. In the first lap, the hinge broke and the wheel came off in Nuvolari's

Italian Grand Prix racing star Tazio Nuvolari struck a stern, if contemplative pose sitting in Piero Dusio's dream car. It became Nuvolari's dream as well and ultimately both men were greatly disappointed when Cisitalia owner Dusio ran out of funds.

The car was similar in size to contemporaries: 102.4-inch (2,600-mm) wheelbase; 51,2-inch (1,300-mm) front and rear track. It used Pirelli Corsa tires, with 5.50×18s at front and 6.00/7.5×18s at the rear.

hands. He steered the rest of the lap using the crossbar, and when he passed his pits—at barely a walking pace—he angrily threw the wheel at the mechanics. Then he roared off. The Cisitalias relied on a simple 1,100cc Fiat engine, and several broke before the race ended. But Dusio won, not because he was best or because it was arranged but because, still a novice, he drove the most cautiously.

The fortune he had made providing millions of uniforms gave him the resources for his dreams, and almost immediately a striking fastback coupe—still using a Fiat engine and drivetrain fitted in a steel-tube frame—appeared in time for the 1948 Paris Motor Show. Designed by his friend Battista "Pinin" Farina, it was designated the 202 and drew instant interest. Actress Ingrid Bergman and her husband, Roberto Rossellini bought one; Henry Ford II ordered a coupe and a cabriolet.

All this fed Dusio's ego and enlarged his fantasy. For 1950, the Fédération Internationale de l'Automobile (FIA) introduced new regulations for Grand Prix racing and a new designation for its most exclusive series: Formula One. And Dusio wanted to compete.

At the end of the war, a number of Germans had relocated to Italy to begin new lives—among them car enthusiast Karl Abarth, who, in keeping with his new home, changed his name to Carlo. He and a few others

The Typ 360 design set the driver slightly forward of the middle of the wheelbase, with the engine snugged-up immediately behind. Porsche engineers specified molybdenum-nickel-chrome tubes for the chassis, magnesium alloys for the various castings, and Elektron, a magnesium-alloy for plates for the bodywork.

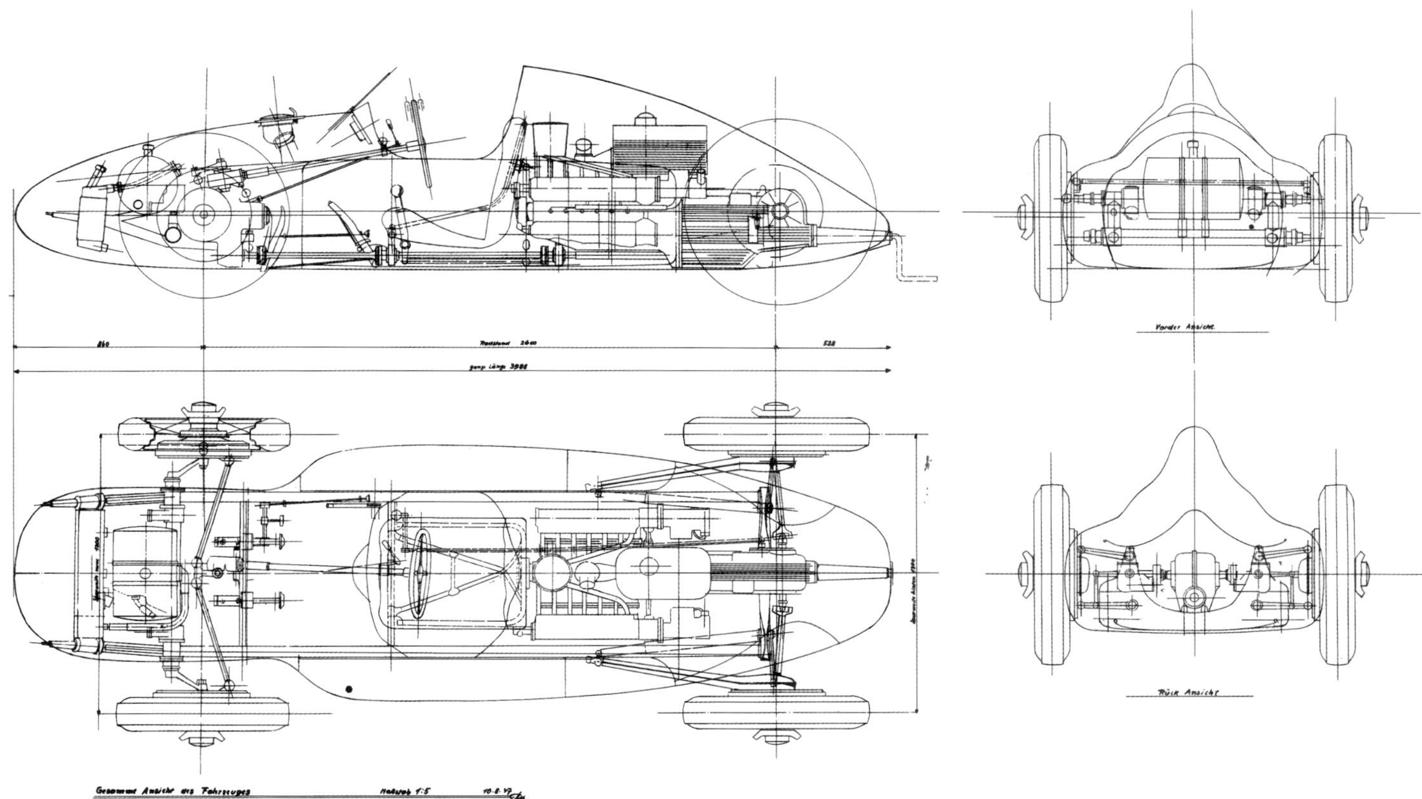

Ferry Porsche's engineers adapted the VW-type trailing-arm independent front suspension and designed an independent rear suspension using radius arms with hydraulic shock absorbers and anti-sway bars.

had settled in Turin, and it was to them that Dusio turned to find the best designer for his Grand Prix car. One name came quickly to the fore: Ferdinand Porsche, whose Auto Unions had raced at Monza and in the Italian province of Tripoli in North Africa.

But Porsche was unavailable. When Germany went to war, it essentially named Porsche its chief engineer, and he and his consultancy worked on countless projects for Hitler's Third Reich, including huge tanks and massive guns. After the armistice, the French government contacted him, asking to meet for help resurrecting their auto industry—at least, that was the story they told him. Once they lured him to French-occupied Baden-Baden, they promptly arrested him and Anton Piëch (who was both Porsche's son-in-law and his company's lawyer) for war crimes. It was while the two men were being moved from prison to prison around France that Dusio approached Porsche's company.

Letters back and forth established Dusio's desires, goals, and ability to pay. In December 1946, Ferry Porsche and Ferdinand's office manager, Karl Rabe, gained permission from the military authorities to travel to Italy. Dusio's Cisitalia operation impressed both men, and they returned to Stuttgart to draw up contracts to begin the design process for a new Formula One car.

The new project became Typ 360. It accompanied other Cisitalia concepts, including a road-going coupe (Porsche Typ 370), a synchromesh transmission (Typ 380) for both vehicles, an agricultural tractor, and an electric generating turbine, all under the same umbrella contract.

Ferry's staff, in the absence of his still-imprisoned father, took elements from their very successful Auto Union Grand Prix cars in designing the 360's chassis, suspension, engine, and drivetrain, with one remarkable addition: they made the car a four-wheel-drive racer, the better to deliver its abundant power to the ground. They devised a V-12 "boxer" engine—that is, just like the VW's flat opposed cylinders—for 1,492cc overall displacement. They specified two Weber carburetors and two vane-type superchargers, one for each cylinder bank, and calculated 400 brake horsepower output at 12,000 rpm. Erwin Komenda designed the racecar's body, inspired by his work on all the Auto Union racers.

Throughout this time, Ferry and his sister, Louise, had regular contact with French authorities, seeking the release of their father and Louise's husband. It became clear to the Porsche family that the charges leveled against Ferdinand were a sham, an effort to extort reparations payments from a wealthy family. Carlo Abarth's influence extended far and wide, and through contacts he had from prewar racing in France, he learned there was a price for Ferdinand's and Anton's releases: 1 million French francs. And when Dusio's first contract payment installment came in, the family had the money.

Because the Allies still considered Ferdinand a person of interest, they released him to a kind of house arrest, living in a hotel in Kitzbühel, Austria. He was allowed visitors, but months passed before he could travel. Ferry, Louise, and Karl Rabe went to see him with the drawings and all the news of the Cisitalia contracts; Ferdinand—as was his style—took a long time examining the drawings in deafening silence. Finally, he looked up and offered his judgment: "Had I received this order, I would have gone about it in the same way as you have done," Ferry later remembered his father saying. For a man spare in his praise, that was as good as it could get.

In the meantime, Piero Dusio, ever the man of vision, had seen his future in far-off Argentina and moved half his company across the ocean, leaving his son to manage what remained in Turin. Dusio's ambition and his now-international operation were already hemorrhaging money, and just as Ferry and Rabe transferred the prototype 360 to Turin, Cisitalia suppliers began withholding parts deliveries as they argued for payment. Dusio, from Buenos Aires, appealed to the Italian government for grants to complete his Grand Prix project "for the glory of Italy." While Mussolini had supported Alfa Romeo, and to a lesser extent Maserati, before the war, times were very different now, and the government repeatedly declined. Dusio's advisers urged him to abandon the hyperexpensive Grand Prix project and instead produce the Porsche-designed Typ 370 coupe. But Dusio single-minded ambition led him to ignore his business sense. When it was clear neither Italy nor Argentina were going to support a racing-car project, he diverted funds.

In the end, Porsche produced just a single Typ 360, an untested prototype that ultimately ended up in Dusio's Autoar (for Automotiva Argentina) facility in Buenos Aires. Neither Autoar nor Porsche did anything with the 370 coupe. In an effort to curry favor with Argentinian president Juan Péron, a known auto enthusiast, Dusio gifted him the race car as part of a

The Typ 360 engine was a "boxer" 12 cylinder with 2.2-inch (56-mm) bore and 2-inch (50.6-mm) stroke providing 1,492 cubic centimeters overall displacement. Dual overhead camshafts operated four valves per cylinder. Engineers expected 370 horsepower at 11,000 rpm.

The transaxle gearbox used a motorcycle-type sequential five-speed gearbox that theoretically delivered a top speed of 200 miles per hour (320 kilometers per hour). Not only that, but the transaxle ran a driveshaft to the front axle, allowing front-wheel drive at the driver's selection. The car's complexity required extraordinary testing, costs for which killed the project.

national plan to develop international racing talent. But the 360, unproven when Porsche sent it to Turin, had mechanical gremlins, and after some frustrating test runs, it went into storage. Its existence was a loosely kept secret, and when Porsche's then racing director Huschke von Hanstein came to Buenos Aires in 1960 for an international race, the Argentinian VW/Porsche distributor helped him "liberate" it from the country, shipping it home to Germany after the race.

This otherwise sad tale had an unexpected effect long before this reunion, however. Ferry's visit with Rabe in 1947 had recalibrated his thinking.

"On the journey back from Turin I became increasingly convinced of the viability of an idea that we had had before the war, namely the construction of a sports car based on Volkswagen components," Ferry told his biographer Günther Molter in their book *Cars Are My Life*. "Our visit to Dusio had rekindled my enthusiasm for the idea, since we could very easily do with Volkswagen components what he was doing with Fiat parts." Porsche's 60 K10 and Typ 64 had been first steps in that direction.

"Cars like that had been my hobby before the war," Ferry continued. "I like a machine that was speedy, that had good acceleration and road holding compared with ordinary cars."

On his drive back to Gmünd with his sister and Rabe, he began to think it was time for the next step.

K 45·286

1947–1948

3

I Didn't See Anything I Wanted

Typ 356/1

Four months after Ferry Porsche and Karl Rabe signed the Cisitalia contract in Turin back in February 1947, Rabe pulled out his company record books and noted the status of the Typ 360 GP car and the 370 coupe for the Italians. Then he went up a few lines and found another number he and Ferry had set aside for internal projects: Typ 356.

Dusio's clever Model 202 road car inspired Ferry. It relied on mechanical components from Fiat—a 1,100cc engine, gearbox, drivetrain, suspension, and steering gear. Dusio had manufactured bicycles for decades, and his designers used tubes to make a frame—a lightweight but cost-intensive method. This they surrounded with a lovely car body produced by one of Italy's masters.

Even while Ferry had helped his father with design and development testing for the VW Beetle, they were thinking of a car of their own, using VW running gear as Dusio had done with Fiat. Ferry set Erwin Komenda to work, and the body engineer completed his first design on June 11. In his four-view drawing—front, rear, side, and overhead—the car was a mid-engine roadster that stepped far beyond simply rebodying a VW V2 cabriolet. Within another month, Komenda had drawn a tubular space frame for the car

Any similarity between the front of Karl Frölich's design for Porsche's Typ 64 and Erwin Komenda's styling for Ferry's personal Roadster was entirely intended. These two vehicles marked the beginning of the Porsche automobile form language, using organic shapes to surround and protect mechanical elements.

with detailed measurements. More drawings emerged, further defining and refining the roadster shape.

Ferdinand Porsche's engineers had fabricated the Typ 64 Berlin-Rome car on aluminum platforms using the standard VW 94.5-inch ((2,400 mm) wheelbase. For the Roadster, Komenda reduced that to 84.6 inches (2,149 mm). Ferry's engineers adopted and adapted the VW steering and its front and rear suspension and installed the 1,131cc Typ 369 opposed four-cylinder, mounting it backward compared to its orientation in the Beetle. Ferdinand had introduced—and then nearly perfected—a torsion-bar/swing-axle rear suspension on the Beetle and the 500-horsepower Auto Union racers, and this, also reversed, went into the Roadster. They increased the basic VW engine output of 25 horsepower at 3,300 rpm to 35 horsepower at 4,000 rpm.

Getting new VW parts from Germany was impossible. Ferdinand's huge plant had ceased all Beetle production during the war, using the floorpans and running gear inside a boxy utility body known as the Kübelwagen, or bucket car—referring more to its low-slung seats than its exterior shape. However, as German Axis soldiers fled Austria at the war's end, they left behind hundreds of these machines, which became parts donors for Ferry's prototype sports car.

1948 Typ 356-001 Roadster In ways, Ferry Porsche's first sportscar resembled the open-wheel Typ 360 Grand Prix car the company was designing for Cisitalia at the time. The driver's seat was slightly ahead of the midpoint on the wheelbase with its VW-derived engine reversed (transaxle aft) to create a mid-engine configuration.

Ferry, years afterward, explained the origin of his 356-001 Roadster, the sports car from VW origins: "I looked around and didn't see anything I liked, so I built my own car."

In the immediate postwar marketplace, most of the cars available were based on late-1930s designs and engineering. Ferry might have considered an Alfa Romeo 6C, which the carmaker had introduced in 1927. Twenty years later, there were coupes, cabriolets, and even race cars with in-line six-cylinder, 2.5-liter engines; but these cars were big (118-inch [2,997-mm] wheelbase), powerful (92 horsepower), and still based on prewar engineering. From Germany, Ferry had BMW's little 44-horsepower, 2.0-liter 321 as a coupe or cabriolet, or perhaps the much more sporting Veritas that used BMW's 321 or 85-horsepower 328 engine. But these required a buyer to bring a 321 or 328 to the manufacturer along with about $6,485 (DM 12,000).

Daimler-Benz, his father's former employer, still offered its 170V, a car Ferdinand had heavily influenced in its design stages. Daimler had adapted it to Kübelwagen bodies during the war as well, but it was a larger car. Materials shortages limited postwar customers to only a four-door sedan body. From France, Ferry knew the prewar Bugatti Type 57 and Delahaye 135MM; they were sleek, powerful, and fast, with the same problem as any of the others: availability of essential parts. Another option was the British MG T series, yet another prewar car only modestly updated as the TC. But with its antiquated ladder frame, it was outdated even compared to contemporary Dusio's Cisitalias or Ferdinand's racing Auto Unions from a decade earlier. Ferry was right. There was nothing to appeal to his trained engineer sensibilities.

And Ferry *was* a trained engineer—his father had insisted on that. Ferdinand was indisputably a genius; many historians rank him among the three or five or ten greatest in the history of the automobile. But in his earliest days he had to prove himself nearly every day as others, with "Dr." or "Professor" ahead of their names, continually challenged his frequently radical innovations.

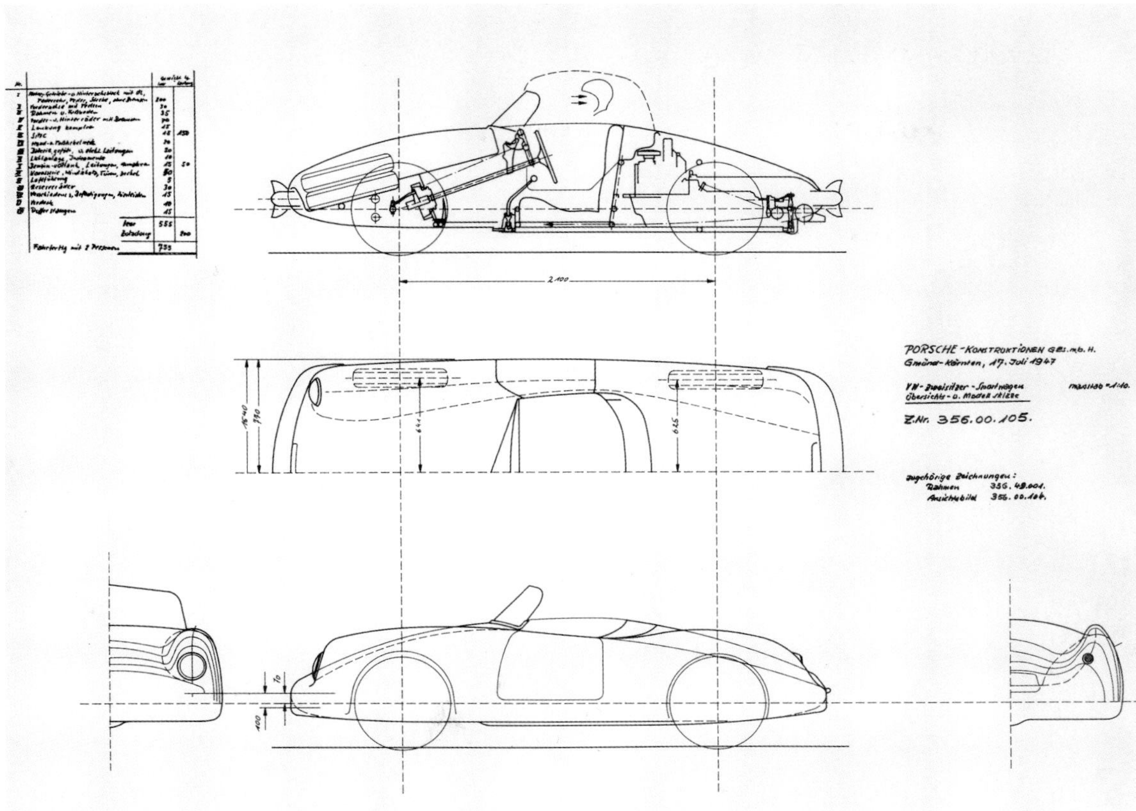

(Left) In this drawing, dated July 17, 1947, designers and engineers were still working out dimensions and details. The wheelbase here is 82.7 inches (2,100 mm) The car was called "VW-Zweisitzer-Sportwagen," Volkswagen two-seater sportscar. The designer had established body width at 64.6 inches (1,640 mm)

(Below) The car grew some from its mid-1947 dimensions. The wheelbase was 84.6 inches (2,150 mm). And width was 65.7 inches (1,670 mm) Final overall length measured 151,96 inches (3,860 mm) and it stood 49.2 inches tall (1,250 mm).

Over time, his stunning accomplishments earned him not one but two honorary doctorates, and these, at last, conferred legitimacy on the older man. However, his seemingly annual job changes jeopardized his son's education—and Ferry admitted he did not particularly enjoy school, preferring to learn engineering by listening to his father's discussions with his staff. However, when Ferdinand joined Austro-Daimler thirty-eight miles south of Vienna, he insisted Ferry stay in school in Vienna to finish his education. Yet even with an engineering degree, Ferry regularly had to prove himself against criticism that "He's just the professor's son! What does he know!" By regularly disproving his critics and proving himself—through the same rigorous engineering methods they used—he patiently earned their respect and support.

As the war had intensified, Stuttgart had become a repeated target of Allied bombing, and German military officials admitted they could not protect Porsche's office from attack. They recommended Ferdinand relocate his business, suggesting first a spot further into Bavaria. Ferdinand and Ferry considered alternatives and chose rural Austria. By this time, Ferry and his wife, Dorothea, had purchased a country estate, the Shüttgut, with a large home at Zell am See, and he and his father learned of a sawmill in the village of Gmünd in Austria's central Alps that was available. It was far enough from the nearest railway to promise them relative safety from misdirected bombs.

Its crude-looking, single-layer soft top was not one of the car's better features, but in a country that got four seasons of weather, it was the bare minimum necessary. The hand-hammered and welded aluminum body sat on a steel grid frame and it weighed 1,289 pounds (585 kg).

When a very accurate bomb had dropped directly through the roof of their Stuttgart offices and exploded in the basement, it incinerated part of their archives. Ferry quickly divided the company in three pieces. Administration remained in Stuttgart; this was home to many of Ferdinand's employees for whom a move presented a hardship. Design and fabrication went to Gmünd. The family and records shifted to Zell.

During Ferdinand's imprisonment, design work continued on Dusio's Cisitalia Grand Prix car at Gmünd, and Ferry's 356 Roadster came together at the same time. His staff had a running chassis ready for road testing in March 1948. Despite lacking a body, Ferry and engineer Emil Rupilius took the vehicle for a test run to evaluate its engine, drivetrain, and brakes. Gmünd is in the heart of the Austrian Alps and just 18.6 miles (30 km) away from the Katschberg Pass, a 5,384-foot (1,641 m) climb with an extremely steep grade—perfect for testing the drivetrain going up and brakes coming down.

"On this road shortly after Heiligenblut [about 450 kilometers, or 280 miles, from Gmünd], Ferry Porsche broke down whilst testing the 356 prototype in company with the engineer Rupilius," Porsche biographer and racer Richard von Frankenberg wrote in *Porsche: Double World Champions, 1900-1977*. "A suspension arm broke on the rear axle, but fortunately a highway maintenance depot was not far away. It was evening, around 7 o'clock, but the sun was still shining. Ferry Porsche went into the building and found the people there very co-operative, especially as they had an old VW desert car for official use. Porsche and Rupilius found in the material store a couple of pieces of U-section steel which fitted near enough. In a very primitive manner they drilled holes into one of these and in just over two hours the car was running again." It was the only mechanical problem anyone ever experienced with the car.

Engineers continued road testing, and Ferry hired a talented body craftsman. Friedrich Weber was a flawed genius whom Ferry had known as an apprentice while his father directed engineering at Austro-Daimler. Ferdinand had recommended that Weber train as a coachbuilder because there was always a need for such craftsmen.

In 1956, Ferry Porsche, standing, encountered his first roadster at a car show. Subsequent owners had trimmed away the front and rear bumpers and bodywork and added paint "spears," the trim around the headlights as well as front lid straps. The car still rode on 5.00 x 16-inch (127 × 406-mm) tires mounted on 3.00 D × 16 steel wheels.

As Ferry recalled, Weber did beautiful work, but he could be a difficult character. Porsche Typ 356 historian Dirk-Michael Conradt discovered a note typed on the back of a portrait of Weber: "Weber, who is highly skilled and remarkably capable, is also headstrong and difficult. He drinks. When thirst strikes him, he leaves his workplace, to return at some later, unpredictable time. In order to build and sell the first Porsche cars it will be necessary to keep Weber in good spirits."

With two colleagues, Weber fabricated and completed the aluminum body within a month's time. "In the first week of May, the new car was ready for its first drive," Conradt wrote in his book, *Porsche 356: Driving in Its Purest Form*. "The roadster was 3.86 meters long, 1.68 meters wide, and only 1.25 meters high."

Ferry was very pleased. "The 356 climbed like a mountain goat and achieved 80 mph without any effort at all," he exclaimed in *Cars Are My Life*. "One day, when Professor Eberan von Eberhorst was visiting us from Turin, we were out testing the 356 on the Katschberg." Ferdinand had brought in Robert Eberan von Eberhorst to run Auto Union race engineering after Ferdinand's contract ended in 1937. After the war, Eberhorst emigrated to Italy and became a liaison between Porsche and Dusio with the Grand Prix car. "I took Eberan with me as co-driver," Ferry said. "He was very impressed with the car's performance, particularly its acceleration, and predicted great success for the car. 'It is essential that we raise sufficient capital to put it into production,' he said."

But Ferry was already a step ahead of him.

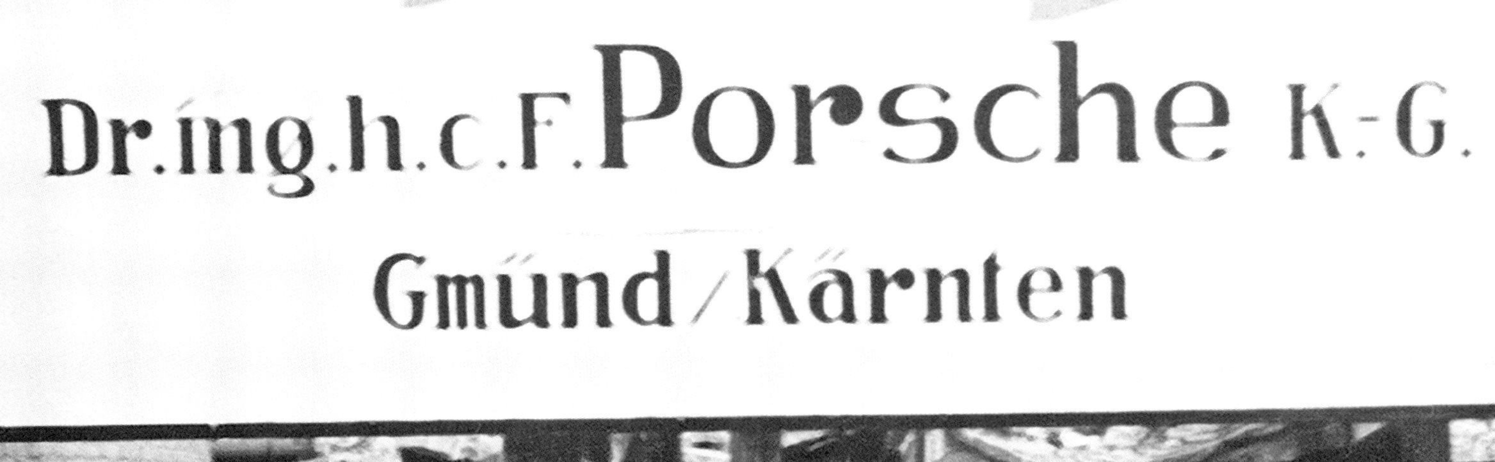
Dr.ing.h.c.F. Porsche K-G.
Gmünd/Kärnten

1945–1950

4

It's Better than Repairing Tractors and Manufacturing Well Pumps!

Rebirth in Gmünd

At Gmünd, Ferry Porsche had nearly 200 employees for whom he felt total responsibility. Some he'd brought with him from Stuttgart, while others had converged from other parts of Austria and Germany. In the aftermath of the war, poverty and devastation were everywhere. Ferry took any work that came into the yard of their *Werk*. They repaired farm tractors; they did the same with war-surplus Kübelwagens, often converting them into tractor-like machines. They took contracts from local communities for water pumps, wind generators, even gas-engine-powered winches for the ski areas that were reopening. At local fairs, they exhibited their machinery. Ferry's car, the 356-001, was, in its own way, a project to keep his staff engaged.

Elsewhere, life resumed a bit more confidently. During the winter, the recently liberated Anton Piëch took wife Louise, Ferry's sister, on a skiing holiday in St. Moritz, Switzerland. While they were there, they met Rupprecht von Senger and his wife. Von Senger was a Swiss architect, illustrator, ad agency owner, promoter, bon vivant, and entrepreneur based in Zürich. When he learned of Piëch's association with the Porsches, he planned a visit to Gmünd. Von Senger and a partner who lived near

1946 Klagenfurt Trade Exposition Before there were cars, there were tractors, water pumps, pulleys, and almost any other kind of design, engineering, and repair work that Ferry could bring in to keep Porsche's employees paid and fed and housed. During a two-week trade exhibition in August 1946, in Klagenfurt where British Occupation Forces headquartered in Austria, the company showed off its products.

Gmünd wanted Porsche to design a lightweight four-seat automobile von Senger could manufacture in Switzerland. When their retainer arrived, Ferry went to Klagenfurt, 200 miles (321.9 km) away, to obtain permission from the British occupation forces to take the assignment. When that came, Karl Rabe wrote in von Senger's name beside "Typ 352," and work began.

Von Senger had unrealistic expectations. He wanted too much car for too low a selling price, and when he and his wife came for a visit the next April, they saw drawings of a car they could not possibly make work. Though the couple left Gmünd disappointed, they had seen Ferry's first efforts at a Porsche car, at this point no more than designs on paper. When von Senger's partner updated him on Porsche's progress, the architect/promoter made another visit at the end of 1947. Within weeks, according to Porsche historian Karl Ludvigsen in his book *Porsche: Origin of the Species*, von Senger "contracted to pay 100,000 Swiss francs in advance—some $25,000—for the first five cars, thus giving Porsche the working capital it needed to source the components and build the cars."

It was as though Robert Eberan von Eberhorst's plea had been answered. With funding in hand, Ferry and his engineers got serious about a production version of his open prototype. On June 8, 1948, he got it registered

Outside the sheds at their Gmünd Works, Porsche engineers prepared a Typ 312 farm tractor with a "two-way" plow (that worked one row on either left or right side), and mud or sand paddles, to support and power the tractor through soft terrain.

Porsche designed and manufactured electric winches like this for the provincial government in Carinthia, Austria. As life slowly returned to normal, these went into use on ski mountains powering chair lifts.

in the provincial capital as "Porsche Sport 356/1" and received a license plate, K 45286.

Ferry had studied Dusio's Cisitalia 201 and 202, both cars assembled around labor-intensive tube frames. He later recalled in *Cars Are My Life*, "The tube frame was too wasteful of space, and too expensive to build. We also needed more space for the occupants as well as their luggage." Recognizing this, his engineers created a simple VW-like floorpan chassis and positioned the engine as it originally had been in the Beetle. Von Senger had access to new VWs and parts for them in Zürich (none were going to Austria yet), and the entrepreneur's payments to Porsche in Gmünd often never left Switzerland, going instead for mechanical parts that von Senger then shipped to the Porsche works.

Von Senger wasted no time getting the car into curious hands. Ferry and his cousin Herbert Kaes had driven the 356 Roadster and Ferry's 64 to Innsbruck, Austria, the previous July for one of the continent's earliest postwar races, a "round-the-park" contest. The two Porsches chased each other around the course between other races, and the local newspapers picked up on the sensational-looking new cars. Well-known automotive artist Walter Gotschke illustrated the weekend event, and his drawings and sketches gave the impression the two cars raced even though it was strictly demonstrations. Journalists who had covered the weekend flocked to von Senger once they learned he possessed the Roadster, and favorable reviews followed. The editor of *Automobil Revue*, based in Bern, wrote about his drive in the magazine's mid-July issue: "It will not be necessary in the future for enthusiastic owners of Volkswagens to tune their cars for extra performance, for the man really able to do this is seeing to it that a special vehicle will soon be available: It is Professor Porsche himself."

Another writer, the Swiss correspondent for Britain's *Motor* magazine, had worked for Ferdinand as an engineer at Steyr in 1929. Now he summarized the Roadster's handling, writing, "The car has really remarkable road holding, combined with a pleasant softness of springing and very light, accurate steering."

Von Senger's purchase included Ferry's 356-001 Roadster as well as the first four aluminum 356/2 coupes and granted him sales and distribution rights for Porsche's cars throughout Switzerland. (Confusingly, Porsche designated Ferry's Roadster as 356-001, meaning it was serial number 1. As the company moved into series production, the designate shifted to 356/2, which represented these second-generation models.)

Unbeknownst to Ferry and Rabe, von Senger was using money from one of his clients to fund the project, a wealthy Zürich hotel owner named Bernard Blank. While Blank was not necessarily passionate about automobiles, he saw the pent-up appetite other wealthy Swiss had developed and had opened a showroom on the ground floor of his hotel, from which he sold British Daimler, Lanchester, and Allard cars.

During the summer and into fall 1948, orders flooded in as Ferry's employees assembled their next generation,

This was Ferry Porsche's trick, naming their Gmünd factory "Wm. Meineke Large-Scale Timber Industry, Berlin – Gmünd Werk Karnerau." He hoped to convince visitors to the village that this remained a family-owned sawmill and lumber yard, not the world manufacturing headquarters of Porsche Engineering of Stuttgart. This photo was taken in 1944.

Inside the sawmill a crew of more than 100 engineers and mechanics assembled Porsche 356 coupes with hand-formed aluminum bodies. But only three men constituted Porsche's entire body-fabrication department, the bottleneck of auto assembly in Gmünd.

the 356/2. "Twenty cars were wanted in Sweden, fifty in Holland, twenty of the latter immediately if possible," Richard von Frankenberg wrote in his book *We at Porsche*. Yet few outside Gmünd understood how small this operation was and how impossible such deliveries were. Crews finished the first 356/2 welded-steel-platform chassis in April 1948. A simple two-page, two-color brochure appeared around the same time, revealing a 356/2 coupe in line drawing, with text in German, French, and English. While the brochure quoted engine displacement at 1,131cc, Ferry quickly standardized to 1,086cc, fitting within the "under 1.1-liter" class for racing.

"The styling of the 356 was influenced by my own ideas," Ferry explained in *We at Porsche*. While he personally preferred an open-wheel race car so he always knew where his front tires were and what they were doing, his road-going compromise provided fenders that were prominent enough to inform any driver where his front wheels were, to give them a feeling for the turn radius. "We followed this idea from the beginning and gave the Porsche front fenders a shape of their own, making them quite distinctive from that of the hood," he added.

Through the winter of 1948–1949, the sawmill completed cars at far from a production-line pace. Part of the delay was parts delivery and aluminum shortages, and the other was panel beater Friedrich Weber's inconsistency. Ferry recognized he needed more capacity, and it arrived quite unexpectedly.

Late in the summer, Anton Piëch had called on von Senger in Zürich. While the two were walking

The compact aluminum bodies used a, 82.7-inch (2,100-mm) wheelbase/152.4-inches long by 65.4 wide by 51.2 inches tall (3,870 mm by 1,660 mm by 1,300 mm). Powered by a 1,131 cubic centimeter modified 40-horsepower VW engine, the car weighed 680 kilograms, 1,499 pounds (680 kg). Porsche quoted a top speed of 87 miles per hour (140 kilometers per hour).

down the main street, they encountered von Senger's backer. When von Senger awkwardly did not introduce Blank, Piëch quickly sorted out where the entrepreneur's money was coming from. Von Senger's relationship with Piëch and the Porsche family evaporated almost immediately.

The first 356/2 was a Weber-body coupe. Through Blank's connections, chassis 002 and 003 went to Gebreuter Beutler Carrosserie, a highly respected shop in nearby Thun. The Beutler brothers, Ernst and Fritz, assembled a prototype and then did five "production" cabriolets, all in steel. But they valued their own working pace and declined to go further when Piëch offered them a contract for more.

The Gmünd works fabricated twenty-nine chassis in 1948, 1949, and 1950, of which fourteen were completed as cabriolets. Two Salzburg coachbuilders completed as many as twenty-two more bodies, and by the end of 1950, the chassis count had reached fifty-two, though more than half a dozen remained uncompleted without a body.

Gmünd, selected for its isolation, was now proving too distant from any railway hub to increase production. Ferry cast a long glance at his former works in Stuttgart-Zuffenhausen, but the US Army had commandeered this facility as a carpool repair depot. He contacted Stuttgart's mayor, a longtime family friend, who obtained a promise the Americans planned to vacate by September 1, 1950.

Then, just when the world thought it was at peace, the United States entered a conflict in Korea, and the Yanks held on to Porsche's shops. Their neighbor,

This was the creative automotive output of the Porsche family in the early 1950s. At left is the Typ 60 Volkswagen Beetle, the Typ 356 coupe, and the 356 cabriolet, a car for which Porsche hired Ernst and Fritz Beutler, coachbuilders in Thun, Switzerland, to fabricate. The brothers took some liberties with Erwin Komenda's design.

Reutter Karosserie, who had fabricated the bodies for the VW prototypes as well as Ferdinand's Typ 64s, offered space, and thus Ferry had a home for his workers to return to Stuttgart. They wrapped up work, wound down production in Austria, and began the move.

Back home in Germany, Ferry and his family believed they were done with auto manufacturing. He intended to resume the engineering consultancy his father had begun; car manufacturing in remote Gmünd had been anything but profitable, though through it, Ferry had supported his employees with regular wages. The family had thoroughly soured on any thought of continuing in the car business. Now, back in Stuttgart, they needed something more reliable and more lucrative.

Then, the company's business manager pointed out a looming problem: shortly after the war ended, Ferry had negotiated a 5-mark royalty from Volkswagen paid to Porsche for every Beetle assembled, covering use of all the designs and patents. That began immediately. Production numbers quickly rose into the thousands and tens of thousands. What was more, the United States had been paying Porsche a healthy rent on its works in Zuffenhausen. Unexpectedly, the family faced an immense tax bill. The business manager pleaded with them to begin manufacturing something—anything—right away to avoid paying a huge sum. Manufacturing, with its huge material expenses, was the answer. His question: Why not continue with the cars?

(Left) Back at the Gmünd Works, engineers and mechanics put Beutler's collapsible cabriolet top through tests. Porsche completely assembled 52 cars, of which around half were cabriolets. Beutler withdrew after seven cars, and Ferry found coachbuilders in Salzburg and elsewhere in Austria to fabricate the desirable open cars.

(Below) At the Geneva Motor Show in 1949, Swiss distributor Bernhard Blank towered over a proudly beaming Louisa Piëch and her brother Ferry (on Blank's left). Porsche and Blank displayed a Beutler cabriolet and a sunroof coupe on their show stand. Heinrich Kunz, far left, Blank's general manager, was most responsible for the car's success in Switzerland.

Porsche's 356 Was Evergreen—and So Was Its Favorite Color

Mass Production in Zuffenhausen

Carefully, diligently, Ferry got his company through the end of the 1940s, reuniting it with the consulting engineering company his father had founded twenty years earlier in Stuttgart. He fulfilled a shared dream of producing a car of their own. Now he needed more of the courage he'd developed in the previous three years. When his financial adviser, Albert Prinzing, warned him of potential tax obligation unless he resumed manufacturing soon, Ferry briefly balked.

"The idea encountered resistance in the Porsche and Piëch families," Karl Ludvigsen wrote in *Porsche: Excellence Was Expected*. "Some members pointed out that so far, the car-building venture in Gmünd had fallen short of roaring success. They also felt that Porsche engineering skills could be deployed more profitably by sticking strictly to design and development, leaving the risks of manufacturing to others." But Prinzing won over Ferry. By fall 1949, they were searching for somewhere to manufacture cars. They literally returned to their roots.

1955 Typ 356-1500 Coupes A pair of drivers pulled out of the Zuffenhausen Works gate for testing miles on the roads and Autobahn around the factory. Between 1948 and 1955, Porsche assembled 9,100 of its 356s, including 52 "production" and 11 SL versions from Gmünd. Ironically, when Ferry committed to ordering 500 car bodies from neighboring Reutter Karosserie, he worried if he could ever sell them all.

1951 Typ 356-1300 Cabriolet (Right-Hand Drive) This is chassis number 10150, the first right-hand drive Porsche sold into England. Porsche offered two engines: a 40-horseppower 1086 cubic centimeter displacement version, and a 44-horsepower 1,286 cubic centimeter displacement model, both sized for the racing classes of the day. At the time, the 1,300 sold for $2,904 (DM12,200 or £1,037) at Zuffenhausen Works.

In Professor Porsche's villa on the hill in Stuttgart, Ferdinand's craftsmen had fabricated the first three Volkswagens. Ferry's new Porsche car-manufacturing company began in the 194-square-foot garage and workroom. Prinzing later remembered space being so tight that if four of them needed to converse, they had to go outside.

For his workforce, Ferry purchased a basic 1,100-square-foot prefabricated wood-framed building adjacent to Werk 1, where the US Army was still operating its motor pool. After considering Prinzing's advice, he embraced the idea with unexpected zeal: he committed to neighboring Reutter Karosserie for five hundred steel car bodies for his Typ 356, just as assembly of the aluminum 356/2s wrapped up in Gmünd.

The family opened the doors on the new company—Dr. Ing h.c. F. Porsche KG, a limited partnership with Ferry and Prinzing as chief executives—in September 1949. They had 298 employees in fabrication (in Gmünd and Zuffenhausen) and 108 engineers, designers, accountants, and secretaries. Their first postwar hire was a mechanic named Herbert Linge, who had apprenticed with them from 1943 to 1945.

The challenge of financing production came next. Banks declined to loan money to a start-up; Porsche's healthy US rent payments and VW royalties weren't sufficient. Ferry launched a bold plan.

In early 1950, Prinzing set out from Zuffenhausen in their aluminum-body demonstrator with another driver in a Beutler cabriolet. Their mission was to call on Germany's top VW dealers, twenty-two in all. The dealers greeted them enthusiastically. The Porsche reputation—established with the VWs as well as the Gmünd sports cars—motivated distributors. Orders ranged from ten to as many as fifty cars at each stop. Prinzing required they pay for the *last* car they would receive. With Porsche's retail price set at roughly $2,030 at the time (DM 9,950), once fees and discounts were factored in, Porsche KG took in nearly roughly $45,000 (DM 200,000). Prinzing not only accumulated capital but also established a credit line for Porsche, which had not yet manufactured its first car in Germany!

Ferry set initial production at eight to ten cars per month, using 40-horsepower, improved 1,086cc VW engines. Ferry's engineer Franz Xaver Reimspiess had designed the engine to Ferdinand's specifications, and they knew it easily could accommodate enlargement to 1,500cc, along with valvetrain improvements. Ferry had hired an Austrian engineer named Ernst Fuhrmann in 1947, and after working on Piero Dusio's Typ 360 Grand Prix car engine, Fuhrmann's next assignment was engine advances for the 356. In late 1950, Porsche introduced a 1,264cc, 44-horsepower engine that fit into the racing class for displacement under 1.3 liters.

1951 Typ 356-1500 Coupe Porsche introduced its new 1,488 cubic centimeter displacement opposed-four-cylinder engine late in the 1951 model year, providing 60 horsepower output. This was enough to propel the, 1,698-pound (770 kg) coupe from 0 to 62 miles per hour (0 to 100 kilometers per hour) in 15.5 seconds, and on to a top speed of 105 miles per hour (170 kilometers per hour).

1951 Typ 356SL-1100 Coupe Porsche, on encouragement from Le Mans co-founder Charles Faroux, prepared three of their carry-over all-aluminum-alloy Gmünd coupes—designated 356 SL for Super Light—for the 24 Hours of Le Mans. Getting there was tough and only one of the three started the race; it finished first in its 1.1-liter class, 19th overall. Its two drivers completed 210 laps, racing 1,765.1 miles (2,840.7 km) at an average speed of 73.5 miles per hour (118.4 kilometers per hour).

A steadily growing group of enthusiastic supporters already were racing Porsches, regularly winning their class in events from Austria to Sweden. An Austrian entrepreneur who had emigrated to the United States and manufactured and sold inexpensive costume jewelry during the war became Porsche's next "customer." Maximilian Hoffman had opened a car showroom on New York City's fashionable Park Avenue in 1947, selling used British and European autos and importing new ones. He ambitiously embraced the VW Beetle but quickly grew disillusioned by its modesty. He'd been selling Jaguars, and the Wehrmacht-green, 25-horsepower VW coupes—with their nonsynchro four-speed transmissions and weak mechanical brakes—paled in comparison. Yet he knew Porsche's name, and after one of the journalists who'd driven Bernhard Blank's Porsche 356/1 raved about it, Hoffman made contact and quickly sealed a deal. The conversation between Ferry and Hoffman has become legend: Ferry said he hoped Max could find buyers for five cars a year, and Max brashly replied, "If I can't sell five a week, I'm not interested." In early autumn 1950, Hoffman's first two cars, both 1.1-liter coupes, arrived in New York. He marketed them vigorously, taking them to regional sports-car races and loaning them to well-known celebrities and sportsmen for demonstrations. It was the beginning of a long, if tempestuous, relationship.

Ferry's relationships in Paris were more mutually respectful. He gained a distributor, racer Auguste Veuillet, and renewed his friendship with Charles Faroux, a founder of the 24-hour race at Le Mans. More important to the Porsche family, Faroux had been a courier and had

1952-53 Typ-1500 540 America Roadster Some racers requested something lighter and sportier than the production cabriolet, so Porsche produced a run of 20 or 21 of these 1,334-pound (605 kg) roadsters strictly for the United States markets. With 70 horsepower, these cars reached 62 miles per hour (100 kilometers per hour) in 10.0 seconds and topped out at 112 miles per hour (180 kilometers per hour). The small run made them pricey: $4,600 US.

1952 Typ 356SL-1100 Le Mans Coupe Porsche returned to Le Mans in 1952, racing three of its 356 Super Lights. One quit in the sixth hour, another was disqualified for running its engine during refueling, and the third won its class with the same drivers as 1951. This year it went further, completing 220 laps for 1,836 miles (2,955.4 km); it averaged 76.5 miles per hour (123.1 kilometers per hour). It placed 11th overall.

delivered the 1 million francs to the French government to buy Ferdinand Porsche's release from prison. He urged Ferdinand and Ferry to enter the big race for June 1951.

Ferdinand, however, never saw his son's first "factory" racing effort. Following a stroke months earlier, he died on January 30, 1951. He was seventy-five and had permanently engraved his name into automotive history. As one historian wrote, if he'd only invented the swing-axle suspension, that would have been enough for a career, but he did so much more.

Within two months of Ferdinand's death, Ferry's brave gamble paid off fully. On March 21, 1951, the 500th Porsche Typ 356 drove out of the Zuffenhausen assembly. Shortly after, Porsche introduced the 44-horsepower 1.3-liter engine. It offered, for its time, bristling performance, reaching 62 miles (100 km) per hour in 19 seconds on its way to a top speed of 96 miles (154.5 km) per hour. Ferry prepared three Gmünd coupes for Le Mans, as 356 SLs, the suffix representing Super and Light. One raced and finished first in its class, registering Porsche's first significant international race win and embedding the automaker in the world of motorsports.

Model year 1952 brought a handsome styling update after Ferry allowed a few extra deutschmarks for one-piece "bent" windshields. The company also introduced right-hand drive models for the United Kingdom and a new 60-horsepower 1,488cc engine with its crankshaft spinning in roller bearings. Model year 1953 introduced a 55-horsepower replacement as the Normal, nicknamed die Dame (the Lady), accompanied by a 70-horsepower Super version. All the cars got Porsche's new fully synchronized four-speed transmission and significantly improved brakes. Performance improved as well, and the Supers reached 62 miles (100 km) per hour in 14 seconds and a top speed of 112 miles (180.2 km) per hour. In response to requests from western US distributor/racer Johnny Von Neumann, Porsche introduced the America Roadster for racers, who quickly snapped up the limited production. The roadster weighed 364 pounds less than the similarly engined cabriolet, and though top speed remained 112 miles per hour (180.2 km), acceleration to 62 miles per hour took just 10 seconds.

Several innovations appeared for 1954, not least of which was an increased-production version of the roadster, called the Speedster. This was another US West Coast–inspired product. Just 200 appeared in 1954, and they all crossed the ocean. Performance was similar to the roadsters, biased toward racetrack acceleration. Customers could order the new 1300 Super engine as well, a 60-horsepower update that also used roller bearings. Model year 1955 marked the end of the Volkswagen-derived engines and the introduction of new three-piece crankcases.

The year 1956 was a landmark one for Porsche. The previous fall, Ferry had introduced the first major update to his 356, designated Typ 356 A. On March 12, the company celebrated twenty-five years in business *and* its 10,000th car manufactured. The "big" engines grew to 1,582cc, corresponding to a new under-1.6-liter racing category, though the 1.5-liter versions remained available as a new Carrera model, intended for ultraperformance enthusiasts and racers. The 1600 Super delivered 75 horsepower; the 1500 GS Carrera (with dual overhead camshafts) offered 100 horsepower using aluminum crankcases, cylinder heads, and cylinder barrels. Suspension modifications improved handling, as did a downsize from 16-inch- (406-mm)-diameter wheels and tires to the more common and popular 15s. Porsche produced a separate parts list for Carrera owners planning for racing or international rallies.

Model year 1957 marked the end of the 1300s when the racing class disappeared. Porsche gave the

(Top) 1954 Typ 356 Speedster To emphasize its sporting nature, Porsche photographed this early Speedster near the timing and scoring tower at the Solitude racing circuit in Stuttgart. Porsche introduced the Speedster in late 1954, sending the first 200 examples to the US; the model remained in production through 1958 with more than 4,100 assembled.

(Above) 1955 Typ 356-1500 Normal Continental Coupe Ferry Porsche learned from his distributor Max Hoffman that his customers in the United States preferred car names to car numbers. The Speedster proved that, so Ferry named a run of 356s it called "Continental." This was fine until Lincoln Division of Ford Motor notified him they had rights to the name and plans to reintroduce it for 1956.

cabriolets slightly taller cloth tops for better headroom and rear visibility. In addition, it added a new Carrera version, the GS/GT, for Grand Sport/Grand Tourisme, strictly in the coupe and Speedster bodies. This engine developed 110 horsepower, and the body used aluminum for the doors and front and rear deck lids. The next technical upgrade arrived in 1958 with the T2, Technical Programme 2. This introduced a new crankcase that provided high oil pressure at low speeds and better oil dispersal across the entire range. Super engines abandoned roller bearings for journal-bearing cranks. Porsche added two new body styles manufactured by Karmann, the Hardtop-Coupe—essentially a cabriolet body with a notchback top welded in place—and the Hardtop-Cabriolet. The company replaced its base 1500 Carrera GS with a more comfortable 356 A 1500 GS Carrera de Luxe. Model year 1959 ended the 356 A series, replacing the Speedster with a new Convertible D available as a 1600 Carrera deluxe with 105 horsepower; the Carrera GS/GT for racers with 115 horsepower appeared only as a coupe. The A series had continued and expanded Porsche's success; Zuffenhausen Works manufactured 20,541 of the second-generation 356s.

1955 Typ 356-1500 Normal European Coupe Whether Porsche's European was Ferry's response to Ford's threat of a lawsuit over the Continental name is unclear. However, the Zuffenhausen Works manufactured a small run of 55-horsepower coupes and cabriolets named for their home continent.

1957 Typ 356 A-1500 GS Carrera GT Speedster Finding an aged Porsche in a barn, let alone a 110-horsepower thoroughbred such as this GS Carrera GT is every collector's fantasy. Porsche assembled around 167 of these 1,498 cubic centimeter displacement Speedsters for a very hungry competition market in the US and Europe. The 1,952-pound (840 kg) cars were capable of 124 miles per hour (200 kilometers per hour) and sold for $4,120 (DM 17,300), at the Zuffenhausen Works.

Porsche's Le Mans commitment continued with class wins in 1952 and 1953 and multiple class victories starting in 1954 with a new racing spyder. Elsewhere, 356 coupes and Speedsters permanently established Porsche's reputation as a production-based race car. Special competition options ranged from gear sets for various tracks to suspension upgrades, numerous lighter-weight replacement parts, and ever-expanding factory and dealer support.

Technical Programme 5 arrived in autumn 1959, designated the 1960 Typ 356 B. Higher headlights and bumpers meant it met world standards for its coupe, cabriolet, roadster, and hardtop coupe models. Porsche simplified engine production to a 60-horsepower 1600 Normal, the 75-horsepower 1600 Super, and a new 1,582cc 90-horsepower Super 90, all with pushrod-activated valves. The Super 90 reached 62 miles per hour (100 kilometers per hour) in 13.6 seconds and topped out at 117 miles per hour (188 kilometers per hour). For racers and the performance afflicted, the company still offered 356 B 1600 Carrera GS/GTs with aluminum doors and decks, aluminum seat shells, and Plexiglas side and back windows. With a new 12-volt electric system, the GS/GT offered customers 115 horsepower

1964 Typ 356 SC Coupe
The SC series, which stood for Super C, culminated Typ 356 production for Porsche. The company's 1,582 cubic centimeter displacement engine developed 95 horsepower, pushing these 2,061-pound (935-kg) coupes from 62 miles per hour (0 to 100 kilometers per hour) in 11.5 seconds and on to a top speed of 115 miles per hour (185 kilometers per hour). Porsche charged $3,917 (DM 16,450) for the coupe, at the factory, and assembled 13,510 coupes and 3,175 cabriolets.

and a top speed of 124 miles per hour (200 kilometers per hour). Porsche fabricated just forty of these coupes.

The Carreras continued in 1961, but the Convertible D disappeared, leaving the Karmann-bodied cabriolets and Hardtop-Coupes as well as the Reutter fastback coupes. Model year 1962 introduced the Technical Programme 6, with several body-design improvements, including a larger front-opening decklid and rear engine cover sporting two vertical air intakes, the so-called Twin Grille lids. Porsche manufactured 31,440 356 Bs and then introduced its final-generation 356, the C and SC, for 1964.

New flat hubcaps betrayed the model's most significant upgrade: disc brakes on all four wheels. Porsche characterized the 356 C as its model for long life and usable torque, while the SC—Super Carrera—was the sports version. The 1.6-liter engines in the C coupe, cabriolet, and hardtop-cabriolet delivered 75 horsepower; the SCs offered 95 horsepower. The 356 C 2000 GS Carrera 2 was a more potent model in standard coupe or cabriolet body style, created to help racing homologation in 1964. This 2.0-liter engine developed 130 brake horsepower, pushing the car to 62 miles per hour (100 kilometers per hour) in 9 seconds and on to a top speed of 124 miles per hour (200 kilometers per hour). Expensive, fast, and demanding to drive, this represented the ultimate 356, and while Porsche manufactured 16,685 356 Cs and SCs, only 126 were Carrera 2s.

(Top) 1958-1959 Typ 356-1600 Normal Hardtop-Coupe In an attempt to provide slightly better accommodations for those in the rear seats, Porsche asked Karmann in nearby Osnabrück to weld steel hardtops onto cabriolet bodies. An alternate version, the Hardtop-Cabriolet provided buyers with the removable Hardtop. Both benefitted from improved rear seat headroom and a much larger rear window.

(Bottom) 1962 Typ 356 B 1600 Super 90 Roadster The "Super 90" designation represented a new 90-horsepower 1,582 cubic centimeter displacement engine while the "Roadster" was a new body Porsche ordered from the Belgian firm D'Ieteren Frères in Brussels. D'Ieteren took over manufacturer from Drauz of Heilbronn, who discontinued their Roadsters in February 1961. In all, Porsche, Drauz, and D'Ieteren manufactured some 2,902 Roadsters from 1960 through 1962.

1953–1962

6

Adventures in the Middle

Typ 550 to Typ 718 WRS

Walter Glöckler was Ferry Porsche's dealer in Frankfurt. He had started with VWs, and when Albert Prinzing called on him to demonstrate the Porsche coupe and cabriolet, he eagerly signed on. Like Ferry, Glöckler was a racer, seeing value in promoting car sales. He sold some 356/2 Gmünd cars, and during the winter of 1949, he got an extra 1,100cc engine and fitted it into a sleek two-seater spyder; his chief mechanic, Hermann Ramelow, fabricated a frame and Wiedenhausen, a coachbuilder literally across the street, produced the body. Unexpectedly, newspaper stories about his racing victories in the "Glöckler Porsche Special" caught Ferry's attention.

Glöckler's spyder was a 990-pound featherweight. Ramelow had tuned the VW-Porsche engine to use methanol, and it produced 58 horsepower, providing startling performance. Glöckler became German champion in 1950, and Ferry sent him an early 1.5-liter engine, which powered the next spyder he, Ramelow, and Wiedenhausen created. On methanol, this engine produced 90 horsepower and won Glöckler his second national championship. It also introduced him to Ferry's distributor Max Hoffman, who purchased the car to race and promote his business in the States.

1953 prototype Typ 550 1500 RS Spyder After watching Frankfurt Porsche/VW dealer Walter Glöckler win races in small, sleek, aluminum-body Spyders in which he fitted Porsche engines—and seeing a pair of racers named Sauter making similar race cars—Ferry authorized this new model. These spyders weighed just 1,510 pounds (685 kg).

(Above) 1953 Typ 550 1500 RS "Spyder with a Roof" Freshly restored, chassis 550-02 races here at the Monterey Reunion. Czech racer Jaroslav Juhan, living in Guatemala, drove this car in the 1953 Carrera. Juhan had led his class for much of the race but in the final leg, the distributor drive on his engine broke. He had carried a spare in his pocket for days but, with the Porsche so reliable, he discarded it the morning of the final leg.

(Left) 1954 Typ 550 1500 RS Spyder Porsche mechanic Sigmund "Siggy" Muyerlin stood alongside the "production" Porsche Spyder with its new 110-horsepower four-cam Typ 548 engine that he maintained for Argentine architect Fernando Segura during the Carrera Panamericana. Segura, with Works racer/mechanic Herbert Linge co-driving, placed fourth in class and finished 12th overall in the 1,908-mile (3,071-km) open-road race through Mexico.

During this time, even as Ferry supported Glöckler with engines and technical assistance, he decided to change those newspaper headlines from "Glöckler Porsche Wins Again" to "Porsche Wins." With production of his Stuttgart steel 356s underway, the second-generation 356 A in development, and a new dual-overhead-camshaft 1.5-liter engine from his employee Ernst Fuhrmann, he urged body engineer Erwin Komenda to develop designs for Porsche's own race car. Komenda and body modeler Heinrich Klie created a slim "Spyder." Inspired by an aerodynamic cockpit cover Glöckler used for record runs in France in late 1952, Porsche's design team produce a fastback coupe as well. Wiedenhausen assembled the bodies, but Porsche used a welded steel-tube ladder frame. For the first time, Ferry's engineers gained access to the University of Stuttgart's wind tunnel.

"Wind tunnel tests carried out on models to finalize the shape of the Spyder produced some unexpected results," according to historian Jürgen Barth. "To improve airflow past the mid-mounted engine under the large one-piece rear bodywork, engineers first installed an air intake behind the seats. At first the opening faced forward, thinking air would be forced in. Then, with the same opening facing rearward, rather surprisingly, this gave better results. Holding a wool thread in the airstream flowing past the car fed itself into the rear-facing opening by itself! When the opening faced forward, the thread fluttered past the opening but never went in." With the one-piece fastback top in place, coupes weighed 1,225 pounds (555.7 kg). Spyders were 1,212 pounds (549.8 kg).

The car, designated Typ 550 1500 RS, used a fully independent suspension with twin trailing arms and adjustable transverse leaf springs with an antiroll bar. The leaf springs served the purpose of Ferdinand Porsche's typical torsion-bar suspension; the rear was more his traditional design, with swing axles controlled by trailing arms attached to round transverse torsion bars. Telescoping shocks all around controlled suspension action. With Ernst Fuhrmann's new Typ 547 twin-cam engine delivering 110 horsepower, the 550 accelerated from 0 to 62 miles per hour (0 to 100 kilometers per hour) in 10 seconds and reached a 137-mile-per-hour (220.5-kilometer-per-hour) top speed.

Following the debut victory at the Nürburgring, Porsche entered a pair of coupes in Le Mans in 1953.

1957 Typ 718 RSK Porsche engineers mounted vertical fins on the rear of the 718s to improve stability for the long, high-speed circuits such as Sebring and Le Mans. The 718 was new for Le Mans with its light space frame and alloy body, improved suspension and brakes, and a five-speed gearbox. Edgar Barth and Umberto Maglioli ran a strong race until the then-seventh-place Porsche collided with a spinning Aston Martin at 2:00 AM, taking out both cars.

Ever cautious, Ferry and his engineers raced with engines "detuned" to 75 horsepower with the goal of finishing. Wearing numbers 44 and 45, the cars took fifteenth and sixteenth place overall and won the Sports 1500 class. A month later, the two coupes went to Mexico for the third annual Carrera Panamericana, earning another class win. Continuing successes in 1955 led Ferry to enter

1957 Typ 718 RSK Edgar Barth headed out on another testing lap at the Nürburgring prior to Le Mans. His son Jürgen, who went on to manage customer racing and win Le Mans himself, looked on with Herbert Linge (both in caps at left), while racing engineer Wilhelm Hild (right) awaited Barth's next round of results and impressions.

three cars at Le Mans. They placed fourth, fifth, and sixth overall and claimed two class victories. Ferry now had a collection of "Porsche Wins" headlines to read.

His Works made subtle improvements in body, chassis, and engine, and assembled thirteen in 1954, including the first group delivered to customers. For 1955, that output rose to eighty-two cars while engineers prepared the next generation Typ 550 A 1500 RS. Four Works race cars and three dozen for customers emerged; engineers replaced the ladder frame with a steel-tube space frame, saving some 35 pounds (15.9 kg) while improving stiffness and rigidity for better handling. They replaced the rear swing axle with a new low-pivot version and added a front antiroll bar. Engine modifications boosted output to 135 horsepower and other changes reduced weight to 1,168 pounds (529.8 kg) with a new five-speed gearbox. Porsche sent two 550 As to Le Mans; one finished fifth and claimed another class win. In 1957, it fell to a private-entry 550 A to uphold factory honor, setting a precedent for future competitions;

(Top) 1960 Typ 718 RS60 Regulations for Le Mans required oversized windscreens; these caused terrible turbulence in the cockpits that increased aerodynamic drag and measurably slowed the cars. Racing engineers fabricated tall side windows and an elevated rear decklid that tricked the airflow into treating the car as a closed coupe.

(Above) 1958 Typ 718 RSK F2 Porsche fabricated something like thirty-five of these 718s and offered a kit to convert perhaps a dozen of the cars to single-center-seat driving for customers racing in FIA Formula 2 races. These 148-horsepower alloy-body race cars weighed just 1,190 pounds (540 kg) and depending on gearing were capable of 155 miles per hour (250 kilometers per hour).

an American entered his 550 A co-driving with a Dutch racer, and they placed eighth and took the Sports 1500 win.

The 1958 update was so substantial it merited a new designation, Typ 718. It was nicknamed the RSK because the configuration of its radically new front suspension resembled the letter *K*—both the cause and the effect of further streamlining the body. Lowering the nose to reduce wind resistance forced a suspension redesign that kept lower suspension arms parallel to the ground but angled the uppers downward toward the car center. One side effect was a new steering linkage using two universal joints to set the steering wheel on the left. But now, engineers had the option to place it in the center or on the right.

Bodywork changed according to the circuits. For high-speed courses such as Sebring, Florida, and Le Mans, the cars sprouted vertical tail fins for stability. Regulations demanded a taller windscreen, so designers elevated the rear engine cover to meet the side windows, which reduced air turbulence in the open spyder cockpits. For some races, engineers fitted a metal passenger seat cover on the car, cutting turbulence more. The engineers further stretched the Typ 547, providing 142 horsepower for 1958 and 148 horsepower through 1959. At Le Mans in 1958, the new cars placed third and fourth behind a

1960 Typ 718 RS60 Porsche entered three such 718s at Le Mans, two of which had new 178-horsepower, 1,606 cubic centimeter displacement engines, but these didn't last. Instead, No. 39 raced the 1.5-liter, 166-horsepower "standard" engine which ran without problem. It was their gearbox that let them down, offering only two gears by the 22nd hour. Barth, driving here, paced it carefully and limped to the finish, winning its class and placing 11th overall.

winning Ferrari and second-place Aston Martin. Each of the RSKs also earned a class win. Out of ten finishers, Porsche had four spots. Newspaper headlines began calling Porsches "the giant killers," which Ferry enjoyed. The company assembled some thirty-five RSKs and, using its new steering configuration, made four with a "center-steering" position. Another handful of RSKs emerged in 1959. After an unexpected first-second-third-fourth finish in Italy's Targa Florio, Porsche then had a very different kind of unexpected experience at Le Mans: none of its cars finished, a startling result in a decade of strong racing accomplishments.

This same year, Porsche introduced the next new Spyder, the Typ 718 RS60. A thin aluminum-body shell encased a welded seamless-steel-tube space frame. Its nose, lower and more rounded than the RSK, helped improve its slice through the air. Designers incorporated a driver's head fairing on the large removable rear deck lid. Just aft of this panel, two very large grilles at the rear of the car fed the engine, breathing and cooling air. For 1959, the next-generation Typ 547 opposed four-cylinder engine provided drivers with 150 horsepower. The front suspension retained the trailing arms/torsion bars configuration, but the rear switched to pairs of angled A-arms on each side, suspended by coil-over Dutch-made Koni twin-acting shock absorbers. Konis at the front also relied on an antiroll bar. At Le Mans in June 1960, one of the new RS60s placed eleventh overall, winning its Sports 1500 class once again.

For 1960, Porsche introduced its 718 RS61. This was not evolutionary but revolutionary. Engineers stretched the wheelbase from 82.7 to 86.6 inches. Pairs of triangular A-arms suspended the rear end, relying on longitudinal radius rods for springing. Racing regulations demanded a wider front end, which influenced the new configuration, though engineers still relied on trailing links. Engine displacement grew to 1,588cc (under 1.6 liters), which gave racers 160 horsepower. A considerably more powerful, radical engine also was available: a new Typ 771 opposed eight-cylinder engine with dual overhead camshafts that displaced 1,982cc. Over its life, its initial 180 horsepower climbed as high as 270

1962 Typ 718 W-RS This spyder, like the GTR coupe, was a test bed for racing engineers who perfected a 210-horsepower, 2.2-liter opposed eight-cylinder engine. In this 1,190-pound (540-kg) package, this combination was so often victorious that the Works raced it for many years, earning it the nickname of *Grossmutter*, Grandmother.

horsepower in the ultralight, highly specialized hillclimb "Bergspyder." This engine was a parallel development through 1961 with a Typ 753 destined for Porsche's future 1.5-liter Formula One car for 1962. But the 771's larger cylinder bore 3 inches (76 mm), (compared to 2.6 inches [66 mm] in the 1,494cc F1 engine) produced success.

The 1961 RS61s were rare machines. Two were spyders, one—designated 718 W-RS— achieving legends on hillclimb courses and earning the nickname *Grossmutter*, Grandmother, for its steady reliability. A third chassis evolved into a coupe, sometimes referred to as the Typ 718 GTR. For Le Mans in 1961, body designers and engineers lopped off the rear two-thirds of the raised engine cover, leaving only an extended hoop. Its height still connected to the side windows, but its sharp trailing edge forced more air into its rear intakes. Body designers worked this configuration to create the GTR coupe, whose roof also ended in an extended hoop. A new championship for GT cars stated in 1961, the *Challenge Mondiale de Vitesse et Endurance*, World Challenge for Speed and Endurance, and the eight-cylinder Grossmutter and GTR were Porsche's weapons of choice. After taking the top three spots at the 1961 Targa Florio, Porsche was hopeful for Le Mans. No one forgot the failure of 1959, but class wins in 1960 had encouraged the team. At the end of 24 hours, the W-RS placed fifth overall and won Sports 2000. The GTR finished seventh and took second in class.

In 1960, Porsche had produced a small run of twenty Typ 756 aluminum-body coupes on 356 B chassis, called the 356 B 1600 GTL Abarth Carrera. Their racing success inspired another prototype GTR coupe with road-going headlamps, brake lights, and a license plate frame. Internally, Ferry and others discussed a hundred-car "production" run with 1.6- and 2.0-liter engines for customer racers. But costly commitments for a different race type ended hopes for the GTR coupe. However, the shapes and forms Heinrich Klie created inspired Porsche's next GT racer.

19

1957–1962

7

Open-Wheel Triumph and Tribulation

Typ 718 to 804

The premier form of motorsports before World War II had been the Grand Prix series. It attracted the world's best drivers, and, by the series regulations, each nation that wished to stage one was allowed one venue. So it was no surprise when, in 1946, racing resurfaced, sanctioned and regulated by the Commission Sportive Internationale (CSI) within the reorganized Fédération Internationale de l'Automobile (FIA). The CSI re-created the two prewar categories, Grand Prix and Voiturette (based on engine displacement), as Formula A and B. By 1950, these were called Formula One and Formula Two. Some of the prewar giants reappeared—Mercedes-Benz, Alfa Romeo, Maserati, Delage, Delahaye—and newcomers joined—Ferrari, English Racing Automobiles (ERA). Attendance and "sponsorship" from tire and petroleum companies supported the races, and the FIA and CSI ran as many as twenty venues a year, with separate races for F1 and F2 at the beginning.

A tragic racing accident at Le Mans in 1955 involving Mercedes-Benz led that company to withdraw from all racing at year end. Financial strain pulled others out, and

1962 Typ 804 Formula One Dan Gurney, driving Porsche's Formula One car (No. 1) qualified second quickest around the Solitude Ring, an 7.1-mile (11.4-km) circuit through hilly suburban Stuttgart. While he may have been studying the Lotus and Cooper behind him, they were no concern during the 25-lap race, which Gurney won by nearly two seconds over Porsche teammate Jo Bonnier.

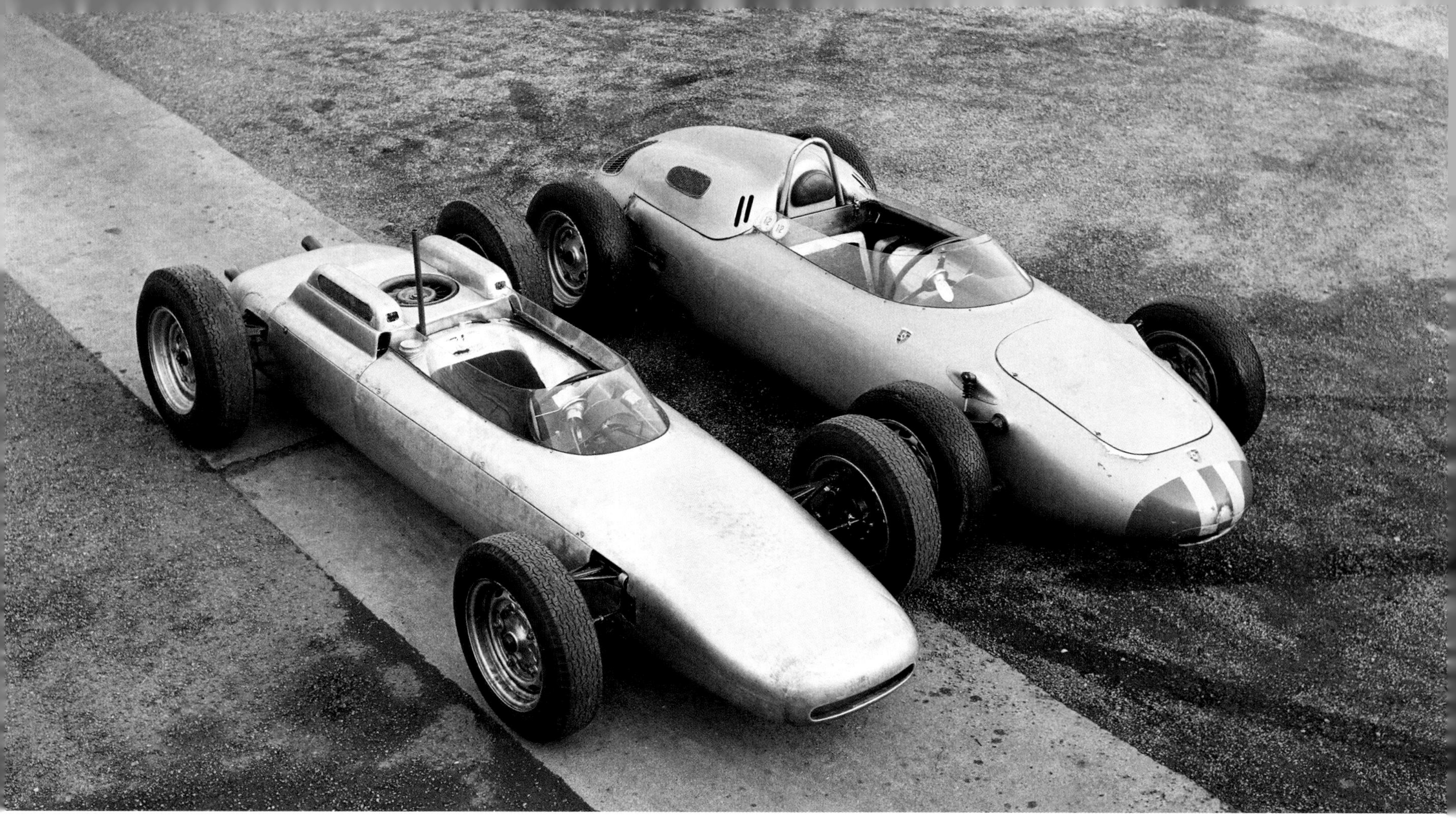

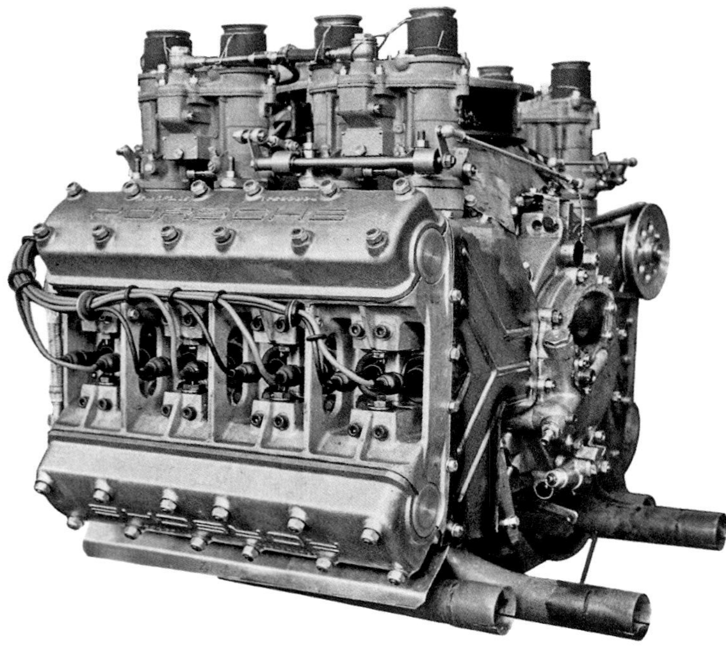

(Top) 1962 Typ 804 Formula One and 1960 Typ 787 Formula Two The two cars came within one kilogram of each other—1,003 pounds (455 kg) for the 804 (left), versus 1,005 pounds (456 kg) for the 787. Both had 1.5-liter engines with 155 horsepower for the 787 and 180 for the 804. Both used a 90.6-inch (2,300-mm) wheelbase. The 804 measured 141.7 inches (3,600 mm) overall versus 134.6 inches (3,420 mm) for the 787.

(Above) Typ 753 Engine The heart of the Typ 804 race car was its complex 1,494 cubic centimeter opposed eight-cylinder engine. Using twin-plug ignition to ensure best fuel burn, it produced 180 horsepower; unfortunately, Porsche needed 200 or 210 to win.

by 1956, it was a challenge for organizers to fill a starting grid; they began positioning F2 behind F1 in a single race. Thus it happened on the weekend of August 4, 1957, that Porsche racer Edgar Barth unexpectedly set the fastest time in qualifying for the F2 group in the German Grand Prix. He drove Porsche's latest sports car, the Typ 718 1500 RSK, whose only modification was that mechanics had removed its headlights. What was more, at the end of the twenty-two-lap race around the Nürburgring, Barth placed twelfth overall but classified first in Formula Two. This started Ferry Porsche and his racing director, Huschke von Hanstein, thinking more about the series as an opportunity to sell more race cars. When the FIA introduced a World Championship for (F1) manufacturers starting in 1958, Ferry made the commitment.

Mechanics modified four RSKs, moving the driving position to the center of the cockpit (F2 and F1 regulations allowed only single-seaters), and Porsche offered these not only to its own Works drivers but also to loyal "privateers," including talented Frenchman Jean Behra. At the French Grand Prix at Reims, Behra won the F2 race. These cars were atypical of Formula race cars at the time; they retained their mid-engine configuration while all the others were more traditional front-engine, rear-drive systems. When, at the end of the 1958 racing season, the FIA and CSI announced new rules for F1 starting in 1961, Porsche felt its time had come: regulations limited engine displacements to 1.5 liters, exactly the displacement of its formidable Typ 547 twin-cam engine.

Porsche's task for 1959 was to shed the bodywork, open and expose the wheels, and lighten the car as much as possible. As engineers and body designers (including Ferry Porsche's young son Ferdinand Alexander, known as FA, and nicknamed Butzi) worked on the project, it assumed the designation Typ 718/2. Meanwhile, Jean Behra had gone to a racing engineer in Modena (the home of Ferrari's and Maserati's operations), who fabricated an open-wheeler—the Behra-Porsche—that relied on all the RSK running gear Porsche was putting into its 718/2s.

For the 1960 season, Porsche sold one of its F2 cars to British racer Stirling Moss, who raced for whiskey producer Rob Walker. Moss scored a succession of second-place finishes before taking first on home ground at Britain's Aintree Circuit. By the end of the season, as many as five F2 Porsches had started the races. Huschke von Hanstein had hired Swedish racer Jo Bonnier and American Dan Gurney to drive Works cars. Bonnier's win at Nürburgring three years after Barth's F2 debut earned Porsche the season Coupe des Constructeurs for the manufacturer's championship and injected extra energy into the program.

As 1961 approached, Porsche found its cars automatically graduated to F1 status, their 1.5-liter engines fitting the new regulations precisely. But the competition in F1 was much stiffer than in F2. Britain alone offered Lotus, Cooper, and British Racing Motors (BRM). All were mid-engine racers, as were the Italian Ferraris and Maseratis. Extra energy aside, it was clear Porsche needed a new car with a more potent engine in order to compete. Engineers and designers began work on an evolutionary car, the Typ 787, and an innovative 1.5-liter opposed eight-cylinder fuel-injected engine for a race car, the Typ 804.

"Porsche's first race in Formula One took place in early April 1961 in Brussels, Belgium," Jürgen Barth explained. "And it was a great disappointment. The Typ 753 engine was not ready, despite delivering 180hp on dynamometer tests months earlier. Both cars, running the old 1.5-liter opposed fours, did not finish." Porsche experienced similar frustration at Monaco in May. There it raced the new Typ 787s with fuel-injected four-cylinder engines; while Bonnier, Gurney, and Hans Herrmann started, only Gurney completed the race, placing fifth.

Still, the Monaco race was not a total loss. It and another disappointing result on Holland's seashore at Zandvoort reinforced what Porsche's engineers knew: they needed more power from a more flexible engine and a more nimble chassis. The rest of the 1961 season was a series of tests, qualifying sessions, race starts, and painful runs to disappointing finishes. Everyone looked

1962 Typ 718/2 Formula Two English racer Graham Hill was as well recognized for his distinctive mustache as for his striped helmet. He was sitting in one of four race cars Porsche entered at Solitude Ring, a venue it considered its hometown track; Hill finished fourth overall.

forward to 1962 and the arrival of the new, purpose-designed Typ 804.

Porsche debuted the car at the Netherlands race at Zandvoort. The car looked the part of a modern, slim, lean, Formula One car. Its engine gave racers Bonnier and Gurney 180 horsepower in a car that weighed 1,003 pounds (455 kg), and measured just 11 feet 10 inches (3600 mm) long. Gearing problems plagued the car, leaving Bonnier in seventh at the finish, and Gurney retired in the pits. The team sat out the next race while engineers attended to hundreds of details.

However, the effort paid off with Porsche's first-ever Formula One victory at the French Grand Prix in Rouen. While others had led Gurney throughout the race, each of them was slowed, sidelined, or retired with problems, and Dan finished first. Bonnier rode the victory lap sitting *on* Gurney's winning car—he had retired on the circuit with gearshift and fuel injection problems, and Gurney stopped trackside to pick up his teammate.

The next race was a non-championship points contest in Porsche's hometown, on the Solitude Ring just outside Stuttgart. By now, the 804s had nearly 200 horsepower. Here again, Gurney was triumphant, and, as he explained in an interview on the 30th anniversary of the race, his lasting memory came during his postrace parade lap, seeing tens of thousands of cheering locals throwing their hats in the air in jubilation.

The next race, at the Nürburgring, was likewise one Gurney remembered all his life. He had qualified fastest of all entries, and Porsche had great hopes for its cars and drivers. Shortly after the start, Gurney's car's battery broke loose from its mounts in the cockpit. The 26-plus-mile Nürburgring is a circuit of seemingly endless curves and elevation changes, and the driver was forced to use his leg to hold the battery against the car-frame tubes. The fuel tank surrounded and supported the driver's seat, and Gurney had no idea whether his battery might spark against aluminum. For most of the race, he worried about explosion. Despite this distraction, he placed third; Bonnier took seventh.

Mechanics performed more modifications in advance of races in Italy at Monza and in the United States at Watkins Glen. Panels of paper-thin fiberglass replaced aluminum bodywork, Porsche's first experiments with the material. The engineers knew they still needed to trim weight and increase horsepower; the Italy and US races made that clear.

Even as it contested the World Manufacturers' Championship for Formula One, Porsche never stopped racing and supporting its customers in GT and sports car races throughout the world. What was more, since 1958, its designers and engineers had been developing a replacement for the Typ 356. When Ferry settled on a design and chassis, he approached his neighbor Reutter Karosserie about manufacturing the new car bodies. But they made a counteroffer: that Ferry should acquire them.

Faced with an unexpected investment even larger than another futile season in Formula One—and acknowledging that the F1 cars brought little in the way of useful advances to his road-going models, the real focus of his car business—Ferry told von Hanstein and his engineers that their Formula One effort was done. There was no announcement; von Hanstein quietly withdrew their entries from the final races of the season. Porsche had assembled four of its Typ 804s and a small run of the intensely complicated Typ 753 engine, all of which moved unceremoniously into storage.

1962 Typ 804 Formula One Porsche debuted the car at Circuit Park Zandvoort for the Grand Prix of the Netherlands, with Works drivers Jo Bonnier (here) and Dan Gurney driving the 80-lap contest. At the end of 208 miles (335 km), Bonnier finisahed seventh, a good first result, while Gurney's gearbox failed, and he retired on his 47th lap.

S-UN 100

1958–1966

8

Replace It? Are You Mad? Replace It! It's Time!

Typ 901, 902, 911, 912

When Erwin Komenda wasn't drawing subtle updates to the gently aging Typ 356 or designing open-wheel and enclosed bodywork racing cars, he was putting forward ideas for the next Porsche. But as early efforts emerged in full-scale models, Ferry wasn't interested. A two-door coupe, designated Typ 530, appeared in 1952; it resembled the Karmann Hardtop-Coupe scaled up 15 percent or so. Ferry shrugged.

The Typ 534 then emerged during the winter of 1953–1954. But it was another enlarged 356 replica, and Ferry, preoccupied with his Typ 550 race car, registered little enthusiasm. Komenda was practicing mind reading. He attended auto shows with Ferry, and as they prowled the halls, Ferry often stopped to admire the General Motors, Ford, Chrysler, and Packard displays. He commented on their size and their rounded shapes, and Komenda made mental notes. Americans introduced four-headlight treatments for their cars, and soon Komenda had a full-scale mock-up of his Typ 644, showing two variations on quad lighting.

Komenda had drawn the Typ 356 on an 82.6-inch (2,098-mm) wheelbase. By 1957, he had stretched his 356 updates to 94.5 inches (2,400 mm). But he was misreading

1964 Typ 901 Ferry Porsche awaited his secretary, Helene Werkmeister, to be seated in the prototype Typ 901. The first production example drove out of the factory on September 14, 1964. A naming conflict with French carmaker Peugeot forced Porsche to renumber the car as 911 after barely a couple dozen were completed

(Top) 1961 Typ 754 T7 The pathway to the next Porsche was littered with dozens of designs, models, and prototypes; each drew closer to the car's final appearance. Under F.A. "Butzi" Porsche's supervision, designer Gerhard Schröder and chief modeler Heinrich Klie created the shape of the car over four years of steady revisions.

(Above) 1963 Typ 901 T8 Factory mechanic, racer, and test driver Herbert Linge took an early 901 out for a spin—literally, and one after another, testing its stability in snow. This prototype, number 4, still used twin exhaust pipes and was testing one of a variety of air intakes in the rear deck.

his boss. Even his modeler, Heinrich Klie, who had perfected Komenda's 550 and 718 Spyders, had fallen into the trap of developing a bigger 356.

To redirect Komenda's interpretations, Ferry hired Albrecht Graf von Goertz. Goertz was a German who in 1936 had emigrated to the United States, where he had rebodied Ford Model As and Bs for clients as well as himself. One of these impressed industrial designer Raymond Loewy, who saw enough promise in Goertz, he put him through school and then to work. In 1953, Goertz opened his own studio and met Max Hoffman. These days, Hoffman was selling Porsche, Mercedes-Benz, and BMW cars, and he steered two commissions to Goertz from BMW. One was a curvaceous 2+2 Model 503 as a coupe and cabriolet, and the other was a new trim and muscular two-seat roadster, the 507. Through Hoffman, Ferry commissioned Goertz to design the next Porsche.

What emerged was unexpectedly avant-garde. No Porsche up to this time had used the "folded paper" hard edges and sharp, abrupt cut lines that were coming into vogue in American styling studios. Ferry remained open-minded—it was strikingly different from Komenda's and Klie's concepts—and brought Goertz to Zuffenhausen to sculpt a model. Ferry *had* expressed interest in a *slightly* larger car with more interior and front storage space, spurred by comments he heard from repeat customers. Goertz followed his orders, but as his model emerged, it was clearly too American, too "Goertz" for Ferry's conservative tastes; for better or worse, Komenda had defined Porsche's style as rounded and organic.

It had been a costly experiment. Goertz introduced Klie and his modelers to Plasticine, a material American studios relied on. It allowed subtle forms revealed by gently scraping away excess material. But it was expensive. One of Ferry's body designers, Eugen Kolb, recalled hearing Ferry complain, "We could have made the model out of butter for what it cost." Klie's modelers swept up the scrapings off the floor to recycle them into the next model.

Ferry asked Goertz to try again. This time, Ferry also put Klie to work. The two worked on opposite sides of the

(Top) 1964 Typ 901 Prototype Porsche has always described its raw car body, before anything is mounted on or attached to it, as the "body-in-white," for obvious reasons. Here, mechanics reckon with how the series car will be assembled.

(Above) 1964 Typ 901 Sales Brochure When Peugeot notified Porsche that it could not use a model designation with a "0" in the middle because Peugeot had registered its trademark in France, Porsche already had printed several hundred of these brochures. But it had thousands more waiting for the press run as Ferry hurriedly changed the zero to a one.

1965 Typ 912 Coupe While Ferry's designers and engineers designed an all-new car body and a 130-horsepower opposed six-cylinder engine, the company had extra engines for its final four-cylinder Typ 356SC. So, Porsche conceived of a lower-priced companion model, the Typ 902 (which became the 912). Porsche priced it at $4,083 (DM 16,250) , compared to the 911 at $5,502 (DM 21,900).

same model, Klie on the passenger side while Goertz shaped the driver's side. By mid-1957, the two versions offered Ferry a glimpse of the future. Goertz's forms introduced a long, continuously sweeping roof line from the top of the windshield to the taillights.

Throughout all this time, Ferry's oldest son F.A. had shown interest and talent in design. F.A., known as Butzi to family and colleagues, attended a prestigious art and design school for the 1957 fall term but returned to his father's Works for a practical education from Goertz, Klie, and Komenda. He immediately commenced an early-days executive training program Ferry instituted for him. He started in engine design and assembly—to understand the heart of their cars. Within a year, he apprenticed with Komenda, who assigned him to the racing department, working for manager Wilhelm Hild. Butzi had a hand in the simple, clean, functional bodies of the company's Formula Two racers, the Typ 718/2 and 787. He was comfortable with Hild, but direct involvement with Komenda proved an awkward fit despite years of acquaintance. Komenda had started with Ferdinand in 1931, four years before Butzi was born. Now the grandson was moving into his job.

By this time, Goertz had returned to the United States, and design of the next Porsche had divided into two camps: Komenda's more traditional 356-inspired efforts and Klie's proposals evolving from Goertz. It was a tricky process; Klie and collaborator body designer Gerhard Schröder worked for Komenda. Yet they were offering counterproposals to their boss's ideas. Things got stickier as Butzi's self-confidence grew. In an interview decades later, he admitted, "I was never convinced that we must build a new Porsche like the old one." Ferry went even further: "No feature of the 356 era should unconditionally be carried over to the new model." Friction between the body engineer and the owner's son was not unexpected.

Throughout the company, these were busy times. Late 1959 brought Porsche's Typ 356 B to the public.

1964 Typ 901/911
Porsche designers invested effort in making the cockpit comfortable and familiar, especially with its instrument cluster. A large tachometer anchored the center with a combination oil temperature/pressure gauge and, at far left, a combination fuel level and oil level gauge. The speedometer sat to the right of the tach, with a clock at far right. Serial production cars arrived with a bright metal "911" mounted at the far right of the wood fascia.

1965 Typ 912
While a passenger sat patiently waiting, a photographer shot the instrument panel of the series production 912 with its three simplified instruments. The fasciawas metal.

Within months, the racing department introduced its new special-body GT car, the Typ 756 Abarth Carrera, and its competition sports car, the Typ 718 RS60, not to mention its new Formula racer, Butzi's Typ 787.

Meanwhile, Zuffenhausen was closing in around Porsche. There was no room to grow, even as Ferry knew the company needed to do just that. He dispatched his cousin, Ghislane Kaes and Hans Kern, his chief financial adviser, to find a site for future growth. At the recommendation of mechanic Herbert Linge who lived there, they went to visit the municipality of Weissach, some 16 miles (25 km) away. A property was available between Weissach and the town of Flacht. The parcel was three times larger than he wanted and much more costly. Ferry was angry, but he quickly recognized he had no alternatives. Although it was more than he wanted to spend, he now had room for a skid pad and test track for developing road-going and racing cars, and room for engineering and design expansion. But one problem nagged at him. Komenda continued offering four-seaters with adult-size rear seats and legroom. Klie, Schröder, and Butzi advocated a 2+2, with rear seats for occasional or emergency use. What was more, the next Porsche didn't have an engine yet!

Ferry's customers had expressed to him their other desire: more power. He set a target of 130 horsepower, the output of his planned 2-liter Typ 356 Carrera 2 and 356 C GS Carrera 2. But this was a race-bred—and, in truth, race-intended—four-cylinder. It was noisy and high-strung, fine for performance loyalists but not for a comfortable GT.

The engine design team had developed one concept through 1959 and 1960, but it failed in all Ferry's goals. It didn't make 130 horsepower, and, a young development engineer named Helmuth Bott reported after his first and only nighttime test drive in November 1960, "It's as loud as a threshing machine. We have to forget about this." It relied on pushrod-operated valves that limited engine speed and meant any horsepower increase for racing required cylinder enlargement. It had no competition potential. Ferry sent everyone back to work.

1964 Typ 901-01 Engine for the Typ 911 Porsche developed and fitted an all-new 1,991 cubic centimeter displacment opposed six-cylinder engine for the Typ 911. It developed 130 horsepower at 6100 revolutions per minute, suitable to push the car from 0 to 62 miles per hour (0 to 100 kilometers per hour) in 9.1 seconds and on to a top speed of 130 miles per hour (210 kilometers per hour).

1965 Typ 616-36 engine for the Typ 912 This 1,582 cubic centimeter displacement opposed four-cylinder engine came from Porsche's previous Typ 356SC model and provided buyers with 90 horsepower. This took the car from 0 to 62 miles per hour (0 to 100 kilometers per hour), in 13.5 seconds and to a top speed of 115 miles per hour (185 kilometers per hour).

It was nearly a year before the body design was resolved. The design department had posted full-size side-view drawings of Komenda's latest 356 notchback roof revision and of a long-roofline fastback from Klie and Schröder for a review in mid-October 1961. Ferry was there with Butzi, Schröder, Kolb, and Komenda. What happened next was so bold and unexpected it solidified Ferry's ideas and changed his company in the same instant.

Komenda walked in, approached the Klie/Schröder drawing that Butzi had supervised, and rewrote dimensions on their drawing—stretching the wheelbase, the overall length, and the rear seat and legroom measurements while Ferry looked on. Then the body engineer turned and, pointing from one drawing to the other, asked, "How do you choose now? This or this?" At that moment, the problems Ferry had heard about between his body man and his son were clear.

"We make this," Ferry said, pointing to the 2+2 design Butzi had supervised with Schröder and Klie.

To protect his choice from further meddling, Ferry rented space in next-door Reutter Karosserie's basement design studios and moved Schröder and his team of body designers into the coachbuilder's building. But Komenda had worked with Reutter for nearly two decades and had friends who kept him up to date on progress in the basement—and occasionally made changes on his behalf. Still, for the most part, the Schröder/Klie/Butzi concept moved steadily toward production.

In other parts of the Works, engineers had developed a new opposed six-cylinder engine. Young racing engine designer Hans Mezger knew overhead cams were crucial for future horsepower development; he had used them in his Formula One Typ 753 and sports car Typ 771 engines, both based on Porsche's Typ 360 Cisitalia Grand Prix car and Ernst Fuhrmann's Typ 547. Mezger collaborated with another young engineer, Horst Marchart, who had invented a chain-driven overhead camshaft system that used a hydraulic chain tensioner.

1964 Typ 901 The profile of the 901/911 has been called "iconic," but also "clean," "simple," and "organic." Many automobile designers used the same words for the 911's predecessors, the 356 series. It's no coincidence that whatever the circumstance, the 911 silhouette is quickly recognizable throughout the world.

The next Porsche engine evolved through Typ numbers, from the "threshing machine" Typ 745 to Typ 821 to Typ 901, a number arrived at from Ferry's agreement with VW for parts distribution through their computer system—the 900 numbers were the sequence available for Porsche, and initially both car and engine shared the same Typ number. Another young engineer arrived in April 1963, Ferdinand Piëch. He was Ferry's nephew and had, like his cousin Butzi, watched and listened to grandfather Ferdinand and uncle Ferry discussing engineering problems and solutions. But Piëch possessed an unassailable desire for only the highest-quality materials. Right from the start, it affected the 901 engine when Piëch advocated for a dry-sump lubrication system, the better for aggressive racing conditions.

There still were details to resolve and thousands of kilometers of testing to complete, but Ferry committed to the 1963 international auto show at Frankfurt to debut his new car, the Typ 901. Journalists saw a yellow one for the first time on Friday September 13, 1963. Even though Ferry announced that production start was a year off and no one but Porsche engineers had ever driven one, the company started recording sales.

Full of hope and excitement, Ferry, motorsports director and public relations boss Huschke von Hanstein, and some sales staff headed to Paris for its international Auto Salon a month later. They never expected the letter that arrived days after the opening.

Automobiles Peugeot had registered with the French copyright office the rights to designate its car models with three digits that used a 0 in the middle. Peugeot's first car, the Model 201, had appeared in 1929, and by 1963, it offered a 403 and 404. The letter advised Porsche it could not designate its new car a 901 in France!

1965 Auto Show Circuit With the 356s remaining in their inventory, Porsche ringed the perimeter of its show booths with S and SC cabriolets and coupes that visitors had to negotiate before seeing what really was new. And that was its startling red racing Typ 904 Carrera GTS and its cool, subtle blue Typ 911. This full line was still street-legal throughout Europe and the US.

Von Hanstein, a baron, was too diplomatic to point out that Porsche's Typ 804 had won the French Grand Prix a year before. He forwarded the letter to Ferry on October 10 and together with sales director Wolfgang Raether, they sorted through solutions. Call it 901 GT? No; sales brochures were ready for printing in German, French, and English, and there was no room to add two letters. But they could replace the middle zero with a one. Ferry contacted Peugeot. His factory had begun assembling the 901 Porsche on September 14. He stopped everything; then with Peugeot's blessing, he began again around November 9. Reports vary as to how many 901s the Works assembled, but reports in the Porsche Archiv reveal barely a dozen. All were pilot production examples requiring more than a full day to assemble. Marketing staff had conceived a companion model using the remaining four-cylinder engines from the 356 C series, and with Peugeot's actions, this Typ 902 became the 912.

Ferry had turned fifty-five on September 9, 1963, five days before assembly began. But another unexpected turn of events likely added to his gray hair. When he had approached Reutter to commission bodies for the 901/911, the owning family balked. The founder had died before the war, and his son and successor had died during wartime bombing in Stuttgart. The family wanted to sell. Reutter knew far too much about Porsche's business for Ferry to risk exposing it to others. Like his acquiring the land at Weissach, he had no choice. He paid roughly $1.5 million at the time (DM 6 million) and almost doubled the size of his Zuffenhausen plant and the number of employees he now directed.

1963–1966

9

Necessity Is the Mother of Invention

Typ 904 Carrera GTS and 906 Carrera 6

In order to control the rivalry between Erwin Komenda and Butzi, Ferry Porsche had named his twenty-eight-year-old son design manager and more clearly differentiated Komenda's title as body construction manager.

When Ferry approached family friend Carlo Abarth about a second run of the diminutive Italian-bodied GTL racing coupes on the new GS 2000 platform, Abarth unexpectedly announced his own new race car, the Abarth Simca 2000. Porsche had essentially owned this class with its GTR and Carrera GS 2.0. When Ferry, racing engineers Wilhelm Hild and Hubert Mimler, and competition director Huschke von Hanstein committed to making a new race car for FIA Group 3 GT and endurance races, the design assignment went to Butzi's team.

"Mr. Hild's staff used to pound every racing driver's seat out of sheet metal," Butzi recalled in the early 1990s. "But they began to use fiberglass because it took so much less time. The driver came in, sat down, and they made a mold. It was done not only for factory team drivers but also customers.

1964 Typ 904 Carrera GTS Assembly Sitting on their welded box-section steel chassis, the fiberglass bodies—Porsche's first—of its Grand Touring Sports coupes awaited completion. When its planned engine wasn't ready, Porsche decided to install its well-proven 180-horsepower Typ 587 two-liter, four-cam, four-cylinder Carrera engine.

1965 Typ 904 Carrera GTS and Typ 911 "Monte Carlo" Porsche entered its brand new 904 and 911 in a grueling road test/road race in the Monte Carlo Rallye. This event started from a dozen cities in Europe, converged on the Mediterranean city, and then ran two brutal overnight trials over snow-and-ice-covered Alpine roads. One 904 placed second overall; the 911 classified fifth.

"When the customers accepted this, we thought, 'Why don't we make a whole car?' At first we simply had made parts out of plastic that had been sheet metal in the past." Butzi had watched Hild's staff replace body panels on the Typ 804 F1 car with fiberglass in 1962. "This was faster," he added.

And speed was necessary. Ferry had authorized the new Group 3 car, but regulations required the manufacturer to complete one hundred examples before it was allowed to race. His chassis engineers designed a radical variable-section ladder frame that narrowed at the front for steering and suspension but stayed wide at the rear to accommodate the midmounted engine, transaxle gearbox, and rear suspension.

Butzi assigned modeler Heinrich Klie and chief designer Gerhard Schröder to work on the car. Before joining Porsche, Schröder had specialized in convertible body design and engineering, and he understood the contribution the car body made to chassis stiffness. The engineers and designers began work in November 1962 when the regulations became clear.

Porsche originally planned to race this new car, designated Typ 904, using a competition version of the six-cylinder engine planned for the Typ 901/911. But delays made that impossible, and Hans Mezger, who by now had designed several of Porsche's racing engines, set to work upgrading the 2.0-liter Typ 587 Carrera four-cylinder. Porsche's racing department had assembled more than 200 of these engines so its acceptance was guaranteed. Mezger devised two versions, a 155-horsepower configuration for road use and a 180-horsepower model for racing.

Klie modeled a very simple body from Plasticine. Schröder almost immediately began making body panel production drawings, knowing the car was to be produced by hand-laying sheets of fiberglass inside female molds of the full-size body.

"We could have improved the aerodynamics," Butzi recalled. "Mr. Tomala [Hans Tomala, Ferry's chief engineer] even meant to elongate the car because the aerodynamics would have been slightly better that way, but there was simply no time."

"And that is also the reason why the car body remained so unchanged," he continued. "This car was four months, working days and nights, from the first Plasticine model to completion of the driving prototype." But it was within a few sleepless weeks from the start that Butzi Porsche really came to understand his role as design manager.

"I think that an advantage was the fact that I was the son, which can entail advantages and disadvantages. People would pay more attention to what I said due to

(Above) 1965 Typ 904 Carrera GTS Coupe Designed and assembled on a 100-day deadline, design manager Butzi Porsche turned the project over to his two most experienced employees, modeler Heinrich Klie and body designer Gerhard Schröder. Years later, Schröder admitted the shape was mostly Klie's, he just drew what the modeler had formed.

(Top) 1965 Typ 904/8 Bergspyder "Kanguruh" Squat, stubby, and mostly unloved, this hillclimber demonstrated Ferdinand Piëch's earliest obsessions in which form followed function. Weighing just 1,275 pounds (570 kg), it used a 210-horsepower 2.0-liter Typ 771 opposed eight-cylinder engine. After hopping and lurching for 447 miles (720 km), over Sicilian mountain roads, it finished second overall.

(Top) 1965 Typ 904 Carrera GTS Coupe Porsche retained a dozen of its 904s for Works racing and testing. It installed the new 210-horsepower, 1,991 cubic centimeter displacement opposed-six-cylinder racing engine. Porsche raced them in Prototype classes, running countless races to develop the engine and their ideas for the next generation racers.

For the car body, Klie relied on shapes he had made for a similar coupe, the Typ 718 GTR.His 904 became the "production" version of the GTR, with 109 assembled. Porsche sold a 155-horsepower road-going version or the 180-horsepower racer for $7,462 (DM 29,700), at the Works.

the fact that I had a direct line to the boss . . . I would be able to work out a proposition, put it in front of him and say, 'See! That's it!'"

Gerhard Schröder remembered the process vividly. In an interview nearly fifty years after their work on the car, he agreed with Butzi's description.

"We were very tight on time. Mr. Klie was shaping the car and I was drawing day and night. We had other ideas but we were told we could not even do a second version. And when we finished, we put it in Butzi's hands and he took it directly to his father. He approved it and I started full-size drawings immediately." The full-size car was 41.9 inches (1,065 mm) tall, 161 inches (4,090 mm) long, and 61 inches (1540 mm) wide. The frame weighed just 99 pounds (45 kg).

The bodies were another matter. They were formed by hand with three layers of glass fiber impregnated with resin at the nearby aircraft manufacturer Heinkel

1965 Typ 906-8 Bergspyder Lessons from the Kanguruh inspired the next generation Bergspyder with a slightly more aerodynamic body that still emphasized weight and efficiency. At 1,102 pounds (500 kg) with its improved 270-horsepower opposed eight-cylinder engine, the 141-inch (3,580-mm) Bergspyders raced on mountains and on road circuits.

Flugzeugbau, and some of the technicians used more material than others—so, while the average body weighed roughly 220 pounds (100 kilograms), some were heavier and some lighter. They completed two each day. The fully assembled car weighed in at 1,633 pounds (740 kg). Its 180-horsepower 1,966cc racing engine shot the car from 0 to 62 miles per hour (0 to 100 kilometers per hour), in 5.5 seconds and on to a top speed of 157 miles per hour (252 kilometers per hour), using its newly developed five-speed transaxle. A year after project start, Porsche unveiled the Typ 904 Carrera GTS at Solitude Palace near Porsche Works on November 26, 1963. Incredibly, the maker completed the hundredth car on March 31, 1964.

The Works assembled 106 cars with four-cylinder engines, and another four, designated Typ 906, debuted the flat-six racing engine with 210 horsepower, which competed as a prototype. Porsche kept 10 cars for its own racing plans. With a large and loyal crowd of racers in the United States, it shipped the first two "customer" cars to the States for races in Daytona, Florida, on February 15 (in which one finished third) and February 16 (in which one placed fifth in the 1,242.7-mile [2,000-km] race and won its prototype class). A month later, five of the cars started at Sebring, Florida, and again, one of these won its prototype class. With Porsche engineers as well as factory mechanics present, the company learned a lot from these events. Porsche had done well for several years in Italy's Targa Florio, and the race in April 1964 really showed the new car's strengths; a pair of "customer" 904s finished first and second overall.

But Ferdinand Piëch already had concluded these 904s were compromised by their capabilities as regular road cars for nonracers. He commandeered some chassis and developed several ultralightweight spyders for hillclimb, a type of racing that penalized

(Below) 1966 Typ 906 Carrera 6 and Typ 911 Coupes The earliest 911s are small cars, until you park Porsche's Typ 906 beside it. The race car stood just 38.6-inches (980-mm), high. Even Ford's legendary GT40 was taller. The 906 resulted from Ferdinand Piëch's drive to improve on Porsche's 904.

(Bottom) 1966 Typ 906 at Nürburgring Bodies for the 904 were sprayed into molds but Piëch insisted his 906s were molded between two presses, insuring greater consistency and less weight. At 1,367 pounds (620 kg), it was 66 pounds (30 kg), lighter than the 904 due also to its magnesium-alloy engine block and other improvements.

weight and rewarded Piëch's style of no-holds-barred and no-expense-spared development. These 904 "Bergspyders" appeared as 1,257-pound (570-kg), 141-inch-long (3,580-mm), stubby projectiles. Fitted with the eight-cylinder Typ 771 engines tuned to 260 horsepower, their handling was so tricky mechanics and drivers nicknamed them "Kangaroos." One placed second at the 1965 Targa, but others crashed because of their twitchy roadholding.

Through 1965, von Hanstein and Piëch had advocated for a stronger, lighter tube frame, and this earned the designation Typ 906. Unexpectedly, Ferrari had introduced the compact mid-engine 2.0-liter Dino, whose specifications suggested domination of Porsche's 904s in either endurance or hillclimb racing. For an important Swiss hillclimb, the two men asked Eugen Kolb to devise a shapely coupe that used British Lotus F1-car suspension and its smaller wheels to get the car lower to the ground.

When Ferry began to consider a second run of 904s to appease customer demand, Piëch essentially refused to cooperate, urging they instead adopt Kolb's body design to a slightly larger tube frame for GT and endurance racing. This became the Typ 906 Carrera 6, using the competition version of the Typ 901/911 engine. To better manage body weight, Kolb and Schröder designed a body assembled from premolded fiberglass parts, which could be rigorously weight controlled. Kolb's body tucked in around the cockpit behind a compound-curve windshield. The cockpit left a broad door sill, and Kolb, Schröder, and others wondered how to get drivers in and out. Engine man Mezger remembered the 1955 Mercedes-Benz 300 SL coupe, which also had massive sills and used gullwing doors. These earned the 906 the nickname "Batmobile." A magazine review at the time described the car as "Shaped from the inside by the regulations, from the outside by the wind."

The hillclimber was low and small, due to its 13-inch (33 cm) diameter Lotus wheels and tires. But as Ferry had anticipated making another hundred 904s, he had preordered 15-inch (38 cm) wheels and tires, and, against Piëch's protests, he insisted the 906 use up this stock. With its 210-horsepower opposed six-cylinder

1966 Typ 906 Carrera Customer Cars By the end of 1966, Porsche had manufactured 65 of the 906s, 52 of which they sold to their racing customers. While the Works team experimented with opposed eight-cylinder engines, the customer cars raced the 1991 cubic centimeter displacement, 210-horsepower engine and five-speed gearbox. Privateers earned many class victories and championships throughout Europe and the US.

engine, the Carrera 6 weighed 1,367 pounds (620 kg), nearly 120 pounds (55 kg), less than the ready-to-race 904 fitted with the same Typ 901 six-cylinder engine. It was only 1 inch (25 mm) taller, but measured 5.5 inches (140 mm) wider, and 2 inches (50 mm) shorter. With standard gearing, it accelerated from 0 to 62 miles miles per hour (0 to 100 kilometers per hour), in 4.5 seconds and reached a top speed of 169 miles per hour (272 kilometers per hour). FIA regulations had changed, and Porsche needed to assemble just fifty for homologation.

As before, Ferry sent the new racers to America first, entering Daytona and Sebring again. At Daytona, a single new 906 went up against the much more powerful Ford GT40s and Ferrari P2s. At the end of 24 hours, the 906 placed sixth overall and won its prototype class. Works-entered 904s took seventh and eighth, winning the Sports 2000 class as well. At Sebring, Porsche entered two Works 906s, and three private owners raced their new cars. At the end of 12 hours, Porsche's team car placed fourth, again claiming the Prototype 200 class win; two private teams finished sixth and eighth.

Porsche's Typ 904 Carrera GTS and Typ 906 Carrera 6 had established a pattern. The company's racers dominated the 2.0-liter classes and held their own, respectably, against bigger, faster, more powerful cars from Ford and Ferrari. But this wasn't enough for Piëch. Not unexpectedly, he had grander ambitions.

PORSCHE
PORSCHE

1967-1974

10

The 911 Perfected, Polished, and Plenty Potent

911 S, 911 R, 911 RS, 911 RSR

There were two variations on the Typ 356 that Ferry knew he had to carry into the 901: a cabriolet and a Super version with a higher-tuned engine. But in the complicated and occasionally dramatic days of 1961–1963, these two variations got lost—though not forgotten.

More than a year before Porsche's former Reutter Works assembled the first 901s, Ferry discussed these delayed desires with Butzi. Butzi's design department modelers, designers, and styling engineers transferred in from Erwin Komenda's body construction department to ensure that everything Butzi's department designed could be successfully manufactured. Butzi also had Gerhard Schröder, who, before joining Porsche, was the cabriolet design engineer for Karmann and perfected the Karmann Ghia convertible for Volkswagen. While Karmann had manufactured hundreds of bodies for 356s, they also had continuously done development work for Porsche even after the 356 line ended.

For a 901 cabriolet, Karmann proposed three options: a padded cloth top similar to the Typ 356 B and C versions; a less sophisticated speedster-style top that unsnapped from removable roof bows and stowed underneath a rear trunk; and a rollover bar behind

1973 Typ 911 Carrera RSR 3.0 IROC Coupes US racing team owner Roger Penske dreamed up a match-race series for a dozen of the world's best drivers—the International Race of Champions—and he convinced Porsche to provide identically prepared 3.0-liter Carreras painted in vivid colors. It proved a tough match because nearly half had never raced a Porsche and had to learn its handling.

(Top) 1967 Typ 911 S Coupe Porsche introduced its most potent series production 911, the S for Super, at the Motodrom Hockenheim where journalists also drove the cars. The S not only provided better performance but also greater luxury in the interior with a leather-covered steering wheel, a woven-texture treatment on the fascia, and leather covered Recaro seats. The S introduced Fuchs five-spoke alloy wheels.

(Above) 1967 Typ 901/10 Engine for the Typ 911 S The S used an upgraded version of Porsche's 2.0-liter opposed six-cylinder engine producing 160 horsepower at 6,600 revolutions per minute. This provided acceleration from 0 to 62 miles per hour (0 to 100 kilometers per hour), in 7.6 seconds. Its top speed was 140 miles per hour (225 kilometers per hour). Porsche sold the new S for $6,135 (DM 24,480) at the Zuffenhausen Works.

the front seat to which removable panels were attached. By mid-1964, designer Hans Plochman and engineer Werner Trenkler had developed two cabriolet prototypes by sawing the tops off prototype 901s. This revealed two irresolvable problems. First, the 901 engine cooling fan sat upright in the engine compartment, filling space that might store a collapsed cloth roof. Fixing this required a new body design or a change in the engine fan; neither was practical. But worse, these topless cars were so flexible they were nearly undrivable. Some additional structure was essential.

This put a rollover bar idea front and center, and by mid-June 1964, Plochman and Trenkler had a new design. Ferry sent this to Karmann for the coachbuilder to fabricate a running prototype. Unexpectedly, developments in the United States entered Ferry's cabriolet considerations around this time. Ralph Nader, a zealous automobile safety advocate, had drawn attention to cars found to be risky. His target was a compact Chevrolet that used an air-cooled engine mounted at the rear; Chevrolet had come to Porsche for engineering help and adopted its recommendation of a swing-axle rear suspension. Chevrolet engineers ordered a transverse bar to limit axle swing, similar to what Porsche fitted, but GM's directors vetoed its $4 cost as too expensive. Nader focused first on the Corvair but soon targeted convertibles universally, and Ferry and others began to worry that the United States—Porsche's largest market—might outlaw open cars. This strengthened the argument for their new innovation. While others wondered about disguising it, Butzi advocated emphasizing it as a safety feature. He wrapped the bar in brushed stainless steel. Marketing named it the Targa, playing on an Italian word that meant shield as well as paying homage to the Targa Florio, which Porsche had won so often. The company offered the semiopen car for 911s and 912s in spring 1966, a few months before Ferry's other variation emerged.

Porsche engineers had proceeded unhindered with plans for a Super model. Upgrading the pistons,

(Top) 1968 Typ 911 R Coupe The 911 R might be called Ferdinand Piëch's "magnificent obsession." He and his engineering staff worked relentlessly to lighten, strengthen, and improve every element of the 911 to form the perfect "Rennsport" competition car. A road-ready R weighed 1,746 pounds (800 kg), while the 911S from which it was derived, came in at 2,270 pounds (1,030 kg).

(Above) 1967 Typ 912 Targa Police Car The German Autobahn Police and their Dutch counterparts were early adopters of these specially prepared 912s using the new Targa body with its removable solid roof panel and soft rear window. While the 912 Targa had a top speed of only 121 miles per hour (195 kilometers per hour) compared to a new S at 140 miles per hour (225 kilometers per hour), nothing was faster than their two-way radios.

(Top) 1969 Typ 911 GTS Coupe As early as 1968, Porsche's racing department began creating a number of hybrids, usually the engine of one car in the lighter-weight chassis and body of another; these earned designations such as the 911 ST and the 911 TR. These usually also received further reinforcement and weight loss; this GTS may be the ultimate version, using a fuel-injected, endurance-prepared S engine in an extremely modified E platform. It worked flawlessly, winning the 84-hour Marathon de la Route race around the Nürburgring.

connecting rods, cylinder heads and valves, timing, and carburetors boosted engine output from the 130 brake horsepower base model to 160 brake horsepower. Acceleration from 0 to 62 miles per hour (0 to 100 kilometers per hour), dropped from 9.1 to 7.6 seconds, and top speed increased from 130 to 140 miles per hour (210 to 225 kilometers per hour). Suspension upgrades and forged alloy wheels improved handling. They reduced overall weight from 2,382 to 2,272 pounds (1,080 to 1,030 kg). Porsche introduced the 911 S in November as a 1967 coupe or Targa model.

With its weight reduction, the S was immediately popular with GT racers. One of the first things competitors did was strip out the luxurious S interior and anything else that might slow the car. But Ferdinand Piëch was already far ahead of them. He set his racing engineers to work on a new variation meant to test every limit of the young 911 for competition; weight and horsepower were prime concerns. To protect his project from interference, he relied on Karosserie Baur, an outside coachwork firm in Stuttgart, to assemble cars he designated the 911 R.

While much of the basic 911 steel structure remained, the doors, front and rear deck lids, front fenders, and front and rear bumpers were molded in thin-gauge fiberglass-reinforced plastic (FRP). Baur fitted a 4-millimeter-thick (0.15-inch) glass windshield and 2-millimeter-thick side windows and backlight. They removed the passenger sun visor, glove box door, interior door panels, carpeting, ashtray and cigarette lighter, and interior heater and reduced dashboard instrumentation from five large dials to three—speedometer, tachometer, and a combination oil pressure and temperature gauge. Overall weight

(Above) Typ 911 Carrera RS Prototype Coupe Despite all the weight saving, 911s still had a problem with aerodynamic lift, front and rear. To keep the rear end down—improving high-speed stability and cornering—engineer Peter Falk devised this tail, the Bürzel. It demonstrably improved handling immediately.

1973 Typ 911 Carrera RS 2.7 Coupe Porsche prepared two Carreras for the 3,293-mile (5,300-km), East Africa Safari by increasing ground clearance to 9.8 inches (25 cm); reinforcing shock absorbers, and adding an aluminum underbody. Björn Waldegård, driving No. 10, had 210 horsepower available, providing him 134 miles per hour (215 kilometers per hour) in his car that weighed nearly 2,425 pounds (1,100 kg), with spare parts, winches, ropes, shovels, spare fuel and oil. But inadequate testing doomed the cars to failure.

dropped from 2,270 to 1,764 pounds (1,030 to 800 kg), for the 911 S coupe to pounds for the R.

For power, Piëch fitted the opposed six-cylinder engine from his new sports car, the Typ 906 Carrera 6. This 2.0-liter, dual-overhead-camshaft engine developed 210 horsepower. The racing shop produced four prototypes, each further refining Piëch's direction and goals. Then Baur assembled twenty Rs as 1968 models. Huschke von Hanstein urged Piëch and Ferry to expand the project. With only twenty examples, the R models were forced to race against other prototypes, including Porsche's 906. A proposal discovered in Porsche Archiv discussed assembling two hundred examples of a "911 R Touring" model to homologate it for production-based Group 4. But Piëch was completely uninterested. This car was his test bed for future ideas for the 911 and other sports cars he already had in mind. Others inside Porsche argued the car was too loud, too crude, too much like a race car to sell to even their most loyal performance enthusiasts. That idea had to wait for several years and a significant change in management.

Piëch's Rs continued racing into the early 1970s—and led to a plethora of alphabetical hybrids. Porsche introduced a new roadgoing model in 1969, the 911 T. It, the base model, and the S had a new chassis whose 2.3-inch (58 mm)-longer wheelbase addressed interior space needs and the car's tail-happy handling. The 911 T weighed 22 pounds (10 kg), less than the base 911, which made it a popular secret among racers and led to a little-known Works hybrid, the 911 ST (S engine on the T platform). There were 911 SRs and even a trio of 911 GTS models, which took weight control to extremes that included forming aluminum headlight buckets to save precious grams and ounces.

1973 Typ 911 Carrera RS 2.7 Right-Hand Drive Coupe Some thought the rear spoiler ugly, and marketing predicted the car would not sell. Porsche needed 500 in production to qualify for racing; marketing was wrong and Porsche ultimately assembled 1,580, including this first of a series of 117 with right-hand drive.

By the early 1970s, Porsche's problems in racing were not in power-to-weight ratio but its cars' aerodynamics and their effect on roadholding, handling, and cornering.

Porsche lost races to Ford and BMW because the 911s lost grip in the turns. Air flowed underneath the rounded nose and over the long fastback, causing lift at both ends. Ernst Fuhrmann, who had left Porsche in 1956 in a dispute over company direction, returned in 1971 as chief engineer and then chief executive. At a race, he watched "his" 911s and promptly set his engineers to work trying to answer his question: "Our cars are losing. Think about it and tell me what you will do?"

1973 Typ 911 Carrera RSR 3.0 Prototype Coupe Porsche entered three of these RSR 3.0s in the Targa Florio 11-lap race this year, over 44.7 miles (72 kilometers), of open roads on Sicily. Their full-width rear spoiler—nicknamed the Mary Stuart collar for the English queen's typical apparel—was one of many other modifications. The effort yielded them first overall, third (with this car) and sixth overall.

The wind tunnel eventually provided the answer: a subtle lip in front at the bottom edge of the front valence that directed air to the sides of the car instead of lifting it. Porsche tested the idea, and Piëch rushed it into production because of its contribution to driving safety.

Rear lift also affected the 911s at high speeds. More time in the wind tunnel delivered a fixed tail wing that did in the rear what the lip had done in front. Designers nicknamed it the Antlers, though the public recognized a duck's upturned tail and called it *Bürzel*.

New design chief Tony Lapine hated the ducktail for altering the 911's otherwise pure lines. After engineers established its optimum height, he shortened it several centimeters to fit his aesthetic. But as with the lip, handling and safety won the battle. To placate the critics, Porsche introduced it on a new series, the 911 Carrera RS 2.7, which resurrected the Carrera name after a ten-year absence on 356 models. The RS was for *Rennsport*,

1973 Typ 911 Carrera RSR Turbo 2.1 Coupe Turbocharging the Porsche required a displacement reduction to meet regulations, but it still developed 500 horsepower in a car weighing 1,746 pounds (800 kg). Massive handling problems required an enormous rear wing to keep the car on the ground. CEO Ernst Fuhrmann hated it and he ordered racing engineer Norbert Singer to "paint it black so no one will see it."

racing sport; the 2.7 designated its 2,687cc engine displacement. Porsche needed to manufacture 500 examples to homologate it for production GT racing. When some inside management held their heads and complained that the ducktail was ugly, that the car was too loud, too crude, and too much like a race car to sell even 50 units, others resurrected a suggestion from Piëch's 911 R: two versions, one for competition and the other for "touring" with a luxurious interior comparable to the flagship 911 S.

Unexpectedly, when Porsche loyalists learned that a "very special" 911 was coming—one that, in its lightest trim (the Sports Kit) weighed 2,115 pounds (960 kg), with an engine developing 210 horsepower—the entire 500-unit production allocation sold out in three months. Ferry authorized another 500-car run, and it sold nearly as rapidly. Porsche assembled something like 200 cars with the Sport Kit option—or RS Lightweights, as the cars became known. When manufacturing finally quit after some 1,580 total cars, Porsche had qualified the Carrera RS in a much more populous Group 4, where it dominated its competition.

For racing customers, Porsche produced an RSR. Initially, just two appeared in 1972, with slightly larger cylinder bore to yield 2,806cc displacement. With significant internal upgrades throughout the 1,984-pound (900-kg), Carrera RSR 2.8, these engines offered racers 300 horsepower. Customer deliveries started for the 1973 season, and Porsche assembled fifty-seven, including those it kept for its Works racing program. For the 1974 season, Porsche introduced the RSR 3.0 with another bore enlargement, yielding 2,993cc overall displacement and developing 315 horsepower—330 horsepower by 1975. Extremely wide wheels and tires added weight and the Carrera RSR 3.0 came in at 2,028 pounds (920 kg). Porsche declined to export either the Sport or Touring 911 Carrera RS 2.7 to the US; it could not pass emissions or safety standards. Meanwhile, the race shops assembled 109 Carrera RS 3.0 "road" cars and 50 (or so) RSR racing or rally versions.

12

1967–1982

Is There Room on the Podium?

Typ 910, 907, 909, 908

While Porsche's Typ 906 Carrera 6 represented an advance from the 904 Carrera GTS, it still left Ferdinand Piëch with the sour taste of compromise in his mouth. He had pushed 906 development with another set of tiny Bergspyders and a trio of longer-tailed coupes to test his ideas for reducing aerodynamic drag in order to increase top speed on long courses such as Le Mans. But the car was still just too big. Its 15-inch tires, a legacy from Ferry's intentions for the 904s, put massive front fenders at the front of the 906. For Piëch, one of the 906's selling points represented the full extent of its compromise: it was another road-legal car for their racing customers. But even before very many of the fifty-some Typ 906s left Porsche Works, he had begun work on its successor. And it was not just a single car but an ever-improving series.

Next in Typ-number succession was the 907, a coupe to stretch every accomplishment the 906 had made. But first, Porsche needed a new hillclimber. With numbers 907, 908, and 909 located within Piëch's imagination, the new steel-tube space-frame Bergspyder claimed number 910. Piëch asked race-car body design engineer Eugen Kolb to create for him a two-seat coupe with a removable roof panel, which quickly made the car a spyder.

1970 Typ 908-03 Spyder at Targa Florio Brian Redman, shown here, co-drove this John Wyer-Gulf Typ 908-03 Spyder with Jo Siffert to overall victory in the 11-lap race around Sicily. The two took six hours 35 minutes 30 seconds to cover 492.1 miles (792 km) at an average speed of 74.4 miles per hour (120.2 km).

(Top) 1967 Typ 910-6 Roadster The 906s drawbacks raced on 15-inch diameter wheels and tires because of leftover supplies from the 904s. With this 910, Porsche adopted 13-inch tires, widely used in Formula One with more compounds available. Eugen Kolb designed the 910 with a removable roof panel (as shown here) to convert the coupe to a roadster. It raced with a 270-horsepower, 1,991 cubic centimeter displacement opposed six-cylinder fuel-injected engine.

(Above) 1967 Typ 907 Kurzheck (Shorttail) Coupe Porsche's race car numbering went astray in the late 1960s as designs and part availabilities sometimes leapfrogged one another. The 907 was the third tube-frame "plastic-body" race car and Eugen Kolb's body paid particular attention to drag, narrowing the cockpit to something like a jet fighter and moving the driver to the right side.

Piëch relegated all remaining 15-inch wheels and tires to the spares piles for 904s and 906s and embraced 13s. This presented two advantages: first, Formula One raced on 13s, and tire makers had developed compounds for that size that didn't exist for the 15s; second, the smaller wheels—although wider—allowed Kolb to reduce and round the front fenders. Wider tires, upgraded upper and lower A-arms, leading and trailing radius arms for the fully independent suspension with coil springs surrounding double-action dampers, and a quick rack-and-pinion steering with two turns lock to lock gave the 910 highly responsive handling.

Porsche fitted its 220-horsepower Typ 906 opposed six-cylinder engine for endurance races or the 270-horsepower Typ 771 opposed eight-cylinder engine for hillclimbs, in which it ran as a prototype. With the six, it weighed 1,279 pounds (580 kg) ; the eight put the car at 1,323 pounds (600 kg).

The 910 spyder proved right for Italy's Targa, but even its carefully managed weight was much too heavy for the weight-conscious Ferdinand Piëch and his hillclimbers. For this, engineers replaced the frame's steel tubes

with aluminum, substituted an impressive number of parts with titanium, and wrapped everything in a tiny open-cockpit body with a low windscreen. The car also carried a 16 liter, 4.2-gallon fuel tank (it only had to climb the hill; it could coast back down). All this kept weight to 1,102 pounds (500 kg), but Piëch drove his engineers to reduce the weight further. Over the course of the 1967 season, they experimented with beryllium brake rotors, which saved 31 pounds (14 kg), but learned the fumes from superheated beryllium were toxic to the mechanic tasked with replacing pads between sessions. Piëch brainstormed with racing engineer Peter Falk, whom he assigned to find a spherical fuel tank that they could then pressurize and so do away with a fuel pump. By the end of 1967, the car weighed just 924 pounds (420 kg).

But Piëch still wasn't done. Engineers eliminated the electric generator and replaced the auto battery with a small one from a motorcycle. Front coil springs came off in favor of a single transverse torsion bar. When two-time World Hillclimb Champion Gerhard Mitter took the car to Montseny, Spain, it was at its lightest: 842 pounds (382 kg). For reliability during the competition weekend, Porsche raced a larger battery and stronger fuel tank and, at 882 pounds (400 kg) the superlight Bergspyder brought Mitter his—and Porsche's—third championship.

Engineers fitted small spoilers to each side of the 1968 Bergspyder rear decklid. These linked mechanically to rear suspension members and reacted to the cornering forces to level the car. As suspension on the outside of the turn compressed, it drew down the outside spoiler and elevated the inside one, which helped increase inside tire grip.

Meanwhile, Eugen Kolb produced his most startling body design yet for the new Typ 907. He drew a car soon nicknamed "Mirage" for its cockpit's resemblance to what was then the current generation of French fighter jet with its slender bubble windshield and compact cabin. Drivers shifted to the right side, which helped them better judge their position inside turns. Kolb designed short-tail 907 Ks (*K* for *kurz*, or short) and, long tail 907 Ls (for *Langheck*, long tail).

(Top) 1967 Typ 907 K (Shorttail) Coupe For racers through terrain like this, these 907s raced with Porsche's 2.0- or 2.2-liter, 270-horsepower opposed eights, with rear wheels 12-inches (30 cm) wide, and a five-speed transmission. A six-speed transmission arrived in 1968 and 907s won countless victories including Porsche's first overall endurance wins.

(Bottom) 1969 Typ 908 Langheck (Longtail) Coupe Porsche's new race car came about as a result of racing regulations that set maximum engine displacement at 3.0 liters. Engineers designed a 2,952 cubic centimeter displacement opposed eight-cylinder that developed 320 horsepower in its first year and 350 in 1969. At Le Mans, this long tail coupe battled a GT40 for the last several hours of the race, finishing second, barely 100 meters, 320 feet behind the Ford.

Piëch's relentless efforts paid off on February 4, 1968, with a stunning debut victory at Daytona's 24-hour race. Regulations limited prototypes to 3.0 liters displacement, so Porsche entered a 2,195cc version of its opposed-eight Typ 771 producing 270 horsepower in 1,323-pound (600-kg), long tail coupes. At Le Mans in 1966, Ford's three GTs had finished in a kind of triangular squadron formation, taking first, second, and third overall and capturing newspaper headlines and photo coverage. The following year, in February 1967, Ferrari's three P3s

1969 Typ 908L Coupe Porsche introduced "active aerodynamics" at the tail end of the 908s with suspension-activated winglets or flaps at the rear edge of the rear wing. In a turn, these pushed down the inside corner and lifted the outside to flatten handling and increase traction to both wheels.

had taken Daytona's checkered flag in perfect formation, three abreast for overall first, second, and third. In 1968, after 24 hours and 2,564 miles, Porsche's three 907s earned first overall and crossed the finish in a modified arrow formation. They repeated the feat at Sebring one month later, two of their cars placing first and second overall. But Piëch still was not yet satisfied.

On the hillclimb circuit, Porsche introduced another number, the Typ 909. As Piëch's 910 spyders shed weight, they grew more challenging to drive—the mid-engine layout still hung the gearbox off the back end of the car. The 909 shifted all the running gear forward, in between the front and rear axles. But moving the gearbox inboard shoved the engine into the cockpit and relegated the driver to sitting on the front axle between the front wheels. The 909, which weighed 948 pounds (430 kilograms) , raced only twice, and its hurried development perhaps doomed its results.

Porsche's next concept was designated 908. Piëch knew of the FIA's plan to limit prototype engine displacements to 3.0 liters (and sports cars, such as Ford's GT and Ferrari's P3 to 5.0 liters), and by July 1967, racing engineers were designing a new 310-horsepower opposed eight-cylinder 2,997cc engine for a new coupe derived from the Typ 907. Tire technology had reversed upon itself, and racing-tire makers now offered a greater range of compounds in 15-inch diameter, so the Typ 908 went back to 15s; this allowed significantly larger brake rotors. The first dozen cars used steel-tube space frames, but after this, all the coupes—short and long—and an assortment of spyders used aluminum tubes. Longtail bodies grew vertical tail fins, which supported a horizontal wing that carried movable flaps at the back edge, just like the hillclimb cars had used. At the April 1968 Le Mans tests, these winged 908 L coupes weighed, 1,543 pounds (700 kg), 1 and reached 200 miles per hour (320 kilometers per hour), through Mulsanne Straight speed traps. The competition debut came a month later in Italy at Monza, where teething problems landed the best-placed 908 in eleventh. (A 907L won its class.) In mid-May at the Nürburgring, a Works 908 K finished first, and hopes rose, but a 908 third place at Spa in Belgium and a sixth at Watkins Glen in New York seemed to steer results back in the wrong direction. Then Austria gave Porsche first and second in 908s, and everyone crossed their fingers for Le Mans. Student riots in France in May and early June 1968 forced organizers to delay the 24-hour race to late September. A slipping alternator belt relegated Porsche's best-finish 908 to third; a privately owned 907 took second (and won the prototype class) behind a 5.0-liter Ford GT.

1968-69 Typ 908/02 Spyder With Porsche, when new racing coupes arrived, open-top Spyders soon followed and, for this model, there were eventually three versions. This first generation variation dipped body panels at the side doors. Subsequent wind tunnel tests indicated this change in surface height adversely affected drag.

1969 Typ 908/02 Spyder "Flunder" The second version Spyder filled in the door panels, prompting mechanics to nickname the car Flunder for the flat-sided deep-sea fish. This particular fish raced at Le Mans with massive motion picture cameras in its nose and tail, filming racing action for actor/producer Steve McQueen's movie "Le Mans."

By 1969, Porsche had introduced a new spyder, Typ 908/02, nicknamed "Flunder" after the flat deep-sea fish that swims in an undulating motion. The first 908 spyder followed Kolb's characteristic cutdown doors, but cockpit turbulence necessitated side windows that arched inwards; Kolb raised the Flounder's door height to near the front and rear wheel bodywork. Four Flounders took the first four places at the Targa Florio in May 1969, and five of them swept the Nürburgring in early June. At Le Mans two weeks later, Porsche ran not only 908 L coupes but also 908/02 long tail Flunders.

Meanwhile, Ferdinand Piëch placed his greatest gamble. Reading the FIA regulations for 3.0-liter prototypes and 5.0-liter sports cars gave him an unexpected insight, and he set his engineers and designers to work on yet another new car for 1969. Unfortunately, as had been the case with other extremely innovative Porsche race cars, insufficient development limited initial successes.

But all along, Le Mans in 1969 was to be Porsche's race for victory in the 908 L. And 23 hours of racing led to a 60-minute game of cat and mouse with Porsche's 908 and a Ford GT. In the last moments, it came down to the courage of a twenty-year-old racing the Ford against the caution of a forty-year-old in the Porsche. The Ford won by 394 feet (120 m), and Porsche again settled for class honors.

Racing year 1970 revealed Porsche's Typ 908/03 spyder as a companion to Piëch's 5.0-liter sports car gamble. Like the Bergspyders, this new open car was as specialized and purpose defined as anything Porsche had yet done. Its ultralight body of polyurethane foam and reinforced fiberglass weighed just 26.5 pounds (12 kg) ; with its titanium tube space frame, the car scaled at 1,201 pounds (545 kg). In many ways, these were Typ 909s with the 3.0-liter engine—driver position was forward again, and handling was stunning. Porsche ran them in only two races during 1970, the Targa Florio and the 1,000km of Nürburgring, finishing one-two in both. They saw more use in 1971, and Porsche, which had assembled thirteen of them, began offering them to trusted customers at year end. Some of these teams continued racing the 908/03s at late as the 1982 season!

ANLAGEN FUR
CIBIE
DUNLOP
917
SHELL
PORSCHE
917
DUNLOP

1968–1975

12

No One Expected the 917

Typ 917 K and L, 917/10, 917/30

Briefly, Ferdinand Piëch was content. His 907s had won major international races; he believed his 908s capable of more. The FIA's new regulations limited Group 6 prototypes to a 3.0-liter maximum displacement and Group 4 sports cars to 5.0 liters. The organization had many hopes: For one, it wanted to encourage teams to race their 5.0-liter GT40s and Lola GTs. And with Formula One currently racing 3.0-liter engines, it sought to inspire a team or two to try prototypes.

To erase any hesitation, the FIA reduced homologation requirements from one hundred to fifty cars, hoping to convince makers who had assembled thirty or forty to add a few more. Some of those, Can-Am builder McLaren most vocally, argued even this was too many. So the FIA halved it again, demanding only twenty-five. This prompted thoughts inside Porsche, which had assembled sixty-two 906s and thirty-five 910s. In various bodies, they had made eighteen 907s. But Piëch felt confident in the 3.0-liter prototype 908. If this performed well through the first half of the season and at Le Mans in June 1968, Porsche planned to continue developing it. If things went differently, it had time—even after Le Mans in June—to develop something for 1969. Piëch did acknowledge

1969 Typ 917 Langheck Coupes After FIA inspectors had refused to approve Porsche's 917s several weeks earlier, Piëch put every capable hand in the company to work assembling the twenty-five copies the FIA wanted to homologate the race car. Was this presentation meant as a bit of intimidation? That's possible.

(Top) 1969 Typ 917L Coupe One of the earliest 917s, the fourth assembled, sat outside the race shops. With almost endless modifications ahead of them, it seemed senseless to assemble 25 identical samples because as soon as inspectors departed, mechanics dismantled nearly all of them.

(Above) 1969 Typ 917 Kurzheck Prototype Eugen Kolb designed the 917 as a transformer; by releasing catches aft of the rear wheels, the long tail came off the car, revealing a short tail race car. But its drooped tail performed like an airplane wing, bringing up the back of the car. During an intense testing session at Zeltweg, Austria, at season end, mechanics built-up a new tail with sheet metal. This immediately cured its rear lift.

to a visiting journalist that if Porsche had known of the FIA's plan to accept twenty-five identical cars with 5.0-liter engines for the World Championship of Makes, he might never have done the 908.

The problem was Group 7, with no displacement limits on the open cars racing in the North American Can-Am Challenge and European Interserie. Ferrari hinted it was developing a 6.0-liter V-12 (and even a 7.0- and an 8.0-liter) for the Can-Am even as Porsche ace Jo Siffert and a couple of private entrants were angling toward 3.0-liter 908/02 spyders for the same contests. Ferrari's bold step was from its 4.4-liter 12-cylinder engines for its 365 P spyders to a new 12-cylinder 7.0-liter displacement 712 for Group 7. Reducing displacement was easy as Inserting cylinder sleeves. Getting a new Ferrari sports car with 5.0 liters was no challenge. In May, Enzo Ferrari sent out word to his customers that said, "If we build this, are you a customer?" His clientele understood "We *are* building this; are you a customer?"

1970 Typ 917K Coupes at Le Mans With its new tail configuration in place (No. 23, far left), one of Porsche's 917 entries at Le Mans races one of its 908 Flunders into the first corner. At the end of 24 hours, the red No. 23 brought Porsche—and Piëch—a long-waited first place overall, winning by five laps over the second-place 917 long tail. The yellow-red Flunder placed third, giving Porsche the entire victory podium.

Ferdinand Piëch understood what sounded to him like a call to arms. It grew louder after the ACO postponed the 1968 Le Mans race because of the student riots. Piëch lost his luxury to see how Porsche's 908s did against Ford and Lola sports cars. He ordered Hans Mezger to design a new engine. With 4.5 liters as overall displacement, he started with the 3.0-liter 908 eight-cylinder and added half again for 12 cylinders. He ended up with 4,494cc, comfortably legal. Mezger used 908 dimensions, cylinders, pistons, connecting rods, and other parts to save design and prototyping time. He took engine output not from one end but from the middle, where flex in a long crankshaft was the least, an idea adopted from the Dusio Typ 360.

By mid-June, Eugen Kolb was scaling up a 908 body to fit a 50 percent larger engine in the lowest drag shape they could imagine. Kolb, Schröder, and Klie—the team that had created the 906, 910, 907, and 908—now undertook a more innovative approach, with Kolb designing a long-tail body (L) with a removable tail

1971 Typ 912-10 engine for Typ 917K racer. By 1971, the 917 raced with a 630-horsepower, 4,999 cubic centimeter displacement opposed 12-cylinder engine using twin sparkplugs per cylinder and dual overhead camshafts. Short tail cars reached 227 miles per hour (366 kilometers per hour). This car uses mufflers for testing.

(Above) 1971 Typ 917-40 Langheck Coupe Porsche sent a long-tail to SERA, a Paris aerodynamics lab, for tuning. The changes, from a new concave nose to rear-wheel covers, were so numerous that the cars earned new designations: 917-40. Here, a designer from the Styling studio applies Martini's intricate color scheme to the car before the start of the 1971 Le Mans. This car, No. 21, retired after just four hours when its large top-mounted engine cooling fan broke its shaft and spun into the air helicopter-like, settling into the trackside trees.

(Top) 1971 Typ 917-20 "Bertha" at Le Mans SERA not only developed the streamlined 917-40 but also proposed this clunky short-tail variation. Internally nicknamed, "Bertha," Styling chief Tony Lapine pronounced it ugly but Piëch told him he could paint it. The ever-irreverent Lapine did, representing the cuts of pork found at the butcher shop. Journalists named it "the Pink Pig."

section to make it short (K). Karl Rabe designated the new project as 912 to confuse outside suppliers about Porsche's plans. The long-tail body measured 189.4 inches (4,810 mm) long, overall, 74.0 inches (1,880 mm) wide, and 36.2 inches (920 mm) tall. The 917 K was 20.5 inches (520 mm) shorter, at 168.9 inches (4,290 mm). Regulations called for a minimum weight of 1,764 pounds (800 kg).

When the late-September Le Mans race ended and Porsche's new 908s followed a then four-year-old Ford GT (but one constantly updated under team manager John Wyer and Gulf Oil) across the finish, Piëch's best guess—or worst fear—proved right. His stress rose in mid-December when Ferrari announced plans to revise its 612 Can-Am spyder as a 512 coupe in order to run the European racing series.

But Enzo Ferrari went a step further. Hearing Porsche's plans, he told a journalist, "With an air-cooled twelve-cylinder, you can never beat a twelve-cylinder Ferrari, never,

1972 Typ 917-10 Can-Am Spyder FIA regulations changes outlawed the 917 coupes at the end of 1971, by which time Works driver Jo Siffert already was enthralled with the North American Canadian-American Challenge, the Can-Am series. The racing shops prepared something like 18 of these Spyders for its Porsche+Audi Works program and for loyal customers.

I say to them . . ." But Ferrari and the FIA never expected Piëch's and Porsche's reaction to these challenges.

By early January 1969, Porsche had scale models in wind tunnels to optimize body design. Piëch confronted Mezger, gauging his confidence in his new engine design, and courageously—if rashly—ordered parts without bothering to assemble and test a prototype engine. It was another of the stunning gambles he took on this project. He booked space at the Geneva Motor Show in mid-March to unveil the car. A press release accompanied the debut, boldly—if deceptively—stating, "4.,5 ltr. Hubraum [displacement] 12 Zylinder 520 PS bei 8,000 U/min." It went on to claim "Twenty-five already assembled and offered to private racers at a price of roughly $35,050 (DM 140,000) at the Works."

A week later, FIA inspectors arrived at Werk 1 to examine the twenty-five completed race cars. Unfortunately, Porsche had finished only two; a third was in the assembly shops, and parts for thirteen more awaited shop space and personnel. Inspectors had been tricked in past years by clever theatrics, and cars had been homologated with only a fraction of the requirement complete. But not this time. Ambitiously, Piëch invited them to come back thirty-one days later. Meanwhile, once that third 917 was completed, it went to Le Mans for testing; there, it exhibited near-treacherous handling and inadequate brakes for a car that topped 205 miles per hour (330 kilometers per hour), along Mulsanne.

As the next inspection approached, Ferry and new motorsports director Rico Steinemann chose to give the FIA a great show. While racing mechanics labored on the 908s, everyone else in the factory—messengers, secretaries, apprentices—was taught just enough to "assemble" the race cars. Steinemann parked them side by side like a parking lot, too close to maneuver. Racing mechanics completed the cars on either end, and on the fateful day, Piëch urged the inspectors to climb in any car, start the engine, and drive away. The inspectors were

stunned; Porsche had shoved the FIA's own regulations in their faces: twenty-five cars did not exist even five weeks before. One of the men drove one of the 917s 100 meters, and they were done and approved. But the celebration was tepid. Development costs had exceeded $5.1 million. Now every car needed to be reassembled properly. If cars sold for $35,000 each, they left the Works trailing some $165,000 in red ink behind them. Relations between the ground-floor race shops and the upstairs executive offices turned frigid.

None of it got better for a while, either. Piëch demanded a car body with minimal drag so that nothing diminished its top speed. While aerodynamics—and the strength of air at high speed to lift an airplane wing—was well understood, no one had connected a teardrop-shaped car racing on the ground traveling faster than some aircraft to these same aerodynamics realities. The 917's drooping tail created a large negative-pressure area that tended to lift the car off the pavement at high speed. Works drivers nicknamed the 917 the Widow-Maker and the Ulcer, among the most potent slurs.

1972 Typ 917-10 Interserie Spyder at Motodrom Hockenheim The Interserie was Europe's variation of the Can-Am. Porsche's 917-10, weighing only 1,653 pounds (750 kg), dominated as it did in the United States. Here, Bosch team racer Willi Kauhsen put the 1,000-horsepower twin-turbocharged 4,999 cubic centimeter displacement opposed 12-cylinder engines to work.

During the 1969 season, Porsche hired John Wyer, whose Gulf Oil team had run the Ford GTs that challenged Porsche for overall victory. They were to come on board for racing year 1970 and 1971. Through the second half of 1969, Porsche raced and tested the 917, and everything improved except its wicked handling. Porsche engineers knew why; they just had a boss who had decreed that nothing should induce drag, including wings that might hold the car down. Engineers Peter Falk and Helmut Flegl recognized that the car's tail sat too low; they also knew announcing it—or acting on it—might be a career-ending move. It took a session in Austria at season's end with Wyer team manager John Horsman and his mechanics participating for the change to happen. This way, as Peter Falk admitted years later, he was able to claim, "They did it!"

"They" elevated the tail end of the car by nearly 18 inches (460 mm), raising it into the air streaming over the car. Then, with a spoiler at the back of this new bodywork, the vague, terrifying handling of the car became predictable and precise. Team racer and test driver Brian Redman summed it up: "Now it's a real race car."

That real race car triumphed almost without misstep through 1970 and 1971. It won repeatedly and set lap records regularly. But Piëch was not happy with someone else racing "his" cars. He unexpectedly created a second Porsche team in his mother's name, Porsche Salzburg. His mother's VW and Porsche distributorship for Austria had the resources to afford such a venture; This gave Ferdinand his own team to run his own way and it clearly vexed the "official" Gulf-Wyer-Porsche team. This operation provided all the competition any factory team could desire. It provoked Horsman to comment decades later, "It was much easier racing against Porsche than for them."

Porsche's 917 Ks and Ls dominated endurance racing. The FIA, irked at Porsche's bravado, regulated the maker out of endurance racing at the end of 1971. But that mattered little. The Can-Am series, which had inspired Ferrari and initiated some of Porsche's

1973 Typ 917-30 Spyder at Riverside Mark Donohue, shown here, wanted a car in which he could spin the rear tires in all four gears, and Porsche gave him exactly that with its ultimate Can-Am car. Donohue's twin-turbocharged 5,374 cubic centimeter displacement, 12-cylinder engine developed 1,100 horsepower for races. Engine builder Valentin Schäffer saw it reach 1,400 horsepower on a bench test.

response to the sports car class, had caught Porsche's attention. It developed a small run of 917 spyders using 917 K engines tuned to more than 600 horsepower for these sprint races and teamed with American racing legend Roger Penske to manage the team and entries in North America. Penske and driver George Follmer won the 1972 Can-Am championship in their turbocharged Typ 917/10.

Porsche introduced turbocharging with this model. Speedway race cars at the Indianapolis 500 had used turbocharging for years, but Piëch's plan was for his cars was so secret that engineer Valentin Schäffer had to be deceptive when he called on turbo manufacturers. When he suggested the horsepower output he sought, they all relaxed: "Okay, we understand; this is a boat." Schäffer's adventures in turbo development were precisely that—adventures—and taming turbocharger lag (the delay between pressing the accelerator pedal and feeling the boost) provided immense challenges.

Porsche returned for 1973 with a new Typ 917/30 with turbocharged output from the 5.4-liter opposed twelve-cylinder engine as high as 1,400 horsepower on a test bench.

The Can-Am series went the way of the FIA World Championship of Makes. Penske and driver Mark Donohue humbled every competitor at every venue and claimed the title a second year in a row; the series outlawed the turbo Porsches at the end of 1973.

The Penske-Donohue 917/30 undertook one more event in August 1975. Penske had believed it might be capable of setting a land speed record, and following upgrades to the car and engine—including introducing an intercooler, a radiator for the fuel mixture to reduce its temperature and increase its density and potency—Donohue lapped the triangular oval racecourse at Talladega, Alabama. Racing to beat a threatening thunderstorm, he set a record at 221.16 miles per hour (356.64-kilometers per hour), which still stands today.

S-M 2383

1967–1976

13

Caught in the Middle

Typ 914-4, 914-6, 914-6GT, 916

In sports car design, midmounted engines were trending. Ferry Porsche's first car had been one, and one of his father's most famous race cars, the Auto Union Grand Prix "Silverfish," had its engines between the axles. Though Ferry had reverted to a rear-engine configuration for his series-production cars, that was for packaging reasons. From the start, Porsche's race cars had their engines mounted amidships. And while Ferry's engineers had started the trend in 1953 with his Typ 550 RS Spyder, by the early 1960s, most race car makers had adopted this configuration. That which excited spectators in racing appealed to enthusiasts for their own cars, and French carmaker René Bonnet introduced his Matra Djet mid-engine road car in 1964. Ferruccio Lamborghini followed with his stunning Miura for 1966, and Enzo Ferrari raced a mid-engine Dino 206 to hillclimbing in 1966 and offered road versions starting in 1967.

Porsche had enough on its mind and on its drawing boards in the late 1960s to avert its gaze from seeming competitors offering "the next new thing." Ferdinand Piëch's mid-engine race cars were climbing ever higher on winner's-circle podiums, and the FIA's new regulations ignited his ambitions. In the meantime, Porsche had bills to pay and a payroll to meet. Its newest 911 S model and Targa variation were selling well. But

1970 Typ 914-4 Porsche put its prototypes and all its race cars through roughly 620 miles (1,000 km), on this road attempting to break the chassis, suspension, and body. If that happened, engineers and mechanics made repairs and fixes in the design and started again until it no longer broke.

(Above) 1970 Typ 914/4. Porsche's chief modeler Heinrich Klie devised the shapes of the Typ 914 as a two-seat sportscar for VW. When VW backed out, Porsche made some changes and introduced it with its 80-horsepower, 1,679 cubic centimeter displacement opposed four-cylinder engine mounted in the middle of the car. Each 914 came with a removable "Targa" top and sold new for $3,006 (DM 11,955), at the Works.

(Right) 1970 Typ 914/6 GT Coupe Porsche's competition version of the 914 used the 220-horsepower, 1,991 cubic centimeter displacement opposed six-cylinder racing engine. The factory assembled twenty-eight in 1970 and another eighteen for 1971, three of which competed in the 84-hour Marathon de la Route in 1970 at the Nürburgring. They swept first, second, and third places.

ever since Ferry and his sister, Louise Piëch, struck their agreement with Volkswagen in 1949 for mutual distribution (as well as a lucrative royalty payment from VW for every car manufactured), those terms had also included VW relying on Porsche for new product research and development.

And by the late 1960s, VW needed a new product. It had improved its image and market share with its Karmann Ghia coupe in 1955 and convertible in 1957. But at VW, body styles got stuck. Improvements to their cars were beneath the skin and thus harder to inspire to repeat customers, let alone new ones.

VW had developed a 1,679cc air-cooled engine for its 411 sedan to replace the Beetle in 1968. VW chairman Heinz Nordhoff, who had negotiated everything with Ferry and Louise in 1949, worked with Ferry again; they conceived a new VW sporty companion to the 411. The assignment came into Porsche's new design/engineering complex in Weissach and put a crowd of people to work. It was designated Typ 914.

VW soon agreed on a mid-engine configuration for a strictly two-seater. Body design went to Butzi Porsche's

styling department, and Nordhoff emphasized it should not resemble current Porsche products. Heinrich Klie set to work developing forms. As the project advanced through Porsche's engineering at Weissach, the 914 assumed two identities: one as VW's project with VW's engine and running gear and the other as a Porsche replacement for the four-cylinder 912. Klie's concept offered generous storage room front and rear and incorporated a large removable fiberglass roof panel in the style of the 911 Targa. Ferry's budgets covered the differences in running gear. The cross-pollination of ideas and the dual applications for the same product were simply a matter of handshake agreement and assumption of continuation into perpetuity.

Nordhoff was approaching a retirement he did not yet want. But VW's board insisted the sixty-eight-year-old chairman find and train a successor. He hired Kurt Lotz, thirteen years his junior, who had been chief executive at the Swiss electrical company Brown Boveri. Lotz was to assume the job at the end of 1968, with Nordhoff available for consultation. But Nordhoff, who had been fighting age and illnesses, unexpectedly took a turn for the worse. Time the two men had counted on for the outgoing chairman to explain VW's operations, and especially its complicated relationship with Porsche, eluded them as Nordhoff spent more and more time in the hospital. He died on April 12, 1968. He had become VW managing director on January 1, 1948, but had known the Porsche family before the war when he was with Opel, fighting for their rights to do the "People's Car."

The familiarity, intimacy, and trust between them never reached Lotz. Newly in charge and wary of making mistakes, he set out to answer confusing questions, legacies of Nordhoff's friendship and trust in Porsche. Why, for example, was VW, known for low-price family cars, embarking on a sports car? Why had it commissioned and paid Porsche for sports car design and development, which Porsche did routinely? As he sorted out the project, he repositioned it as a Porsche-designed VW from which it derived the profit.

But VW backing a new Porsche was one thing; VW still needed a new lineup. He commissioned a mid-

1969 Typ 914/8 S-11 Coupe
Ferry Porsche, holding the window frame, stands among well-wishers beside his 60th-birthday gift, a special 914 fitted with a 260-horsepower, 2,996 cubic centimeter displacement opposed eight-cylinder engine derived from the racing Typ 908. Ferry used the car daily for several years, putting on thousands of kilometers and enjoying its 155 mile per hour (250 kilometer per hour) top speed.

engine family car and a kind of camper van from Porsche, both using an air-cooled engine mounted under the rear seat. Ferry, who was using VW's funds to construct with research and design campus at Weissach, designated the new project EA 266, and his engineers saw in it possibilities for their own sport coupe.

This recast the 914 as a kind of stepchild. Its body and chassis offered tremendous versatility, with room to accommodate VW's original 411 engine as well as one of the 911 variants. Longtime mechanic and racer Herbert Linge was in charge of testing and development and recalled the 1.7-liter VW engine giving adequate performance and fuel economy. But when racing engineers considered competition versions, they sent the car to a wind tunnel, where its good results surprised nearly everyone. The 914 created slightly more rear lift and slightly less front lift than the flagship 911; Klie's body needed only a simple rear spoiler to give the 911 a challenge, something no one expected. Or wanted.

Kurt Lotz and Ferry Porsche addressed questions of marketing and sales. For US customers, the 914 was marketed through a newly formed subsidiary Porsche+Audi as a way for VW to promote its Nordhoff-era acquisition of Audi. In the States, the 914 wore a Porsche badge on the nose and the designation 914/6 VW-Porsche on the rear. In Europe, VW-Porsche VG was born as a 50/50 partnership between the two, and the 1.7-liter car was named the Volkswagen-Porsche. This resulted in an unexpected—and unwelcome—nickname, the VoPo, which was the abbreviation for the East German Volkspolizei, the people's police. Notwithstanding the unfortunate connotation, the companies unveiled the VW-Porsche 914 and VW-Porsche 914/6 at the 1969 Frankfurt Motor Show. The 1.7-liter engine offered buyers 80 horsepower in a car weighing 1,984 pounds (900 kg). In order to protect the primacy of the 911, Porsche fitted its 110-horsepower Typ 911 T engine in the 2,072-pound (940-kg) Typ 914/6.

Despite its nickname, the 914/4 found a ready market. It sold for $3,275 in Germany at introduction; the 53-horsepower Karmann Ghia convertible had been $2,445 two years earlier.

The 914/6 met a more skeptical response. By the time the convolutions of contracts and distributions and badging were settled, Porsche had to introduce its version of the car at $5,475. This hurt sales because, with no family resemblance, potential customers wondered why they should pay $4 *more* for this car than

the 911 T, which sold for $5,471. In the first three years of life, VW manufactured 65,351 of the four-cylinder models. The 1973 model 914/4 upgraded to VW's 100-horsepower 1,971cc air-cooled four-cylinder. VW assembled another 32,522 of these. A companion 914/4-1.8 arrived in 1974 and 1975, and its 1,795cc engine offered 85 horsepower, and 17,773 of these sold. In contrast, Porsche manufactured just 3,388 of the 914/6 from 1970 through 1972.

Ferdinand Piëch embraced the vehicle and he commissioned two 914/8s. One he kept for himself; it used a 2,996cc 300-horsepower Typ 908 opposed eight-cylinder racing engine in the 2,535-pound (1,150-kg) car. He had the second built as a sixtieth birthday present for Ferry using a more mildly tuned 260-horsepower engine. Ferry enjoyed it, ultimately driving it more than 6,000 miles (10,000 km). Engineers welded a steel roof in place of the removable fiberglass panel to enhance stiffness.

Porsche also produced a run of eleven steel-roof Typ 916s. Fitted with the 2.4-liter 911 S fuel-injected opposed six, these 2,200-pound (1,000-kg) cars offered their exclusive owners 190 horsepower. These ran with noticeably flared fenders (an option for the racers who acquired one of the handful of 914/6 GT models). If you knew the right people and had $10,953, you might have gotten one of the 916s.

The world economy and German politics are part of this story. VW chairman Kurt Lotz had acquired NSU, a nearly hundred-year-old company with success in front-engine, water-cooled, front-wheel-drive autos. However, it had invested heavily in rotary engine development, and its production cars' reliability and warranty problems nearly broke the company. VW used NSU's four-cylinder internal combustion engine (ICE) successes to develop the Golf, its Beetle successor. It did the same thing soon after with Audi technology for the VW Passat. Once VW went to front engines and water cooling, it never looked back.

All this led to turmoil within and outside VW. Lotz *had* reauthorized the VW-Porsche EA 266, the mid-engine air-cooled car, yet his strategy pushed water-cooled engines. He lost the support of his labor unions and then, fatally, his supervisory board. When 1971 sales figures appeared, VW clearly was struggling. Lotz resigned on September 13, 1971.

VW replaced him with Rudolf Leiding, an abrasive, aggressive cost cutter. Within three weeks of taking over, he stopped the EA266. VW had already invested $4.6 million (DM 16 million), and the car was production-ready; its resemblance to the new Golf was striking. But it was a huge investment that was steering VW away from its new direction. While some saw Leiding rejecting the ties between VW and Porsche, Leiding simply aimed to save, simplify, and turn around the company.

That process was like turning a ship. VW suffered a $323 million (DM 833 million) loss, in 1974. That was the year the Golfs reached European dealers, but Leiding hadn't turned the ship quickly enough; at the start of 1975, just as the Golf arrived in the United States as the Rabbit, Leiding left. The board replaced him in August with Toni Schmücker. Unexpectedly, watching sales rise to a record $7.5 billion (DM 18.45 billion), for 1975, Schmücker felt the company needed something sporty in its lineup. One of his first calls was to Porsche.

1974 Typ 914-1.8 "Bumble Bee" As 914 production wound down, Porsche's North American distributor created two special 914s—this black/yellow "Bumble Bee," and a white/red "Creamsicle" to commemorate Porsche's outstanding Can-Am career. The company fitted its 99-horsepower, 1,795 cubic centimeter displacement fuel-injected four-cylinder engine. This accelerated the car from 0 to 62 miles per hour (0 to 100 kilometers per hour), in 12.0 seconds and on to a top speed of 110 miles per hour (178 kilometers per hour). Porsche assembled 500 of each.

Carrera
911 TURBO

1974–Present

Exhaust Gas Makes You Go Faster!

Turbocharging the 911

VW's corporate activities caught Porsche management unprepared. Projects that had been resurrected were killed, then new ones initiated were killed, too. Revenues Porsche counted on to operate Weissach evaporated. In Zuffenhausen in 1971, Ferry confronted a management crisis of his own. He responded by removing all the Porsches and Piëchs from their jobs in the company and hiring trained professional outsiders in their place.

Ernst Fuhrmann had designed Porsche's dual-overhead-camshaft Typ 547 engine for the Typ 356. He quit Porsche in 1956 when Ferry promoted a recent arrival to an executive position Fuhrmann believed he had earned. At his next employer, he had risen to management board membership. Now Ferry invited him back as CEO. Fuhrmann was in Zuffenhausen barely two weeks when VW upended the tables.

The same financial hurdles that affected VW also impacted Porsche. The German government had devalued its mark by 9 percent. And the US government, responding to Detroit automakers' cries of unfair advantages for imports (particularly VW), imposed a 10 percent import duty on all automobiles manufactured outside the country. The

1974 Typ 930 Turbo Prototype Porsche introduced its first turbocharged series production model as a 1975 model in early autumn 1974. This car, destined for the international auto show circuit, ran with the new 260-horsepower, 2,994 cubic centimeter displacement opposed six-cylinder engine. This accelerated the 2,513-pound (1,140-kg) coupe from 0 to 62 miles per hour (0 to 100 kilometers per hour), in 5.5 seconds and on to a top speed of 155 miles per hour (250 kilometers per hour).

(Top) 1974 Typ 930 Turbo Series Production Number 001 Ferry Porsche was a thoughtful and considerate brother who gave his older sister Louisa Piëch the company's first production Turbo coupe. Louisa was a dedicated amateur painter, so Ferry deleted tinted windows; thus, as she drove, she saw true colors. To non-family members, Porsche sold the Turbos for $25,503 (DM65,800) .

(Above) 1977 Typ 930 Turbo Targa When Porsche engineer Rolf Sprenger, in charge of customer service at the time, saw cars such as this return to Werks 1 for service, he wondered why Porsche was not doing these kinds of modifications rather than sending his customers to other shops. Ferry agreed and Sprenger established *Sonderwunsch*, German for "Special Wishes," to take these projects in house. After several years, Porsche changed the name to *Exclusiv*, a word more easily pronounced worldwide.

combined impact at Porsche was profound: VW's decision left Weissach's development center with neither a project, a revenue stream, nor a successor for the 911.

Over the years, Fuhrmann had concluded that, for motorsport to continue it had to maintain a connection to series production. He had been impressed with Porsche's turbo Can-Am cars, which he learned about from a distance. He considered "his" company's dilemmas: a 911 approaching the age at which Porsche had discontinued the 356, a campus full of engineers and designers with more time than work, and no new revenues. To reenergize the 911, to keep it alive and make it interesting again, he asked his engineers about turbocharging it.

"Oh, it was tried already!" It had been; Ferdinand Piëch had directed experiments with a turbocharger hung off the back end of a 911 prototype and another that emerged from the deck lid of a 914. His department shelved the ideas, judged to be premature.

"It was refused by management!" "It was impossible!" "There was not enough room!" Engineers had a litany

of reasons, but, as boss, Fuhrmann ignored that. He had to put his people to work; he had to reinvigorate the 911. As he summed up his two careers at Porsche in 1991, he explained, "This was my contribution to turbocharging the Nine-Eleven: I looked in the engine compartment and said, 'There must be room!'"

Fuhrmann also understood that racing improved cars and successful races sold them. There was no more possibility for a Porsche prototype—if Porsche hoped to race, it was left with the 911. But the only way for it to compete against 450- to 480-horsepower cars from Matra and Mirage was to turbocharge. The FIA permitted 3.0 liters maximum displacement and imposed a multiplier rule on turbos that meant actual displacement multiplied by 1.4 must be no more than 3,000cc. Porsche's engineers devised an opposed six-cylinder engine of 2,142cc. Still, the car was too big, too heavy. A brutal weight regimen, similar to what Piëch had imposed on his 911 R, got it down to 1,819 pounds (825 kg). But with the FIA minimum at 1,433 pounds (650 kg), Fuhrmann, Norbert Singer, and engineering director Helmuth Bott realized they only could erase the weight penalty with more power. Any further help had to come from their engineers Valentin Schäffer and Hans Mezger. And they delivered—by the end of the 1974 season, they had pulled 500 horsepower from the 911 engine using one large KKK turbocharger. (Engineer Singer had joined Porsche in March 1970, tasked at first with cooling gearboxes on the 917s; success there, including World Endurance, Can-Am, and Interserie championships led to his next assignment, turning the 911 into a race car and managing the process of turbocharging it.)

But now, with its rear engine, turbocharger, and transaxle, when engineers weighed the car with full fuel and oil tanks, 70 percent of the weight sat on the rear axles and only 30 percent rode up front. To maintain any kind of control of the nearly 500 horsepower with that weight imbalance demanded exceptionally large tires riding on extremely wide wheels. Still, this didn't remedy all the problems.

Racing engineers now recognized aerodynamics as another villain in race-car stability. What had tamed impossible handling was front air dams and rear spoilers and wings. With this new racer, the Carrera RSR Turbo 2.1, Singer and company broke new ground. And stunned Ernst Fuhrmann as he recalled in the 1991 interview with the author:

(Top) 1979 Typ 930 Turbo Coupe By 1979, Porsche already was in its third generation Turbo. The rear wing, known as "the Antlers" to its designers and the Whale Tail to outsiders, gave way to the more beneficial "tea tray" with its upturned edges to better manage airflow. Engine output grew to 300 horsepower and the price, due to currency revaluations, had risen to $73,688 (DM 134,850) .

(Above) 1983 Typ 930S "Slant Nose" Coupe One of Rolf Sprenger's first Exclusiv creations was an adaptation of the flat nose on the company's racing Typ 935s, the so-called "slant nose." Flattening the nose relied on retractable headlights from Porsche's new Typ 944 model; it enabled an increase in top speed from 162 miles per hour (260 kilometers per hour), to more than 171 miles per hour (275 kilometers per hour) .

(Top) 1990 Typ 930S Cabriolet Officially, Porsche ended 930 production in 1989. However, one customer had ordered an extraordinarily optioned version, especially when he learned he was getting the very last 930. Slant nose options cost a premium— $41,135 (DM 77,330) without the car, which was $85,585 (DM 160,900). The options list for this car ran 11 pages and may have added a bit more to the price.

(Bottom) 1990 Typ 965 Turbo Prototype By this time, Porsche's startling Typ 959 had come and gone, but engineers wanted to rekindle the magic that car created with enthusiasts and journalists. They envisioned an all-wheel-drive Turbo with special body treatments, the Typ 965, but the economy had collapsed. The few prototypes went into storage.

"Why must it be so big?" Fuhrmann demanded. He'd missed days spent perfecting aero on 917 coupes and spyders so effectively that even cars with seemingly large drag lapped faster because downforce and grip improved handling. "Okay! But it's an airplane wing! It's ugly. Paint it black so nobody sees it," he protested.

When the car appeared at Le Mans June 15 and 16, its silver, red, and blue Martini livery contoured a 911 shape swollen with huge, flared fenders—the rear of the car was 15 inches (380 mm), wider than the series 911 in 1974—and culminated in a vast black wing. It led the race for a while, but its production-based five-speed transmission proved inadequate for the car's 405 pound-feet of torque. It finished second overall, having steadily held that position behind a 1,400-pound (635-kg), 480-horsepower Matra for 15 hours.

Fuhrmann gave his production engineers the same assignment: to homologate the car for racing, put a turbocharger on the series 911. Throttle response had plagued Schäffer, who tamed the first turbos for Porsche racing 917 spyder. However, race-car use was straightforward. Racers either ran full throttle or were braking. No one coasted in a racing car.

BMW had introduced a turbocharged 2002 for 1973, derived from a system that outside engineer Michael May had developed. May sold aftermarket kits to Ford enthusiasts for its 2.3-liter Capri models; Porsche acquired one, and Herbert Ampferer took his first drive. (Engine designer Ampferer joined Porsche in 1970 and worked first on VW's underseat engine, then followed on the Typ 924. His next task was to follow Valentin Schäffer's work turbocharging Porsche's race cars and bring it to the street in series production 911s.)

"The response was horribly bad," he recalled in an interview with the author in 2012. "I made a tour out of Zuffenhausen and after a while, I made a u-turn in a small road. I gave the gas pedal a push and the car made a huge jump. I was [pointed] in the direction of a huge concrete wall." He returned to Weissach with a clearer understanding of the challenges he faced. Unexpectedly, those grew more complicated.

Looking in the engine compartment of a 911, it was not immediately clear where the turbo and its necessary plumbing might fit. He asked his boss, "Tell me, do we need air conditioning for that car?"

"No, we don't need it."

"Do we need a rear wiper and motor for this car?"

"No, we don't need that. This is only 200 cars or something like that. Forget it!" Coincidentally, the FIA required 200 examples for homologation.

Then sales and marketing got involved. Lessons from Porsche's unexpectedly successful 911 Carrera RS 2.7

1993 Typ 964 Turbo 3.6 Coupe
When the next-generation Turbo arrived as the 1991 Typ 964, it carried over the previous 320-horsepower, 3.3-liter engine. A new engine arrived in December 1993, delivering 360 horsepower from 3.6 liters, pushing the car from 0 to 62 miles per hour (0 to 100 kilometers per hour), in 4.8 seconds and up to a top speed of 174 miles per hour (280 kilometers per hour).

had sunk in. "We think we can sell many more cars," they told Ampferer. "But we need air-conditioning. And a rear wiper."

I threw away all my drawings and started all over," he said.

Down another hallway, others reckoned with the future Porsche, too. Weight and balance issues that had enormous impact on the racing 2.1-liter RSR were still considerations, even though the series turbo engine developed barely half the output of the racer—260 horsepower in a car with air-conditioning, luxury interior, rear wiper, and 2,635 pounds (1,195 kg), of weight. The standard Carrera coupe was 65.0 inches (1,652 mm) wide; the turbo grew to 69.9 inches (1,775 mm). But it was the spoiler at the back that, like Fuhrmann's "airplane wing," drew comments. Two newcomers were responsible: designer Harm Lagaay, recently arrived from BMW and Ford, and head modeler Peter Reisinger, an import from Opel along with new design chief Tony Lapine. Reisinger and his colleagues quickly nicknamed their creation the Antlers, though this became better known as the Whale Tail. Again, Fuhrmann was shocked; when he ordered his first turbo as his factory test car, he specified a normal 911 Carrera body with no rear wing.

Production passed the 200 homologation units, and by the end of model year 1977, Porsche had turned out 2,850. Incredibly, it did this in an economy that unexpectedly got much worse just before introduction.

Porsche unveiled the Typ 930 Turbo Carrera at the Frankfurt International Auto Show in mid-September 1973. From there, it went to Paris for the International Salon in early October. It excited enthusiasts even through Porsche had explained first deliveries were a year away. Then, unexpectedly, world politics stepped in just as the Paris show closed.

On October 16, the Organization of Arab Petroleum Exporting Countries—OAPEC—announced it was increasing the per-barrel price of crude oil from $3.00 to $5.11. The next day, the OAPEC presented its embargo on oil exports to nations sympathetic to Israel. It reduced crude oil deliveries 25 percent to the same countries immediately. By March 1974, five months before the first 930 Turbo appeared, crude oil was selling at $12.00 per barrel. Gasoline prices at US pumps doubled and then tripled; shortages caused long lines, and buyers were allowed only 10 gallons (37.85 liters). Germany briefly prohibited private driving on Sundays.

Porsche did not change course. Engineers already were developing updates for the 1978 model that raised output to 300 horsepower. Longer-range plans included a turbocharged Targa and a cabriolet, based on the 911 SC Cabriolet. By the end of its first decade, Porsche had manufactured 14,476 turbos. It introduced the next-generation model, the Typ 964, in 1989, and its 320-horsepower 964 Turbo debuted in 1991. An optional performance kit delivered 355 horsepower for 1992 and 1993, and a limited-edition Turbo S in 1992 provided some eighty-six owners with 381 horsepower.

Porsche's Typ 993 Turbo crossed an important threshold: offering customers 408 horsepower (but only in an all-wheel-drive platform) starting in 1996. Chief engineer Helmuth Bott's involvement with the Typ 959 had convinced him that for driver safety and control, Porsche vehicles with more than 400 horsepower were to be delivered with all-wheel drive. That decision unleashed a steady growth in horsepower.

(Opposite top) 1997 Typ 993 Turbo S Coupe Porsche introduced the next generation 911, the Typ 993 as a mid-1994 model. By 1997, its Turbo used all-wheel drive and with Exclusiv's help in this "S" version, provided customers 450 horsepower. Porsche assembled just 345, selling these coupes for $175,085 (DM 304,650) .

(Opposite bottom) 1997 Typ 993 Turbo S Coupe The 3,600 cubic centimeter displacement twin-turbo, twin-intercooler "S" engine shot the car from from 0 to 62 miles per hour (0 to 100 kilometers per hour) in 4.1 seconds and on to its top speed of 186 miles per hour (300 kilometers per hour). This was previously territory visited only by Porsche's rarest race cars. The cars, loaded with luxuries, weighed 3,307 pounds (1,500 kg).

MAX MORITZ PORSCHE
VALVOLINE
8

1975–1981

15

Freeing the Whale

Group 5 and Group 4 Silhouette Racers

FIA/CSI regulation changes for 1975 shifted the emphasis away from Group 6 prototypes and spyders to Group 5 "silhouette" coupes. These were race cars *derived* from series production, and the organizers established a World Championship for Manufacturers (WCM) for this class. There was no minimum production for Group 5. However, regulations for Group 4—cars closer to pure series-production models—required 400 assembled over two years for homologation. These two groups, 5 and 4, were the reasons Fuhrmann pushed his engineers to turbocharge the 911. Porsche had manufactured 274 of its Typ 930 Turbos in 1974 and 1,176 in 1975, qualifying the cars by a large margin. As a result, two development programs were underway at once.

Norbert Singer's Group 5 car had to originate from series-production roots that—at least fundamentally—had to remain apparent to any scrutineer. Singer's team started with a completely stripped Typ 930 shell with no rustproofing, sound-deadening, or interior trim. They fabricated fenders, doors, and front and rear deck lids of thin fiberglass-reinforced plastic (FRP). Body designer Eugen Kolb created a one-piece nose, including fenders and front air dam, for easy removal during pit stops. He created two versions: one with headlights in the normal position and another, aerodynamically cleaner, with flat fenders and lights mounted in the air dam.

1977 Typ 934/5 Coupe Edgar Dören and Jürgen Barth shared flight duties in the Valvoline Racing Typ 934/5 at the ADAC 1000-Kilometers of Nürburgring in May 1977. The 934/5 designation arose when private teams mated 934 front ends to 935 engines, rear suspensions, and bodywork to race in Group 5.

(Top) 1976 Typ 934 Coupe Bob Wollek was on his way to overall victory as he accelerated out of a turn on the Norisring city circuit in Nürnberg. Kremer brothers Manfred and Erwin prepared the car for Wollek and sponsor Vaillant, the German manufacturer of heating, ventilation, and hot water equipment.

(Above) 1976 Typ 935-01 Porsche's first Typ 935—in its second-generation slanted nose—underwent a frustrating May 1976 debut at the Nürburgring when a distributor cap broke in the engine after nine laps and drivers Manfred Schurti and Rolf Stommelen were disqualified for receiving outside assistance.

At the rear, Kolb devised a long tail that fit without modifying the original body. This included a very large and aggressive rear wing, had an adjustable trailing edge, and used vertically mounted "fences" at each end to contain airflow.

The interior was spare in the extreme—no headliner, a driver's titanium racing seat, minimal padding, no spare tire or wheel. The instrument panel retained the tachometer front and center. The roll bar and gear-shift lever were aluminum. While the windscreen was safety glass, all other windows were Plexiglas. Singer got the Typ 935 down below 1,984 pounds (900 kg), but the CSI had held off solidifying details in the specification until the season start. Vehicle weight was one part of the equation; the other was the scale rulemakers had established determined by engine displacement. Porsche's turbocharged 2,856cc opposed six required the 1.4-times "supercharging factor," setting adjusted displacement at 3,998.4cc. Minimum weight had to be 2,138.5 pounds (970 kg). Unexpectedly, Singer had

the luxury of placing more than 154 pounds (70 kg) of ballast where it best helped balance. He took the car to Circuit Paul Ricard in southern France in December 1975 to conduct countless tests, including ballast placement. When they finished, the car sat, race ready, with 47 percent of its weight at the front and 53 at the rear. The 31.7 gallon (120 liter) fuel tank, oil reservoir, fire-extinguishing system, and battery were in the nose of the car.

Porsche's racing Typ 935 engine evolved from the series Typ 930. Hans Mezger and Valentin Schäffer carried over the production crankshaft, crankcase, and valves but replaced the camshafts, exhaust, lubrication system, and connecting rods. Five electric fuel pumps served the Bosch high-pressure fuel-injection system with its intake-mounted injectors. Engineers mounted the turbocharged engine's air-to-air intercooler in the rear wing, relying on airflow across the wing to extract heat. The engine delivered 590 horsepower at 1.5-bar boost (22 psi).

Singer knew of the new Group 5 regulations in plenty of time. He had nearly completed work on his car, designated Typ 935, evolved from the 2.1-liter Carrera RSR Turbo. But Porsche was the only carmaker so far along in this process, and unexpectedly the CSI pushed the series launch back to 1976. With more time available, the engineers moved on to the Group 4 companion, the Typ 934. Rules here were far more limiting. Engineers were permitted to modify the suspension, replace some parts with others for reinforcement, and use race-car brakes.

Externally, the car resembled its series 930 donor but with notable upgrades. Lateral plastic fender extensions grew roughly 2 by 4 inches (50 by 100 mm), out from each wheel well to accommodate permitted wheels. An aggressive nose fed air to two intercooler water radiators, a center oil cooler, and, at the edges, the brakes for cooling. CSI regulations required Porsche use the production Whale Tail, or Antlers, rear spoiler.

Singer's team did not gut the 934 cockpit quite as brutally as they had for the 935; rear and passenger seats came out, and an aluminum roll bar went in. Regulations required them to use production glass windows. Group 4 minimum weight was 2,469.2 pounds (1,120 kg), based on

1977 Kremer 935 K2 One of the characteristics of the 935s that spectators most enjoyed was their tendency to spit flame as the cars decelerated. Here, Bob Wollek briefly steers his Vaillant-Racing Kremer 935 K2 into a turn on the Nürburgring 1.4-mile (2.3-km), Grand Prix circuit. He finished third overall.

DUNLOP
ADAC
TEXACO
VAILLANT · KREMER
TOYOTA
51
Vaillant
MAX MORITZ PORSCHE
Jägermeister
Jägermeister
DUNLOP
GEORG LOOS
LOOS
Shell
GOODYEAR

the 934's engine displacement, and this allowed one of its conversation pieces: with this much weight allowance, Singer concluded the electric window motors used in the series car were barely heavier than manual cranks, so the car raced with power windows.

Testing Porsche had done on the 934's air-to-water intercoolers paid a bonus when, unexpectedly—during the 1976 racing year—the CSI "reinterpreted" its own regulations on rear wings. It had previously accepted rear airfoils that were different from production. Then it insisted that while the spoiler might differ, it must be interchangeable with the Typ 930 standard version. Porsche had successfully debuted both the 935 and the 934 at Mugello, Italy, in late March; the 935 won overall and a private 934 finishing fourth and had won the Grand Touring class. It had repeated the same feat at nearby Vallelunga fourteen days later. Now, at Silverstone, England, another week later, Singer learned his wing was illegal because he had modified the rear panel.

Changing wings demanded hours in wind tunnels and on tracks to prove a new shape. Mezger and Schäffer had gone for a bulky-but-lighter air-to-air intercooler because they had had the luxury of space in that vast rear wing. Now, they adapted the air-to-water system they had devised for the Typ 934 to use it on the 935. As Singer explained to the author, "This required us—in the space of barely eight weeks—to design and test new water intercoolers with all their plumbing and connections and pumps, retuning the engine for this system, developing a new space cam for the fuel injection pump, and developing and testing an entirely new throttle linkage."

For years, a good finish at the 1,000-kilometer race at the Nürburgring was crucial. Expectedly, this proved impossible for the 935. As an interim step, engineers fitted it with the 934's coolers; balancing all these

Typ 935 Coupes from Kremer, Max Moritz, Loos, and others Bob Wollek in the Green Vaillant-Kremer 935 No. 51 (far left) finished second in the October 1977 Bilstein Supersprint at the 'Ring. Manfred Schurti drove the Jägermeister No. 52 to third overall; and Rolf Stommelen in the Georg Loos Gelo-Racing No. 66 was overall winner of the 44-lap, 62.5-mile (100-km) race.

variables was tough, and internal vibrations in the engine broke distributors in both entries.

By this time, however, a clever hybrid had appeared. Known as the Typ 934/5, it arrived at Silverstone as Singer learned the bad news about his 935. This racer was mostly 934 but used the 935's wider rear fenders and—coincidentally—the wing; this allowed it to race in Group 5. One finished third overall. Two privately entered 934/5s placed second and fourth at the 'Ring.

Le Mans, with its own regulations, was a better story for Porsche's 935. While its performance in the 24-hour race was far from flawless, with small troubles here and there, the car finished the race in fourth overall, winning its Group 5 class. The race finished with a massive Porsche sweep, showing victories across four classes *and* overall. The next several races continued 935 development and 934 dominance, and the cars delivered Group 5 and 4 titles for 1976 to Weissach.

Through the 1976 season, Porsche entrusted its second 935 to the Kremer brothers, Manfred and Erwin, in Cologne to operate and develop the car. Their finishes aided Porsche's championship. But for 1977, the field expanded exponentially, as Porsche began selling 935 customer cars. At some venues, as many as five of 935s started. The 934 entries proliferated as well; ultimately Porsche assembled some forty-two of them for European and US customers in 1976 and 1977.

Group 5 races had become Porsche shows; by midseason, German TV decided to ignore the bigger cars and devote coverage to the more competitive under-2.0-liter classes. This caught Ernst Fuhrmann's attention, and he commanded Singer, Mezger, Schäffer, et al. to create an under-2.0-liter 935. If remedying all the intercooling problems in 1976 had been difficult, this was off the scale.

Yet they did it. They started in March 1977 and had an entry for the season's sixth meeting, at the Norisring, on July 3. It ran a turbocharged 1,425cc engine (1,995cc with the multiplier) that developed 370 horsepower in a scaled-down 935 body of just 1,653.5 pounds (750 kg). It had virtually no testing time and lasted thirty-eight of the seventy laps of the race. But three weeks later, "Baby," as they nicknamed the Typ 935/77 2.0, finished 52 seconds ahead of the second-place car in the small-displacement division of the widely broadcast German Racing Championship (Deutsch Rennwagen Meisterschaft, DRM) and claimed class victory. That satisfied Fuhrmann, who retired the car to the Porsche Museum for display. At season end, with one more Group 4 and 5 championship, Porsche withdrew from actively

Typ 935/78 "Moby Dick" Coupe Looking very much like a great white whale, Norbert Singer's rule-bending 1978 version of the company's Group 5 car sat in the pits at Circuit Paul Ricard in Le Castellet, France, before resuming exhaustive testing. Ricard was the winter-testing home for Porsche racing at times when Weissach was snowed in.

1979 Kremer 935 K3 Americans Bill and Don Whittington arrived at Le Mans in 1979 with a suitcase of cash and acquired this latest iteration of Kremer's aerodynamic bodywork on Porsche's Typ 935 on practice day. Together with Kremer team driver Klaus Ludwig, the three won the 24-hour race. It represented the first and only win at Le Mans for a production-derived Group 5 car.

1980 Kremer Typ 935 K3 Long-time Porsche racer and Le Mans participant Dick Barbour entered two of his Kremer-prepared K3 935s at Le Mans in 1980. Barbour's race car partner Bob Garretson had brought in Apple Computer sponsorship for the Group 5 season. Garretson and co-drivers Bobby Rahal and Alan Moffat completed 134 laps before retiring.

racing the cars. It continued to support its customer racing teams except for the occasional "statement" entry.

If Baby was sublime, Singer's 1978 candidate was . . . not. As Group 5 regulations relaxed, he continued studying and finding areas for interpretation. By the time his Typ 935/78 emerged from his shops, it was like no 911 anyone had imagined.

"Because under the Group 5 regulations, I could not alter the roof line, I made a new one, keeping the original inside it," he told the author. "Rules meant to help front engine cars with their front exhausts allowed me to lower my entire car 2.36 in (six centimeters) so I completely cut away the floor pan and, with an aluminum tube frame that basically carried the entire car, replaced the floor with thin fiberglass. We turned the gearbox over to reduce stress on driveshafts and made a completely new suspension. We developed a new engine of 3.2-liters which we water cooled—the first time for a Porsche—and we developed a new body." The bodywork, another Kolb creation, stretched the air-dam-mounted headlights and nose far forward and drew out the tail to lengths reminiscent of the 917 L. By the time chassis designer Horst Reitter, body designer Kolb, race-engine wizard Schäffer, and chief engineer Singer finished, they had a 911 that was 192 inches (4,890 mm) long, on its regular 89.2-inches (2,279-mm) wheelbase; it weighed 2,260 pounds (1,025 kg), and its engine developed 650 horsepower. It was long, wide, and white with modest Martini racing stickers on the doors and front hood. It first appeared at Silverstone, and observers quickly named it "Moby Dick." It won its first race by a convincing seven-lap margin (21 miles [33.8 km]). In tests before Le Mans, its true destination and purpose, it clocked 227 miles per hour (365 kilometers per hour). But during the race it suffered small indignities, from a sticking throttle to a leaking water radiator to an ailing fuel-injection pump and a broken distributor. It finished seventh overall, earning third place in Group 5. Its impact on other racing teams, however, was immense.

Singer worked on another Moby Dick for 1979; it was canceled before the race, but private teams developed their own. By 1980, nearly a dozen whales in various colors reflecting other sponsor logos appeared at every Group 5 contest. This helped Porsche reclaim the WCM title 1978, 1979, 1980, and 1981. Its 935s continued racing well into the 1983 season even after regulators had done their best to outlaw them.

MARTINI

1976–1981

16

There's a Car in the Museum?

Typ 936

Norbert Singer and his team hurried to get their new Typ 934 and Typ 935 to their racing debuts. CEO Ernst Fuhrmann met with them regularly to assess progress. Unexpectedly, he asked them what they thought about new regulations for Group 6. All eyes looked everywhere but at Fuhrmann, and the room fell silent. Fuhrmann's gaze settled on Singer.

"We're preparing the 935 for the world championship. We know, of course, there is a sports prototype class," Singer related to the author. Fuhrmann also knew there was a World Sportscar Championship (WSC) for prototypes. In his usual way, he spoke slowly and asked everyone what it might take to construct a car for a WSC program.

"We still have a lot of spare parts from the 917 in stock," he reminded everyone. "It should be easy to make a sports prototype out of the parts."

The room erupted in noise. "We're already doing Group 5!" "We're supporting the privateers in Group 4!" "Adding another series? There is no time!" Singer remembered everyone had a good excuse.

1976 Typ 936 Spyder at the 'Ring To keep the new Group 6 entry secret from competitors, Ernst Fuhrman ordered it painted black. It worked too well at its April debut during the Nürburgring 300-Kilometers, raced mostly under rain and fog. Sponsor Count Rossi de Montelera of Martini loved the stealth appearance until racing photographers had trouble shooting it and few pictures appeared.

(Top) 1976 Typ 936 Spyder in the Nürburgring Pits Sitting in the pits before the start of the 11-lap race at the 'Ring, its flat black paint delivered a striking statement of confidence. Ultimately, Works driver Rolf Stommelen finished the 156.1-mile (251.2-km), race in fourth place. Poor news coverage of the new car prompted Martini sponsors to repaint it white before its second outing.

(Above) 1976 Typ 936 at Le Mans It's hard to say that repainting the car white made that much difference, but, at the end of 24 hours, No. 20 was first overall, finishing 11 laps ahead of second. Jacky Ickx and Gijs van Lennep completed 350 laps, 2,963.9 miles (4,769.9 km). They drove an average speed of 123.5 miles per hour (198.7 kilometers per hour).

But Fuhrmann knew Renault was working on such a car. As was Alfa Romeo. Le Mans still invited sports prototypes. It spurned FIA title races to form its own series, a Daytona-Le Mans Trophy, and the Endurance Triple Crown, with Daytona and Sebring.

"Okay, I'll tell you," Fuhrmann said to no one in particular. "We do it."

Two weeks later, he heard the same excuses: "We do it. Take parts from stock, make a new space frame, just make a body . . ."

Singer saw an opening: "A new body needs wind-tunnel time."

But Fuhrmann blocked it. "You have a lot of experience, Herr Singer. You don't need a wind tunnel. Just make it!"

Fuhrmann assigned the project to Helmut Flegl, who had developed the 917 coupes to success and the 917 Can-Am and Interserie spyders to domination. Group 6 set a 3.0-liter engine displacement limit, so Flegl adopted Porsche's 2,142cc RSR Carrera Turbo

engine; with the multiplier, this yielded 2,998.8cc. The engine developed 520 horsepower running at 1.5-bar boost (22 psi). A pair of air-to-air intercoolers straddled the five-speed 917 transaxle. Horst Reitter designed an aluminum-tube space-frame chassis using the engine as a stress-bearing element—a first for Porsche. Eugen Kolb drew an open single-seat body blending elements from his 908/03 and his 917/10 spyders. Formed in polyester for strength and weight management, the body split in three segments so that the front and rear sections were completely removable. It weighed 1,543 pounds (700 kg). The CSI allowed Group 6 cars 42.3 gallons (160 liters) of fuel; Reitter fitted the tank between the driver and engine. In keeping with the Typ 934 and 935, this was designated Typ 936.

"'The car was a real secret, nobody should know Porsche is doing a Group 6 car,' Mr. Fuhrmann told us. So he had the funny idea to paint it black so no one would see it in its earliest testing around Weissach," Singer recalled.

(Top) 1976 Typ 936 at Dijon The 936 repeated its overall victory from Le Mans again at Dijon in early September. Jacky Ickx, ready to climb in, and Jochen Mass drove the car to first, completing the 152-lap race in two hours, 41 minutes, 23 seconds. They covered the 310.64 miles (499.93 km), at an average speed of 115.5 miles per hour (185 kilometers per hour).

(Above) 1977 Typ 936-77 at Le Mans Porsche returned to Le Mans in June 1977 and again finished triumphantly as well as dramatically. Co-drivers Hurley Haywood, Jürgen Barth, and Jacky Ickx together accumulated 342 laps. But the last three occurred at a slow pace with the engine running on five cylinders. Just 200 meters from the finish, the engine belched white smoke but Barth kept it going and, jubilantly waving his fist, crossed the finish line. Within a dozen meters the engine seized and the car lurched to a stop.

1977 Typ 936 and Typ 911 SC Safari Entries This was a typical view of the always-busy Weissach Rennabteilung race shops. Mechanics ready the next-generation 936 Spyder, which still needs its elevated rear wing. In the background, a pair of Africa Safari 911 SC 3.0-liter coupes await final prep before shipment.

Following successful Weissach tests, Flegl and Singer scheduled endurance tests at Paul Ricard immediately. Officially, Porsche was renting the track to test the 935; the secret 936 was hidden in the trailer. Until it wasn't. The day before, Formula One teams had done open testing, and journalists crowded the track. On Porsche's day, the F1 teams were gone, but some journalists lingered. Porsche unloaded the 935 and had rolled out the 936 when a reporter from Germany's *Sport Auto* rounded the corner.

"With it, all painted black, no signs on it, it was unbelievable. It was on the lift of the truck, just there!" Singer laughed. "Then a writer from France's daily sporting newspaper *L'Équipe* came around the corner." Fuhrmann planned to debut the car at Nürburgring in three weeks. Singer promised the German journalist that if he got rid the Frenchman, he could have an "exclusive" on the prototype. *Sport Auto*'s publishing schedule meant the story appeared just before the race. The Frenchman left, leaving the scoop to the German.

When Porsche's racing sponsor, Count Gregorio Rossi di Montelera, saw the car in Fuhrmann's stealth paint, he fell in love. His company's usual stripes and logos appeared on the flat black spyder at the Nürburgring on April 4. Driver Rolf Stommelen raced the completely unexpected Martini & Rossi "Black Widow" to fifth place overall. But this early-April race took place in gloomy rain. Photographers had trouble seeing the Black Widow, and for its next race, the 936 assumed traditional Martini livery.

The 936 story was what Porsche had expected from its 935 and gotten with its 934: overall victory at Monza, Imola, Le Mans, Enna, Dijon, and Salzburg, and a third in Canada and the World Sportscar Championship. With Fuhrmann's curiosity satisfied, Porsche gave the 936 a

1981 Typ 908-80 at Nürburgring Longtime Porsche-privateer Reinhold Joest had tried to assemble a Works 936, but Ernst Fuhrmann declined the offer. So, Porsche racing helped Joest assemble his own that he named 908/80. Works driver Jochen Mass co-drove with Joest to finish second overall at the 1,000-Kilometers of Nürburgring in May 1981. They finished second overall in a tragically shortened race following a horrific crash.

"retiree" schedule, one race a year at Le Mans. And while the 936/77 won that one, there was nothing easy about the victory.

With 45 minutes to go, a huge lead in hand, driver Hurley Haywood pitted with a seized piston. The pit crew cleverly disconnected the spark and fuel feed, and factory test and development driver Jürgen Barth drove the final laps on five cylinders. He needed to complete two laps within a certain amount of time, and mechanics taped an alarm clock to his steering wheel. He motored noisily out of the pits and stuck to the inner edges of the circuit, letting other race cars pass. But he was 10 seconds early as he crossed the finish the second time. Now he had another 8.47 miles (13.63 km)! Exiting the final curve, Barth's engine trailed white smoke. He crossed the finish line. There was a bang. The rear tires locked. The engine seized a handful of meters past the finish line. Porsche had won by nine laps with the final three on five cylinders.

Between 1977 and 1978, Flegl, Singer, and company improved aerodynamics. That car had reached 205 miles per hour (330 kilometers per hour), along Mulsanne in 1976. In early 1977 tests, it was 15 miles per hour (24 kilometers per hour) faster using a slightly longer tail. It sat 2.3 inches (60 mm) lower. By race start, Porsche had completed a second 936, and both ran 540-horsepower, twin-turbocharged engines. One, race No. 3, lost its engine in the fourth hour; No. 4 won by eleven laps— nearly 100 miles (152 km)!

The two "old" Typ 936s returned to Le Mans for a third go in 1978 with all-new engines. Weissach wizards Mezger and Schäffer adopted the four-valve, water-cooled cylinder heads from Singer's Moby Dick for the 580 brake horsepower 2,142cc opposed six. Flacht

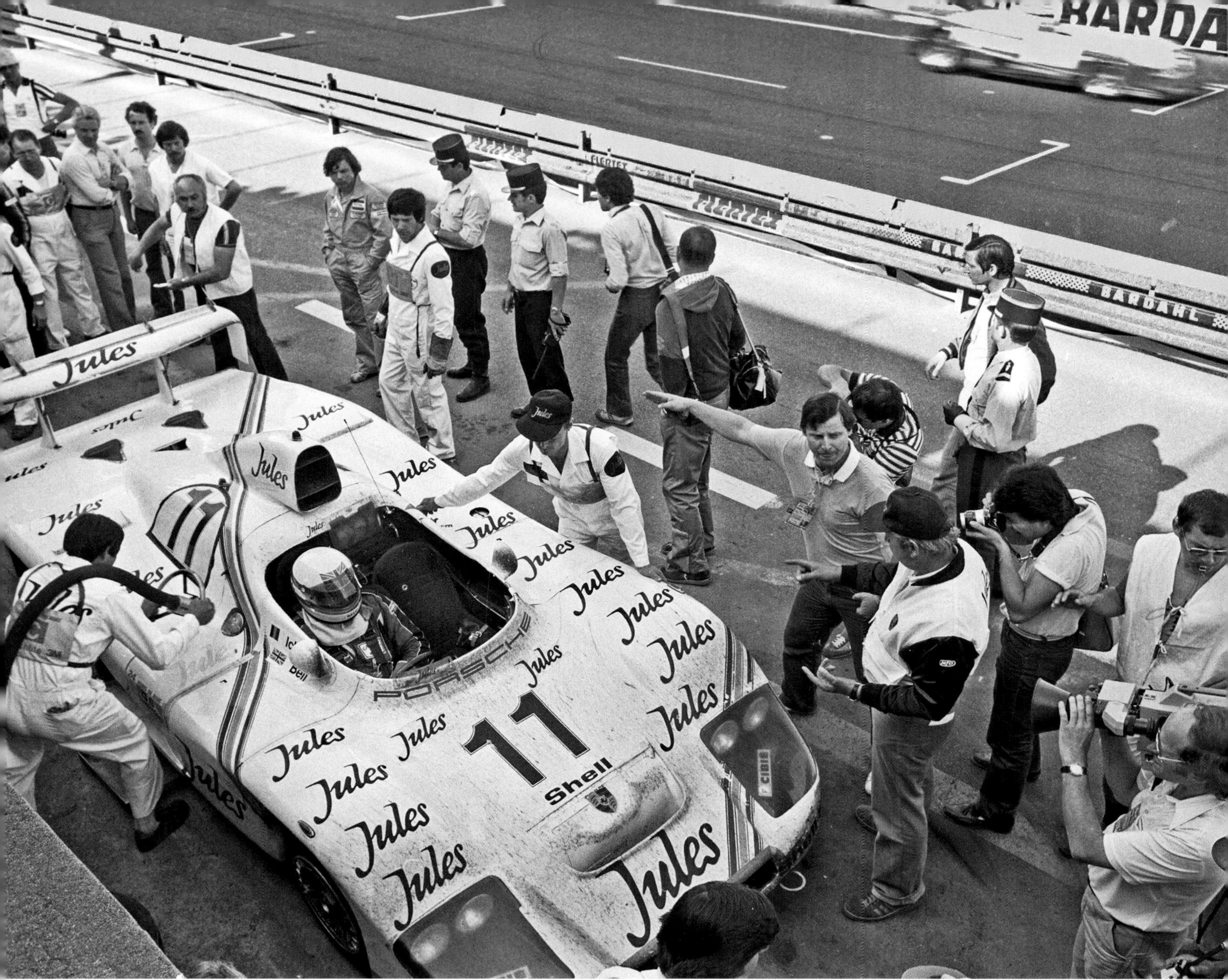

1981 Typ 936-81 in Le Mans Pits Porsche was a longshot for 1981. It was only last-minute sponsorship from Christian Dior introducing a new men's cologne, Jules, that got them to the circuit. Co-drivers Jacky Ickx and Derek Bell put the No. 11 car in the pole position on the grid. A second 936, No. 12, for Hurley Haywood, Jochen Mass, and Vern Schuppan, qualified second fastest.

workers fabricated a third 936, using the earlier two-valve engine for insurance. The engines necessitated new gearboxes, and despite successful 40-hour endurance tests at Ricard, they gave trouble at Le Mans, leaving their best finish at second and third overall behind the popular favorite Renault-Alpine; the third car retired in the 20th hour after an accident.

For 1979, because Porsche's 935s were strictly customer teams, Works racing was on a hiatus. Flegl, Singer, and their team, reassigned to series car development, were called back to racing. The 936s remained largely unchanged from 1978. The lack of ongoing development extracted a cost because other race-car makers weren't distracted by production models. In fact, they pulled one of the four-valve engine 936s out of the Porsche Museum for minimal preparation. The race was a disappointment. A rear tire blew on Brian Redman's second place 936 in the third hour, tearing off masses of left rear bodywork. Using the toolkit knife on board, Redman cut away the remains

of the tire and limped the car to the pits; that crawl took 38 minutes. Repairs required another 53 minutes. They returned to the race in 38th but by midnight, had climbed back to seventh. Jacky Ickx was still running seventh early in the morning when his alternator drive belt broke. He replaced it, but a few kilometers later it flew off, stranding him. A Porsche mechanic took a nighttime stroll; when he spotted Ickx, he casually dropped a new belt over the fence. But Le Mans is ringed with marshals who see everything. Ickx got the new belt on and made it back to the pits, but several hours later, race management disqualified it for receiving outside assistance. As for the other car, a gearbox failure forced retirement in late morning.

For 1980, the Works raced their new front-engine, water-cooled cars, and Porsche left Group 6 to collaborator Joest Racing's team. An extremely experienced driver and team manager, Reinhold Joest had won in Porsches for decades, more than once beating Works entries to the checkered flag. With Porsche's backdoor assistance, he assembled a 1977 replica 936 and hired Jacky Ickx to co-drive with him. Joest Racing entered the car as a Typ 908/80. The team led from the early evening, but, exercising too much caution, they never built a significant cushion. When an alternator belt broke again, Ickx was ready and fitted the new one perfectly. But that and the necessary pit stop cost half an hour.

Their next problem was equally familiar, but much bigger: on Sunday morning, fifth gear broke as it had in 1979. With six hours to go, mechanics miraculously replaced the gearbox in 25 minutes, and Ickx ran the car to catch up. By the final hour, he had taken the lead. Then a sudden hard rain fell, and Ickx pitted for wet tires. Unexpectedly, the squall blew over, the sun returned, and Ickx had to slack his pace to save his tires. The Joest Racing 908/80 took second overall, two laps behind the winners.

Year 1981 marked thirty years since Porsche's first Le Mans appearance. Ernst Fuhrmann had retired in 1980, and Ferry hired Peter W. Schutz. Schutz, born in Berlin to American parents and educated in Chicago, had most recently run Germany's largest diesel truck maker. As he had neither carmaking experience, sports car knowledge, nor any understanding of racing, Ferry dispatched him to Sebring to watch the 12-hour race. Schutz returned a convert. A positive, optimistic man, he had a proven ability to motivate others. Ferry needed that; Fuhrmann had suggested killing Porsche's most profitable—and beloved—car line, the 911, a prospect that had murdered morale. Schutz, in an interview with the author, explained that he acted quickly: during a presentation Norbert Singer and others were making about Porsche 1981 Le Man entries, he asked about their chances of winning.

There was no chance. As production-based cars, these 924s were racing for marketing, they explained. "I'll tell you what," he said to them. "So long as I am chairman here we will never enter a race without the intention to win it. But because I do not know how to do that, let's meet again here tomorrow and you will tell me what you're going to do." Morale, which had been nearly moribund at Porsche, soared overnight. Unexpectedly, the company was going back to Le Mans not just for marketing but to win!

The two 936s emerged from retirement again. New engines were upgraded derivatives of the air-and-water-cooled, four-valve, dual-overhead-cam engines Porsche had run in 1979. These displaced 2,649cc, and with twin turbos and intercoolers, they produced 620 horsepower. Entry in the race was in doubt until fashion house Christian Dior stepped in with advertising funds for its new men's cologne, Jules. Jacky Ickx topped 380 kilometers per hour, 236 miles per hour in one of the cars along Mulsanne in practice and won the pole starting position. The race had troubled and tragic beginnings, with a crash early in the second hour in which flying debris killed a course marshal. An hour later, another crash killed a driver. Each crash slowed cars for 30 minutes, controlled by newly introduced pace cars. Then it all opened up and ran cleanly under a clear, hot sky. One 936 had all the bad luck, suffering spark-plug, clutch, and fuel-injection problems and finishing twelfth overall.

DE CADENET
BP
les mutuelles du mans
OCEANIC
26
PORSCHE
Jules
11
Shell
DUNLOP
BOSCH Shell
Shell BOSCH BILSTEIN

Ickx and co-driver Derek Bell experienced the opposite: they took the lead in the fourth hour and won by fourteen laps. Peter Schutz, the great motivator, was jubilant. He had insisted Ferry Porsche come to Le Mans, an activity Ferry abandoned during the Fuhrmann years. Hesitantly, Ferry had agreed. Schutz brought him to the victory platform for the trophies; Ferry wept when the public address system played the German national anthem to honor the overall winners.

1981 Typ 936-81 at Le Mans Once they reached Le Mans, it only took Jacky Ickx and Derek Bell (No. 11) to add another overall victory to their logbooks and the 936 record. They completed 354 laps, finishing fourteen laps ahead of second place. They drove 2,998.3 miles (4,825.3 km), at an average speed of 124.9 miles per hour (201.1 kilometers per hour). Sister 936, No. 12, suffered clutch problems and finished 12th. The Joest Racing 908/80, No. 14, retired after an accident on its 60th lap.

S-CL 849

1975–1995

17

I Need Antifreeze with a Porsche?

Typ 928, 924, 944, 968

In the revolving door of relations between Porsche's Weissach engineers and designers and Volkswagen's ever-changing chairmen, Porsche had accepted a new contract to design and develop a "replacement" for the just-introduced Volkswagen-Porsche Typ 914. It entered Porsche's record books as Project EA 425. Unlike the 914 and the ill-fated EA 266, this new car was meant to be VW only.

Development at Weissach included adopting an engine from VW's pool, this one an Audi 1,984cc water-cooled in-line four-cylinder that produced 125 horsepower at 5,800 rpm. Porsche gave it a single overhead camshaft, Bosch K-Jetronic electronic fuel injection, and a new dual exhaust system for a sportier sound. For vehicle balance, Weissach developed a gearbox based on the rear-mounted transaxles of Porsche's race cars. But these required long driveshafts to transfer engine power, which were prone to vibrations. Porsche encased the slender driveshaft in a near-body-length rigid tube.

Young Porsche stylist Harm Lagaay designed the body, which Lotz personally selected from all the Weissach candidates. It was handsome, if crude—it was Lagaay's

1976 Typ 924 This former VW project set new precedents for Porsche's sports cars in several ways. It put a water-cooled four-cylinder engine in front with a four-speed manual trans-axle gearbox at the rear. It also delivered one of Ferry Porsche's long-wanted large glass rear hatch. The 924 debuted with a price of $9,222 (DM 23,240) at the Works.

(Top) 1974 Prototype 924 Harm Lagaay's prototype had enough potential that VW liked it until they didn't; Porsche happily took it back. Porsche modified a 125-horsepower in-line four-cylinder from the Audi 100 using Bosch K-Jetronic electronic fuel injection. The car rode on an all-new platform with a 94.5 inches (2,400-mm) wheelbase. It measured 165.9 inches (4,214 mm) long, 66.3 inches (1,865 mm) wide; and stood 50 inches (1,270 mm) in height.

(Above) 1978 Typ 928 As early as 1968, Porsche management considered a new model either to replace or supplement the 911. By 1971, Ernst Fuhrmann, who viewed the 911 as dated, encouraged a water-cooled front-engined GT car. To that end, engineers designed a 4,474 cubic centimeter displacement V-8 that developed 240 horsepower, with easy growth possible beyond 300 horsepower. When the 924 returned to Porsche, progress on this Typ 928 moved to a side track.

first full car body design, and years later he admitted there were design tricks and techniques he simply didn't know yet. Thus, in January 1975, when VW moved out Rudolf Leiding as chairman and brought in Toni Schmücker, who promptly returned the project to Porsche, Lagaay was thrilled.

Schmücker acted perhaps prematurely, and certainly brashly. While he sold the EA 425 back to Porsche, he also laid off 25,000 employees. And, of course, with the way things work, at the end of 1976, VW declared its largest profit ever, DM 1 billion. This earned him the nickname "Toni der Trickster." Meanwhile, Leiding hardly could be faulted for honoring—perhaps against logic or other voices—VW's obligation to Porsche's sports car. In his previous job directing VW's Brazilian operations, he had approved and supported "Project X," a two-seat sports car whose shape resembled Lagaay's EA 425. It went into production as the SP2, standing for São Paulo 2. There had been an SP1, using a VW variant 1.6-liter air-cooled engine in the rear, but with only 65 horsepower, it was woefully slow. The SP2 provided 75 horsepower—still anemic—when it finally appeared in 1972, by which time Leiding was gone.

With the EA 425 back at Weissach, the styling department finished Lagaay's body design and engineering further modified Audi's four-cylinder engine. The now-Porsche Typ 924 received 911 seats, and, with contracts in place with VW's factory in nearby Neckarsulm, the car began production in 1975 as 1976 model.

Porsche already had followed a similar path: front engine, water cooled, rear-wheel drive. But it conceived its concept, the Typ 928, as either a 911 companion or replacement. By 1971, then-new CEO Ernst Fuhrmann had approved 928 development with a 300-horsepower V-8 engine, 2+2 seating, and a clear orientation toward Grand Touring.

American politics impacted the 928 as well as it had the EA 425/924. The US Congress had turned its attention to its auto industry. This was the time when Fuhrmann worried the United States might outlaw any car with an engine in the rear. Even in the tight-money days of the early 1970s, nearly half of Porsche's production went to customers in the United States. It was an essential market.

Tony Lapine joined Porsche as its new styling chief at the same time. Lapine had headed design at Opel, the GM subsidiary in Rüsselsheim; he had transferred to that job from Detroit and had brought with him several designers and modelers with from GM's studios in Warren, Michigan. When he moved on to Porsche, he again insisted those individuals accompany him.

One member of that team, Wolfgang Möbius, won the assignment to design the 928. He started with the design language that body engineer Erwin Komenda, modeler Heinrich Klie, and body designers working for Butzi Porsche had developed. But his shape went beyond evolution, past the point of revolution, and finally settled between stunning and startling. Yet this was consistent Porsche design—the 356 and the 911 had done the same.

Engineers designed a new 240-horsepower, 4,474cc, water-cooled, overhead-camshaft V-8. Porsche planned to introduce the car as a 1976 model; it was not to compete against the one-year-old, 260-horsepower Turbo for the title of flagship of the fleet. Porsche planned the 928 with either its own five-speed manual gearbox or a modified Mercedes-Benz three-speed automatic. Where the Turbo focused on Ferrari and Lamborghini buyers, the 928 appealed to BMW and Mercedes-Benz sport coupe owners, to say nothing of those Americans who wanted a "continental" Corvette.

Porsche's work on the 924 delayed 928 introduction until 1978. Then, its 143-mile-per-hour (230-kilometer per hour) top speed, its 6.8-second acceleration from 0 to 62 miles per hour (100 kilometers per hour), its arresting looks, and its space-capsule-like interior promptly won it the Car of the Year title from the European motoring media—the first and only time a sports car has won such acclaim. Where Porsche had introduced the 924 in 1976 at $9,220, the 928 debuted at $27,500. At the same time, the 1978 911 SC coupe sold for $19,950, and Turbo buyers needed $39,250 to take home a 1978 Typ 930.

Regular power upgrades and new designations followed. Porsche introduced a turbocharged 924, the Typ 931, as a 1979 model with 170 horsepower and a 140-mile-per-hour (225-kilometer-per-hour), top speed. The Typ 928 S arrived as a 300-horsepower midyear 1980 model with a 155-mile-per-hour (250-kilometer-per hour) top speed. By this time, Porsche also had unveiled competition versions of the 924 for the European FIA and American SCCA racing classes. A small run of 924 Carreras emerged as a lightened and enhanced Carrera GT (310 pounds [140 kg], lighter with 210 horsepower). Porsche assembled 400 for general homologation purposes, then dialed that up with a 50-car run of 245-horsepower Carrera GTS. Porsche entered three at Le Mans in 1980; while cooling problems led two of the cars to finish on three cylinders, they placed sixth, twelfth, and thirteenth overall and won their classes. These led to a 375-horsepower version, the 924 Carrera GTR. Two of these, plus a new prototype designated 944 LM, went to Le Mans in 1981. These were the three cars that inspired new chairman Peter Schutz, upon learning they had no chance for overall victory, to challenge his engineers

(Top) 1978 Typ 928 While Styling chief Tony Lapine asked Wolfgang Möbius to design the exterior of the new Porsche, he also requested interior designer Vlasta Rujbr to create an upholstery that stylized a checkered flag waving in the wind. The Pascha cloth became as much a design statement of the car as its exterior shape.

(Above) 1979 Typ 931 (924 Turbo) Cries from customers for more power for the 924 led to the 1979 turbocharged version. The 1,984 cubic centimeter displacement in-line four-cylinder engine developed 170 horsepower. This 50-horsepower increase reduced acceleration from 10.5 seconds to 7.8 to reach 62 miles per hour (100 kilometers per hour), and raised top speed from 124 miles per hour (200 kilometers per hour), up to 140 miles per hour (225 kilometers per hour).

1981 Typ 944 GTP at Le Mans Porsche under Fuhrmann expanded the front-engine car line up quickly and took them racing. Typ 924 Carrera GTs (the Typ 937) raced at Le Mans in 1980 and this 944 GTP, the successor, ran in 1981. Cooling problems plagued two of the three 924s whose best finish was sixth overall in 1980. In 1981, this 944 GTP with Jürgen Barth and Walter Rohrl driving finished seventh overall and won its prototype class.

1982 Typ 944 Months after the Le Mans class win, Porsche introduced the road-going 944 which blended body forms from the 924 Carrera and 944 GTP. For Porsche enthusiasts, the 944 presented one big difference: while the 924s still used Audi-derived power, the 944 ran with a new Porsche engine of 2,479 cubic centimeters displacement. It was essentially one-half of the latest V-8 engine used in the luxury GT 928. The engine developed 163 horsepower.

to bring out something that could do so. The 944 LM placed seventh and won its class, and one of the GTRs finished eleventh and won its class.

The previous fall, Porsche had introduced the series-production 944. Its body was a more muscular version of the 928 Turbo, with flares around front and rear wheel wells, a handsome rear spoiler, and—to silence 924 critics who complained of a sedan engine in their sports car—the introduction of Porsche's 2,479cc in-line four (derived from one-half of the latest 928 V-8). This engine offered buyers 163 horsepower and a top speed on 137 miles per hour.

The 928 sat at the other end of the spectrum. From its concept as a luxury GT, it was never subjected to any of the design and engineering compromises necessary to pull a race car out of its shell. Its competition was other luxury GTs. Thus, the 928 S gained another 10 horsepower, to 310, by 1984.

In January, the 944 Turbo arrived, offering 220 horsepower and a 152-mile-per-hour (245-kilometer-per-hour), top speed. By 1986, the 924 S ran with the normally aspirated 944 engine, detuned to 150 horsepower from the 944 version's 163-horsepower configuration. Then a 944 S appeared for 1987 with 190 normally aspirated horses, followed by a 944 Turbo S delivering 250 horsepower. Its five-speed gearbox drove it to 162 miles per hour (260 kilometers per hour). Porsche assembled 1,635.

Even after discontinuing the 924 in 1988, Porsche supported three separate product lines—actually four, counting the 959 supercar derived from the 911. In an economy that was once again contracting, this felt risky, if not downright irresponsible.

The 928 line introduced the 320-horsepower S4 in model year 1987. Engineering was developing a new 2,990cc in-line four-cylinder for the 944 S, due for introduction as a 1990 model, but not until a more potent 928 emerged: the 330-horsepower, 171-mile-per-hour (275-kilometer-per-hour), Typ 928 GT luxury rocket.

Porsche unveiled the 944 S2 cabriolet for 1989, along with a new 944 Turbo coupe and then, in 1991, a 944 Turbo cabriolet. This 944 Turbo delivered 250 horsepower.

A year later, for model year 1992, a handsome new Typ 968 coupe and cabriolet replaced the 944 series. Updating the 2,990cc engine produced 240 horsepower and offered buyers a top speed of 157 miles per hour (252 kilometers per hour). The 968s remained in production through 1995, culminating in a nearly mythical Turbo S coupe created primarily as homologation for racing purposes. These extremely potent coupes weighed 2,866 pounds (1,300 kg), offered 305 horsepower, and accelerated from a standstill to 62 miles per hour (100 kilometers per hour), in 5 seconds. Porsche produced just fourteen during model years 1993 and 1994.

Model year 1995 marked the end of the 928 line as well, ending Porsche's initial examination of water-cooled front-engine sports cars with transaxle gearboxes. Theultimate 928 was its most aggressive. The 350-horsepower, 5,397cc V-8 GTS cruised effortlessly at 171 miles per hour (275 kilometers per hour), via five-speed manual or four-speed automatic transmission. But the risks of supporting these car lines for too long became clear when accountants did their arithmetic: Porsche manufactured 61,056 Typ 928s from 1976 through 1995 but only 2,831 of the GTS. During healthier times, the company had produced 130,937 of its nonracing 924s and 140,286 of the 944 in all its variations. Yet starting in the mid-1980s, currency fluctuations and other economic factors pushed chairman Peter Schutz and his co-brain and chief collaborator, Helmuth Bott, out of the company before their scheduled departures. Four years of the 968 saw only 11,245 cars leave the factory. But worse, the 911, 928, and 968 didn't share a single part in common. They required three separate assembly lines with incompatible training for assembly line staff.

Things had to change. And once again, Porsche's board called back a former engineer to do the job.

(Above) 1995 Typ 928 GTS This was the ultimate 928 V-8 from Porsche. With 350-horsepower,and a top speed of 171 miles per hour (275 kilometers per hour), it provided driving enjoyment with a five-speed manual trans-axle rear-mounted gearbox, or a four-speed automatic for these high-speed luxury cruisers. Porsche sold these cars for $117,406 (DM 167,890). In all, Porsche assembled 61,056 of its 928 models.

(Below) 1994 Typ 968 Turbo S Coupe While a total of 11,245 of the 968 models emerged from the factory in Ulm, the company assembled just eleven of these 305-horsepower coupes. This limited-run, pricey coupe— $122,378 (DM 175,000), at the factory—higher than the flagship 928 GTS, was the company's ultimate four-cylinder, turbocharged, intercooled sports car. It was capable of 174 miles per hour (280 kilometers per hour).

Shell
Shell
1
ROTHMANS
DUNLOP

1982–1995

What Do You Mean It Can Stick to the Ceiling?

Ground Effects

By January 1981, FISA's Technical Commission was developing regulations for its next racing championship. Porsche engineer and racer Jürgen Barth represented Porsche in FISA, and he urged management to participate in Group C, which was due to launch in 1982 and replaced the former Group 5 silhouette cars and Group 6 sports cars. Barth circulated a memo enumerating questions the commission faced: new engine or existing one? Turbo or natural aspiration? Water or air cooled? What displacement? Output? Gearbox? Chassis? Barth wondered whether Porsche was adapting existing elements to these new regulations or planned to start from scratch. And if the latter, at what cost? And where were these funds to come from?

Some inside Porsche thought this was premature. CEO Peter Schutz had just arrived, and his racing knowledge was limited. Cautiously, Porsche's engineers proposed two engine options. They liked the idea of a new 3.0-liter V-6 using water-cooled four-valve cylinder heads, which they planned as a stressed member of a new chassis; the V configuration certainly eased the design challenges of underbody aerodynamics ground-effects tunnels, legal in this new car. But new engines cost money and took

1982 Typ 956 at Le Mans Jacky Ickx and Derek Bell streaked past the Le Mans Ferris Wheel, a fixture of the circuit just as the 956 became one. Ickx and Bell driving No. 1 won the race, finishing three laps ahead of teammates Jochen Mas and Vern Schuppan, No. 2 in second and No. 3 with Jürgen Barth, Hurley Haywood, and Al Holbert finishing third.

(Top) 1982 Typ 956 Roll Out at Weissach Jürgen Barth put the first few laps on the brand-new Group C prototype. He was surprised by the ground effects which allowed cornering speeds so much higher he felt it in his neck. Chief engineer Norbert Singer was surprised by the dirt under the car and asked Bath if he'd gone off? No, the ground effects had vacuumed the track surface.

(Above) 1982 Typ 956 Christening in the Rennabteilung Racing manager Peter Falk anoints 956-001 with champagne after the development team had their sips. From left, Norbert Singer, chief mechanic Klaus Bischof, chassis designer Horst Reitter, Jürgen Barth (in drivers suit), and others of the team watch with pride.

years to develop, equally certain to delay Porsche's entry to 1983 or even 1984.

The second option was to revise and update the 2,857cc opposed six-cylinder with water-cooled four-valve cylinder heads created for Moby Dick. Recent electronic developments ensured engineers that 650 horsepower was feasible from either engine. All they needed—in either case—was approval from the new boss.

After seeing his first race, Schutz the novice returned as a zealot. He had separated the *Rennabteilung*, the motorsports shops, from the rest of engineering, more decisively dividing engineers and others strictly between the two purposes of series-production and racing cars. The zealot matured into a disciple when Porsche won Le Mans with cars from the museum in 1981.

Norbert Singer didn't wait for approval to start on the new Group C car. Horst Reitter began designing an aluminum monocoque chassis; years before, they had considered a monocoque for the 936, but there was no time. Now, Group C regulations demanded "crushable structure" for the front, rear, and sides of the car. While nearly every requirement and goal for the new car was still possible with an aluminum tube-frame structure, crushability was not.

Race-car body designer Eugen Kolb drew a body around known specifications, including overall length, wheelbase, height, and width. On August 1, 1981, Schutz's new budget for 1982 included funds to develop the new racer, designated 956.

Fuel-consumption regulations were extremely strict. Cars were allowed a 26.42 gallons (100-liter) fuel tank. FISA provided 158.52 gallons (600 liters) for a 6-hour endurance race and 600.48 gallons (2,500 liters) for Le Mans. Refueling rigs were to pump only 13.2 gallons (50 liters) per minute, which guaranteed pit stops required at least 2 minutes. Singer felt fortunate that Porsche already had an engine, the "Indy" engine it had revised for the 1981 Le Mans–winning 936.

This engine, the Typ 935/76, displaced 2,649cc. With the FIA's 1.4-times multiplier rule, the four-valve opposed six-cylinder engine yielded an adjusted 3,708.6cc displacement. Run with a 7.2:1 compression ratio and low boost for endurance, it developed 620 horsepower. But everything else for the car was new.

That included, most dramatically, ground effects. These came about primarily from two tunnels underneath the bodywork that opened from minimum ground clearance under the front axle to large venturi tunnels at the rear of the car. Reitter's monocoque and Kolb's bodywork accommodated these crucial aerodynamic upgrades.

From Reitter's chassis drawings, a full-scale seating buck emerged for Singer to test-fit the driving position

(Left) 1982 Typ 956 Debut at Silverstone Jacky Ickx and Derek Bell co-drove the 6-hour race at Silverstone, finishing second overall. Here the car led Ford's C100 Group C entry (No. 7) and Reinhold Joest's Group C Porsche Typ 936 (No. 4). The Silverstone victory frustrated the drivers who had to carefully manage fuel consumption. Gone, it seemed, were the days of all-out racing.

(Below) 1982 Typ 956 at Spa Porsche sent two cars to the Belgium round of the World Endurance Championships—WEC—one for car makers and the other for drivers. After 624 miles (1,000 km), No. 1 took first place with Jacky Ickx and Jochen Mass driving. Derek Bell and Vern Schuppan in No. 2 were third overall, second in class, three laps back.

1982 Typ 956s for Le Mans As Porsche had done with its 907s, 908s, and 917s, Norbert Singer, Horst Reitter, and Eugen Kolb created a "long tail" version of the 956 for Le Mans. Regulations strictly restricted overall length and the engineers' solution was instead to lower the rear wing. In the wind tunnel this had the effect of lengthening the car body.

and driver's sight lines over the front fenders. Reitter's concept once again set the fuel tank transversely behind the cockpit seats. With the opposed six-cylinder engine mounted behind that, the greatest portion of the car's weight sat between the axles. With maximum vehicle height of 43.3 inches (1,100 mm), Reitter and Kolb succeeded in giving the Typ 956 a low center of gravity and low polar moment of inertia, tremendous aids to vehicle agility.

The work pace was familiar, as grueling and fast-paced as it had been with any of Porsche's past race cars. It proved too much for many of its competitors, few of whom were ready by January 1, 1982; FISA regulators relaxed the rules, declaring 1982 a transition year. It permitted teams to race previous-generation Group 4, 5, and 6 cars to fill starting grids. But Porsche pressed on.

Reitter's technicians completed their first 956 monocoque on November 23, 1981. Singer already had one-fifth-scale models of Kolb's race-car body in the wind tunnel. He ultimately ran some 400 variations through the University of Stuttgart and Volkswagen wind tunnels during the next eighteen months. As Reitter completed the monocoque, Singer and his team saw measurements of 4,237.9 pounds (1,922.3 kg), of downforce. The completed car had to weigh at least 1,763.7 pounds (800 kg); these numbers hinted that if a race driver could somehow get the car up to the ceiling of a long tunnel, the "downforce" vacuum could hold it up there. By mid-December, Singer, Kolb, and Reitter were satisfied with the wind-tunnel data, and technicians began preparing body molds. Porsche envisioned racing four to six 956s through 1982 and then offering a customer run beginning in 1983.

That plan hit a snag just two weeks later. The North American International Motor Sports Association (IMSA) also had new regulations, and two of these directly conflicted with Singer's 956. First, IMSA required all engines to originate from series-production power plants, and the Typ 936/956 was purebred competition. And it required the driver's feet and pedal box to be behind the front axle, but Reitter had designed the 956

(Right) 1982 Typ 956 Scale Model Norbert Singer, left, explains the shapes of the 956 to motorsports and press manager Manfred Jantke and CEO Peter W. Schutz. The model was milled from a laminate of woods to 1:5 scale for extensive wind tunnel testing. The milling machine operator stood by.

(Below) 1983 Typ 956 Customer Car at Diepholz Reinhold Joest was an early 956 customer. His driver Bob Wollek raced the car in Deutsche Rennwagen Meisterschaft (DRM) round at Diepholz Airport, the sixth and final round of the season. Wollek finished fourth in this finale, good enough to earn him the championship title for a second year in a row.

to FISA specs, which allowed the feet ahead of the axle for vehicle balance. Neither side could compromise; Porsche was too far along in its development program to stop and redesign the car. The solid, fixed confines of the monocoque made it impossible to simply slide the driver back 11.82 inches (300 mm). And IMSA could not be seen making an exception for a single manufacturer when it, too, was well along in establishing its new Grand Touring Prototype (GTP) class. For now, 956s were confined to non-US venues, greatly reducing the market for the car. Singer knew he had the burden of change.

In February, Valentin Schäffer's crew ran their first dynamometer test on the Typ 956 engine. Schäffer's modifications not only achieved the expected 620 horsepower output but used 5 percent less fuel than the engine consumed in 1981. He set his goal at 3.92 miles per gallon, meeting the FISA allowance of 60 liters per 100 kilometers. Kolb's body design width helped Schäffer reposition the turbos from the rear of the 936, improving throttle response and exhaust flow.

Then, on March 27, the complete car—a prototype in a mosaic of mismatched body panels ready to run—emerged from Porsche's new shops in Flacht at the lower end of the Weissach circuit. Motorsports director and chief testing engineer Peter Falk assigned Works racer and customer racing manager Jürgen Barth the driving duty.

"It was a car built specifically for Jacky Ickx, who is one meter seventy [centimeters] tall, where I am one-eight-five. So I was jammed inside," Barth told the author with a laugh.

"No one had driven a ground-effects sports car before. The cornering forces were simply incredible. I went out and did about five laps and came in to check fluids. And Professor Bott looked around at the rear of the car and asked me if I had gone off the road?

"'No!' I told him!" Bott pointed out the dust clinging to large venturi tunnels under neath the rear of the car. This unexpected discovery surprised everyone. "The tunnels under the car had vacuumed the track!"

The ride was very stiff, crucial to maintaining the underbody airflow for ground effects to function as conceived. Le Mans was eighty-four days away. Singer took the car to southern France, to the Circuit Paul Ricard in Le Castellet, for extensive testing. He relied on Derek Bell and Jacky Ickx, drivers Porsche had contracted for the season. By the time they finished, they'd run 373 miles (600 km), without incident.

To further prove the car, Barth and development engineer Roland Kussmaul put the car through 623 miles (1,000 km), over various sessions on the "rough road"—essentially a cobblestone road after a minor earthquake—including a 6-inch (150-mm), jump. Through all this time, Singer kept fine-tuning the body in wind tunnels. Kolb had designed a long tail, though, it still fit within overall length regulations. He lowered and lengthened the elevated rear wing. When they finished, they had reduced drag by 25 percent and managed another 4.5 percent improvement in fuel economy. By May 6, the prototype had accumulated 4,244 miles (6,830 km), of testing. Ten days later, it had one more 6-hour test. But first, it needed paint.

1983 Group C at Monza Bob Wollek and Thierry Boutsen shared the drive in Reinhold Joest's No. 11 Typ 956, winning the 624-mile (1,000-km), opening round of the 1983 WEC season. They beat the Works No. 1 Porsche (hidden behind No. 11) of Ickx and Mass by only 0.07 seconds. Bell and Holbert (No. 2, far left), finished seventh. The Martini Lancia LC2-83 placed ninth.

FIAMM
Shell
Marlboro

1983 DRM at Norisring Keke Rosberg raced the Kremer Racing Typ 956 at the Norisring city circuit in Nürnberg. Rosberg placed fifth in the Norisring Trophy race, a non-championship support event to the main contest, the annual 200-mile DRM race.

Through all this time, the cars had been white. Just before their race debut at Silverstone, England, the British tobacco company Rothmans signed on as a multiyear, multiprogram sponsor. The cars emerged in blue, white, and gold, colors that became as much Porsche identity as Rothmans.

Silverstone was not the first race of 1982, but for many teams it was the final contest before Le Mans, and thus the place to test the cars' readiness for 24 hours by racing them for 6. Ford brought its C100, Lola came with its T610, Jean Rondeau entered his M482; there was a Peugeot-powered car, several others with Ford Cosworth power, and a number of sports racers, including new Lancias, that began to bridge the gap between Group 6 and Group C. Porsche arrived, ready to race, with the well-tested prototype 001.

Peter Falk's practice strategy was to confirm chassis setup and determine fuel consumption to set his plan for refueling and for tire and driver changes. As a result, first sessions in the 956s failed to impressive outsiders. But then, with his data confirmed, Falk released Ickx. Ickx sliced more than a full second off the fastest (and former pole-sitting) Lancia, a margin so great Lancia put up no challenge.

In the race, the Group 6 Lancias, under no fuel restrictions, ran away. Eventually, they enjoyed a five-lap lead over Falk's Porsche drivers, who were obeying orders to conserve fuel. One Lancia broke down; another won, finishing three laps ahead of the Porsche, which still won its Group C class. What was more, the 956 unexpectedly finished with 10.8 gallons (40.9 liters), in the tank, having averaged 5.67 miles per gallon (41.48

liters per 100 kilometers). It beat Schäffer's target by 1.75 miles per gallon (18.5 liters per 100 kilometers)!

Singer, ever the perfectionist, returned with the cars to Weissach and a list of fourty matters to rectify. Those done, the car went for its final exam: 30 hours on the rolling road—a chassis dynamometer onto which the car is chained and vented with massive fans and then run for the full length of Le Mans, plus 6 hours. Test drivers followed a precise script for negotiating the 8.48-mile (13.64-km), Circuit de la Sarthe, including 30 seconds flat-out in top gear to simulate the Mulsanne Straight. The car finished without a problem by dusk on May 22, barely a month before Le Mans.

Just before Le Mans week, Singer brought Bell and Ickx back to Weissach for initial tests of the three cars Porsche had entered for Le Mans: 956-002, -003, and -004. Once in France, Porsche discovered competitors similar to those at Silverstone—just many more of them. The maker measured itself against its competition and confirmed its theories. The 956s reached 230 miles per hour (370 kilometers per hour), along Mulsanne, some 10 miles per hour (16 kilometers per hour), slower than the 917s a decade earlier. But their ground effects made them *much* faster through turns. Drivers felt considerably more strain on their upper-body muscles and necks than before.

Jacky Ickx and Derek Bell won, though their victory was not without some worries. Their engine experienced fuel-mix and cooling gremlins, but Sunday morning, everything seemed to fix itself.

Jochen Mass and Vern Schuppan took second, finishing three laps behind their teammates, but for the cameras it was more like 20 feet (6 m). Another 20 feet (6 m), behind them, Porsche Typ 956 No. 3, Haywood/Holbert/Barth, placed third; it was nineteen laps behind the winners. The three cars' finishing order followed their race numbers—almost 30 minutes before the checkered flag.

When the officials and the journalists completed counting, Porsche cars had won the Group C class, IMSA GTX (Grand Touring Experimental), IMSA GTO (Grand Touring over 2.5 liters), Group 5, and Group 4, taking each class victory and filling seven of the ten top places. In addition, Ickx/Bell won the Index of Energy Efficiency, with Mass/Schuppan second and Barth/Haywood/Holbert fourth. And in a final data point of significance, Ickx/Bell and John Fitzpatrick and David Hobbs in Fitzpatrick's customer car each set class records for distance completed. (Fitzpatrick and Hobbs, both British racing drivers had long histories with Porsche and Fitzpatrick, as team owner, was an early customer for the 956.)

After the race ended, the Automobile Club de l'Ouest (ACO) released its official results, publishing actual fuel consumption for each car. Bell and Ickx had used 618.55 gallons (2,341.3 liters), to win, meaning they left 68.35 gallons (258.71 liters), in their reservoir. Could they have gone faster? Probably. Driven farther? Probably.

But Porsche's theory of racing, starting with Ferdinand Porsche and continuing through such outside practitioners as John Wyer, Roger Penske, and others, has been that you go as slowly as you can to win. Your goal is to cross the finish line on fumes and roll to a stop 1 inch (1 meter)—beyond it. An amusing corollary is that you should build your race car so efficiently that it crosses the finish line as it runs out of gas, whereupon it promptly falls apart completely, every item, every element, every ingredient completely spent.

But the Porsche men were not dreamers. Le Mans was, in its way, the be-all and end-all of any racing season. Still, championships required many successful finishes. Porsche won the World Endurance Championship (WEC) following victories at Spa, Fuji, and Brands Hatch. In addition, the drivers' championship went to Jacky Ickx.

Porsche looked forward to 1983. Customer Racing manager Jürgen Barth was already busy, handling orders from private teams who were ordering 956s for the next WEC season.

S LL 7731

1983–Present

Anyone Bring Sunblock?

911 Cabriolet

Before reporting for CEO duty in Zuffenhausen in January 1981, Peter Schutz had interviewed Porsche's dealers and customers about its cars. He came away dismayed and confused, especially about 911s: too expensive; plagued with problems Porsche refused to solve; soon to be discontinued; most profitable car line; customers extremely loyal despite drawbacks.

"If you want to build a business, you've got to connect with the dreams of your customers," Schutz explained in an interview some fifteen years after leaving Porsche. "You've got to understand your customer and build whatever it is they dream of. If they can't discover their dream, you show it to them. Porsche is in the business of selling memberships in the dream." Schutz found that dream and business in jeopardy.

Hoping to understand more, Schutz went to meet Weissach director Helmuth Bott soon after arriving. Bott had a bar chart on his office wall, tracking lifelines of Porsche's autos. The 924, 944, and 928 ran out four years or beyond. The 911 stopped in 1981—within months. Schutz examined the chart, grabbed a marker from his desk, and extended the 911 line off the end of the chart, onto the wall, around the corner, and on to the next wall.

1993 Typ 964 Speedster The original Typ 356 Speedster from 1954 through 1958 established a true cult following. So Porsche followed up the 1989 Carrera version with one on the Carrera 2 platform. In its narrow body configuration— 65.0-inches (1,652-mm), wide—the Works assembled 930. The Exclusiv department also delivered about fifteen wide bodies.

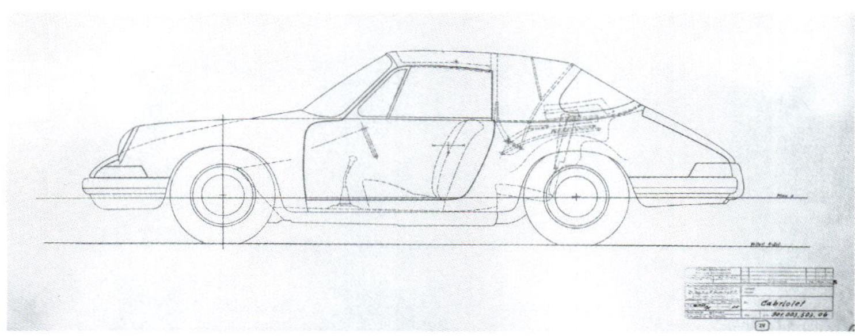

(Top) 1983 Typ 911SC Cabriolet After eighteen model years without an open Porsche, the company reintroduced the cabriolet in the final year of the SC series. The project required significant chassis reinforcement but yielded a manual-top convertible capable of 146 miles per hour (235 kilometers per hour), making it one of the fastest in the world. Porsche assembled 4,096 in this first year.

(Above) 1964 Typ 901 Cabriolet Ferry Porsche had asked for an open car body on the 356 replacement from early in the process. The request got lost in internal politics but designs and testing revealed the need for chassis platform strengthening. What was more, the engine's tall vertical fan left too little room to stow a collapsed cloth top.

"I wrote on his wall with an indelible marker," Schutz told the author, wearing a Cheshire Cat grin. "And I said, 'Mr. Bott, do we understand each other?'

"He sat there beaming! He said, 'You can do that, Herr Schutz?'

"I can do that, Herr Bott.'"

Within moments, Bott showed Schutz *his* dreams for the car: a cabriolet. He led Schutz deep into the garage below his office and uncovered an open 911, dubbed "Bott's Speedster," which Fuhrmann had ordered destroyed. As the two men brainstormed taking the open car to series production, Schutz asked how they could inform dealers and customers that the 911 was very much alive.

"The poor morale, and the reason the revenue was down was because they were losing their 911," Schutz continued. "I don't think I'd even sat in one by this point. I wasn't really even sure what it was, but that didn't matter. It was my role as chairman to get the company going again, and that was the surest, easiest, fastest way." Bott's proposal came in promptly, as did Schutz's approval.

"A few days later I went back to see Professor Porsche. I told him I believed everything he had told me about the conditions of his company and that I decided

1967 Typ 912 Targa Porsche's immediate solution to the convertible top obstacles was this integrated roll-over bar that supported a removable top panel over the cockpit and a zip-out rear window. Porsche offered these on four-cylinder 912s through 1969, and the full line of 911s included a Targa through model year 1993.

to build a convertible out of the 911. His response was, 'I think we should have done that five or six years ago. You know why we didn't? We were afraid of regulations that never came."

Bott wasted no time once Schutz committed to producing the 911 cabrio. It was nothing as easy as simply cutting off the steel roof section and fitting a piece of cloth in its place; still, within a month, his experimental department had created a prototype that he nicknamed the Roadster. By mid-April, he was driving a prototype around Weissach. In an interview three years after he retired, he said it had reminded him of his first drives in the Typ 911 Targa and how he had insisted the back window be fully removable. He made a note to tell his engineers he wanted a zippered-in rear window for the cabriolet as well. A bit more than two weeks after Bott drove the prototype, he put Schutz in it and earned the chairman's blessing.

"It was an interesting challenge," body engineer Eugen Kolb told the author. "When Schutz saw the first prototype, he said, 'Okay, let's go to series production!' And the date was clear when Schutz wanted it: to debut at Frankfurt."

Kolb, who, as a race-car body designer, was familiar with extremely short deadlines, also had expertise in kinematics, the operations of an object in motion. In this case, he had to fabricate a convertible top that opened, stowed behind rear seats, and closed, sealing tightly.

"Schutz saw the prototype and expected they could make it very soon," Kolb said. "It was just impossible. He did not understand how much work was needed." If there was a single problem with Schutz as chairman, according to colleagues, it was his naïveté—how his enthusiastic responses to proposals were usually interpreted as approval, if not outright orders, with no sense of the complexity involved.

Now they needed to inform the world of the 911 resurrection. If it weren't enough to cut off a steel roof and stiffen an open car, they leapt much further. Following Schutz's cabriolet endorsement, he and Bott had conceived the idea of displaying it at Frankfurt on an all-wheel-drive chassis to hint at directions Porsche was going with future products. By early July, Bott's staff began assembling Porsche's first four-wheel-drive prototype, designated 911 A4. The days between early July and the September show flew past. Yet on September 17, when the Frankfurt doors opened, journalists and invited guests saw a white Porsche 911 Cabriolet prototype with matching white interior sitting on a mirror platform.

The team involved in the show car had hastily cobbled together a cabriolet using a Porsche Turbo 3.3-liter platform. The mirrors showed off the driveshaft running *forward* from the engine to the front axle, to startle

1989 Typ 911 Carrera Speedster Contemplating uses for a sizable number of 3.2-liter Carrera cabriolet bodies at the end of the model run, Porsche resurrected the Speedster name and appearance. It was strictly a two seater with a fiberglass tonneau covering a rear storage area. Zuffenhausen assembled 171 of these narrow-body Speedsters and another 2,103 on the 4.85-inch (123-mm), wider Turbolook body.

visitors with another unexpected discovery: this 911 Turbo Cabriolet was also four-wheel drive. Porsche announced the unexpected, "Not only are we not killing the 911, we are taking it in directions you have not yet imagined!" The car was a sensation, appearing in newspapers and on the covers of enthusiast magazines around the world.

Remarkably, following a summer filled with exhaustive tests and modifications to rebuild the stiffness of a 911 coupe in the open cabriolet, Zuffenhausen assemblers completed the first series-production Typ 911 SC Cabriolet on October 6 as a mid-1982 model introduction. Owners raised and lowered the cloth top by hand. Under Fuhrmann's direction, Porsche had introduced the 911 SC (for Super Carrera) for 1978, reducing the 911 lineup to this normally aspirated 2,994cc opposed six with Bosch K-Jetronic electronic fuel injection, which produced 180 horsepower. While this was 20 horsepower less than the final Carrera, engineers reworked the engine to produce more torque: 195 pound-feet, versus 188 in the Carrera, for better urban drivability. The SC was also slightly wider than the prior

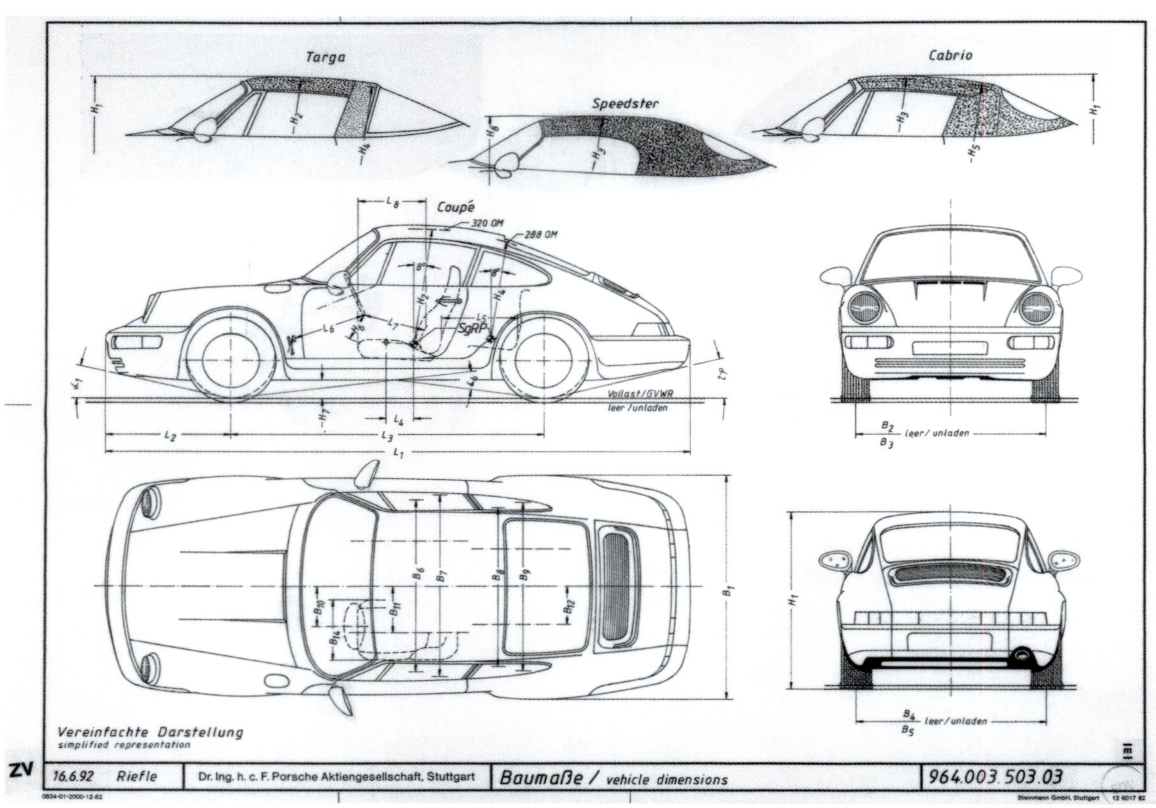

(Above) 1992 Typ 964 Carrera 2 Cabriolet Turbolook Porsche offered a wide-body cabriolet through 1992 and 1993, marketed in the United States as the Carrera 2 America Roadster. It used the same 70-inch-wide (1,775-mm) turbo body which was 4.85 inches (123 mm), wider than standard cabriolets. Zuffenhausen assembled 702 of these over the two-year production span.

(Left) 1992 Typ 964 Cabriolet and Targa Plans revealed Porsche's intention to continue not only its Targa and Cabrio bodies through the Typ 964 series run, but also proposed another Speedster with its lower-profile roof line. Porsche introduced the Typ 964 Carrera 2 Speedster as a 1993 model.

Carrera models—65.0 inches (1,652 mm), versus 63.4 inches (1,610 mm). Buyers found chrome-plated window frames, door handles, and headlight bezels among the subtle bodywork evolutions. Underneath, standard front and rear sway bars further improved handling. Porsche offered the turbo front and rear spoilers as options on the Carrera, leading to winged Targas and Cabriolets as special orders.

Porsche replaced the SC with the new 3.2 Carrera series for 1984, in coupe, Targa, and Cabriolet body styles. The new 3,164cc opposed six-cylinder engine developed 231 horsepower, using Bosch's Digital Motor Electronics system to control ignition spark and fuel injection. Stiffer emissions regulations in the United States and Japan reduced output to 207 horsepower for these markets. Turbo-look spoilers and wider fenders along with Turbo wheels, tires, and brakes reappeared as options with the 1985 model year. Porsche reworked its synchromesh five-speed transmission to reduce gear forces and altered gear-lever geometry to provide shorter gearshifts and designated the new gearbox G50.

The company introduced its first retro concept at the 1987 Frankfurt show, offering a speedster body style thirty years after discontinuing the 356 variant. For 1988 and 1989, Porsche assembled the 3.2 Speedster on its Turbo platform and wide bodywork (though some "narrow-body" cars emerged) as strictly a two-seater with a twin-humped tonneau cover over the rear package area. While SCs now boasted an electric lift for the Cabriolet's top, the Speedster was faithful to the original with its hunkered-down manually operated cloth top. However, the Speedster did carry over the 3.2 Cabriolet's electric windows, replacing the crude plastic side curtains from the 1950s.

At the 1989 Frankfurt show, Porsche revealed the all-wheel-drive Typ 964 Carrera 4, with antilock brakes, a new 250-horsepower, 3,600cc opposed six-cylinder engine, and its new coil-spring suspension. In early spring 1990, the company also introduced a companion rear-drive Carrera 2 and Targa and cabriolet body models. A Turbo-look Carrera 2 Cabriolet appeared as a 1992 and 1993 model; for US markets, Porsche resurrected another resonant "old-timer" name, calling it the America Roadster. At the same time, Porsche introduced its rear-wheel drive, 355-horsepower Turbo Cabriolet. Near the end of 964 production, it offered its next Speedster in narrow body only.

Porsche's 1994 Typ 933 in Carrera, coupe, and cabriolet bodies replaced the 964s. Updated 3,600cc engines delivered 272 horsepower. This new model presented the first front-to-rear body redesign of the venerable 911 of 1964. The Cabrio appeared in spring 1994. Electric roof lifts had evolved through the 964; those had required stopping the engine, but 993 drivers needed only to apply the parking brake to release the interlocks.

Porsche's one millionth series-production car drove off the Zuffenhausen assembly line on July 15, 1996, the total including 356s, 911s, and the front-engine transaxle variations. For this model year, engineers raised engine output to 285 horsepower and introduced not only a wide-body, normally aspirated coupe but also an ingenious Targa that featured a large all-glass retracting roof.

The 1998 Typ 993 marked the end of a long era at Porsche: this model ran with the last of Porsche's legendary, long-lived air-cooled engines. Exhaust emissions and noise pollution necessitated a change some engineers had wanted for decades—and some loyalists simply refused to accept.

1997 Typ 933 Cabriolet The Typ 933 ticked off several checkmarks for Porsche enthusiasts. Engineers and designers felt the predecessor Typ 964 had veered too much toward comfort. So, under Peter Falk's direction, the 993 aimed toward nimble handling. A new rear axle assembly helped.

SAIMA
SAIMA
SAIMA
Marlboro
8
HERCULES
HERCULES
UNIPART
MP4

1982–1987

20

Open Wheels to New Horizons

TAG P01

Decades had passed since Porsche's last foray into open-wheel racing in Formula One and Two at the start of the 1960s. But curiosity still lingered. No matter how Porsche cars did in the variously named World Endurance Championships, there always was a sense that open-wheel racing was really the top tier and everything else was either training ground or retirement activity.

The United States Auto Club (USAC) and Championship Auto Racing Teams (CART) series in the US carried some of that cachet. Thus, when Ted Field approached Porsche with the idea of using its engines for an Indy assault, Helmuth Bott and Ernst Fuhrmann were intrigued. Field had successfully raced Carrera RSRs and 935s with his Interscope team, based in California. Field and co-driver Danny Ongais had raced a pair of black 935s in IMSA and at Le Mans. Field had acquired some open-wheel chassis, and Porsche offered the services of Valentin Schäffer and Hans Mezger, who modified one of their 2,650cc Typ 935 engines to run on alcohol, the specified fuel for the American series.

Unfortunately for Field and Porsche, this took place just as a number of other team owners, including Porsche friend Roger Penske, were in a dispute with USAC over

1984 Typ TAG-P01 and McLaren McLaren Formula One star Niki Lauda was extremely anxious to get Porsche's engine into his McLaren. He had strong faith in Hans Mezger's design and Valentin Schäffer's turbocharger mastery. He was right, and in its 1984 debut season, the F1 drivers' championship became a battle between Lauda and teammate Alain Prost with Lauda winning the title.

1980 Typ Indy P6B Interscope
The engine men converted Porsche's 2.65-liter opposed six-cylinder engine to run on methanol, required at Indy. Mounted in Interscope's Parnelli P6B chassis, the engine produced 630 horsepower. The 1,499 pound (680 kg) racer turned test laps that were fast enough, but they severely threatened one important competitor. He spoke to sanctioning body officials and, rather than lose him, they changed the rules which made the Interscope car uncompetitive.

racing's future. Dissatisfied with USAC's answers, they formed Championship Auto Racing Teams. CART had more in common with Porsche's own direction than the older, tradition-bound USAC. However, the flagship event of the series—the Indianapolis 500—belonged to USAC. This complicated things.

Porsche assembled its engine to USAC specs, and its test in Field's car were extremely promising. So promising, in fact, that some of USAC's old guard threatened to join CART if USAC didn't find a way to slow the Porsche. In the last few months before the 500, USAC assessed its options and changed the rules on Porsche. The change was so drastic it left neither Porsche nor Field any chance of success. USAC retained its old guard, and Porsche withdrew.

Then, unexpectedly, a year later, McLaren International approached Porsche about producing an engine for Formula One. McLaren, like many other teams, ran normally aspirated 3.0-liter Ford Cosworth engines. But since 1977, Renault had competed with turbos. While early efforts had stumbled, or exploded, by 1981, the message was clear: to win in F1, one must race with turbos. McLaren knew of Porsche's success in Can-Am, the Interserie, and Group 4, 5, and 6. Recognizing significant differences between USAC and the FIA, which sanctioned Formula One, Bott and Mezger met with McLaren VP Ron Dennis and designer John Barnard to determine their needs.

Bott wrote a proposal, but McLaren suggested Porsche fund it entirely. Ferry Porsche refused. Unexpectedly, an organization called Techniques d'Avant Garde (TAG), which sponsored a competing F1 team at that time and had universal interests in long-term technology development programs, stepped up as McLaren's sponsor. This solved the problem of money. On October 12, 1981, Dennis and Peter Schutz signed contracts.

For one very busy year, Mezger, turbo *Meister* Valentin Schäffer, and their teams worked on a new twin-turbo 1,499cc V-6 engine with intercoolers. The contract between TAG, McLaren, and Porsche established strict deadlines; McLaren intended to begin testing the engine in Barnard's latest cars in 1983 and campaign them from 1984 through 1987. Porsche's first prototype engine ran on a test bench on December 18, 1981. Mezger's target had been 600-plus horsepower, which the first run exceeded. This meant it offered plenty of potential for future development. Curiosity led Porsche to install the new engine in one of its Typ 956 endurance racers for testing turbo lag, throttle response, and engine performance under a real-world load. But this went against McLaren's contract, which stipulated the engine was only ever supposed to run in McLaren race cars; Ron Dennis viewed the aerodynamics, and especially the weight, of the 956 as nothing close to real Formula One World. It took masterful diplomacy on the part of Bott and Schutz to calm the hot-tempered Dennis.

Porsche got an engine into a McLaren MP4 on March 28, 1983, and it steadily accumulated 4,000 miles (6,400 km), of testing at Weissach. Meanwhile, Porsche began assembly of ten more development engines. McLaren planned only testing through 1983, but team driver Niki Lauda, who had done much of that testing, had other ideas. McLaren's principal sponsor was Marlboro tobacco, which also had a personal services contract with Lauda. Lauda ran an end run around Dennis and Barnard, convincing Marlboro's chairman that McLaren was essentially wasting time. By now, the engine developed 700 horsepower, a 200-horsepower advantage over the Cosworths and close to the turbo Renaults. Marlboro flexed its contract muscle; over

(Top) 1983 Typ McLaren MP4/1D and TAG-P01 At Weissach McLaren and TAG transporters and support vehicles moved onto the Weissach test circuit as part of the team's extensive testing and development program. Porsche's 700-horspower, 1.5-liter twin-turbocharged, twin-intercooled V-6 engine ran more than 2,485 miles (4,000 km), of tests there.

(Above) 1983 Typ 2623 TAG-P01 Engine Hans Mezger specified 82-millimeter cylinder bore and 47.3-millimeter piston stroke in the V-6 for 1,499 cubic centimeters total displacement. The 330-pound (150-kg), engine initially developed 600 horsepower, 11,200 revolutions per minute (rpm) at race boost of 3.3-bar, 48 pounds per square inch (psi).

1984 Formula One at Österreichring Alain Prost, No. 7, qualified second but got ahead of pole-sitter Nelson Piquet, No. 1, at the start. Niki Lauda, No. 8, started from fifth but shot up the inside to pass Elio de Angelis, No. 11. Lauda, an Austrian, won the race on his "home" circuit. This was the 12th race of the season and marked the 400th Formula One Grand Prix since the series started in 1950.

(Top) 1984 McLaren MP4–Tag P01 Testing McLaren personnel surrounded Alain Prost during a pit stop while testing at Circuit Paul Ricard in February 1983. Michelin and Bosch technicians also were on hand. The efforts paid off well; Prost won seven races during the 1984 season.

(Above) 1985 Typ TAG-P01 and McLaren Alain Prost joined McLaren in 1984 and finished second in the championship behind Lauda. Here Prost drove his McLaren-TAG to second place overall in the Grand Prix of Holland, the 11th round in the 1985 season. Prost won the championship.

Barnard's and Dennis's protests, Lauda tested at Silverstone and then raced the new McLaren MP4 with TAG P01 engine at Zandvoort in the Netherlands, Monza in Italy, Brands Hatch in the United Kingdom, and Kyalami in South Africa.

It was perhaps a premature effort, though everyone agreed testing under racing conditions taught them more. Porsche had fit its engines into a chassis designed for Cosworth engines with all the compromises Barnard could handle. Room for intercoolers was inadequate, but the brakes were worse. These had been fine for 500 horsepower, but Lauda and teammate John Watson learned to start braking 500 feet (150 m), earlier than everyone else—and with the engines idled down under long braking, it took them longer to climb back up in speed. By Kyalami, Barnard had resolved so many of the problems that Lauda ran the race's second-fastest lap, but he finished only eleventh due to continuing electrical gremlins.

Just as it had in Group C, the FIA began enforcing fuel-use restrictions in F1 starting in 1984. Limits of 220 liters, 58.1 US gallons per race led Mezger to increase engine compression to 7.8:1, and Bosch developed a new, highly efficient sequential fuel-injection and spark-ignition management system. That, plus a new chassis from Barnard, changed the course of McLaren Racing. New teammate Alain Prost (who replaced Watson) won the season opener in Rio de Janeiro. When officials inspected the car after his victory, it still had 5.3 gallons (20 liters), of fuel. The season's second race, at Kyalami, went to McLaren one-two, with Lauda winning and Prost in second. The rest of the season proved the brilliance of Porsche's engine design, Barnard's chassis, and TAG's support. When the racing year ended, McLaren-TAG had won the World Constructors' Championship, and Porsche's engines had given Niki Lauda a World Drivers' Championship; Prost placed second.

For the 1985 season, the FIA reduced the fuel allowance to 51.5 US gallons (195 liters). Mezger responded by increasing compression to 8.0:1 and raising turbo boost from 3.3 bar (48 psi) to 3.4. This produced 850 horsepower. Bosch provided its third-generation Motronic engine-management system for injection and spark, and Barnard repositioned the turbos to improve throttle response. McLaren took its title again, and the drivers' championship went to Prost, who had won six of the sixteen races. Lauda, frequently plagued by vibrations from electronics malfunctions, retired more often than finishing and placed tenth; he retired from racing at year end.

Keke Rosberg joined the McLaren team with Prost for 1986. And another newcomer joined an equally

(Top) 1984 British Grand Prix at Brands Hatch The United Kingdom had banned tobacco-product advertising back in 1971. For Marlboro-McLaren racing, this meant obscuring the sponsor name on British circuits. Niki Lauda, No. 8, qualified third fastest but at the end of 71 laps, was the overall winner, finishing 42 seconds ahead of the second-place Renault.

(Above) 1989 Typ 2708 Indy at Mid-Ohio This was another frustrating open-wheel adventure for Porsche. Planned as their next assault on the legendary Indy 500, Weissach began a program with Porsche Motorsports North America. Hans Mezger prepared a new 2.6-liter methanol-fueled V-8 that produced 700 horsepower at 0.6 bar boost (8.7 psi). The chassis was the ongoing problem, but endless testing paid off with the car's first—and only—overall victory at Mid-Ohio Sports Car Course in September 1989. Porsche withdrew at the end of 1990.

established team on the sixteen grids of the season: the Williams team began using Honda engines. TAG, which had sponsored Williams, offered the Porsche-TAG engine to them as well, but owner Frank Williams was reluctant to share information with competitor McLaren International or to compromise on his needs because it was likely Porsche was providing a one-size-fits-all engine. Williams approached Honda instead.

Prost won four of his starts and took the Drivers' Championship again. Rosberg placed sixth. But in a sign of the changing times, McLaren-TAG placed second in the Constructors' Championship behind newcomer Honda.

For 1987, Porsche's final year under contract with TAG and McLaren, Mezger cranked boost to 3.5 bar (51 psi) and raised compression to 8.7:1. This gave Alain Prost and new driver Stefan Johansson 900 horsepower in races. Over the years, Mezger also had been able to increase engine speeds with redlines that climbed from 11,200 rpm in 1983 to 12,600 by 1987. Drivers were even permitted 13,000 rpm for short bursts. The Porsche engine controls had continually allowed drivers to alter their turbo boost; for 1987, the Motronic system allowed drivers to vary their fuel mixture from inside the cockpit with a three-position selector.

According to Jürgen Barth, as far as that selector was concerned, Alain Prost left it alone. It was Prost—sharply intelligent, deeply thoughtful, cleverly insightful, and known by other drivers as the Professor—"who, among all of the drivers used the least amount of tire rubber, brake pads or fuel—never had to change the setting," Barth explained. "He always raced with the mixture set a little bit rich, because more internal cooling through fuel evaporation meant less risk of engine damage."

There is a saying in motorsports: sometimes, a race is lost by a ten-cent part. A succession of simple, low-cost parts that failed during the 1987 season frustrated McLaren, TAG, and Porsche in their final season. McLaren won just four of sixteen F1 races; Prost finished the year in fourth place in drivers' standings, and Johansson classified sixth. It had been an impressive run. Between late 1983 and the end of 1987, the Porsche engine had given McLaren and TAG three world championships and earned twenty-five Formula One Grand Prix victories from sixty-eight starts.

For 1988, McLaren joined Williams in using Honda engines, which the Japanese manufacturer provided at no cost. Porsche could not afford such generosity—TAG had paid all the costs. Frustratingly, Weissach had entered the agreement expecting to find downstream uses for a 1.5-liter V-6. But its running characteristics made it impractical for endurance racing and absolutely impossible for any future series-production applications.

1990 Typ 3512 Footwork-Porsche Formula One This proved to be a very frustrating project for engine designer Hans Mezger. Porsche's client, Footwork Racing, had commissioned an engine for the new Formula One regulations: 3.5-liter maximum displacement with natural aspiration. Footwork needed 700 horsepower in an engine no heavier than 331 pounds (150-kg) engine. The engine fell short at 670 horsepower and was overweight at 364 pounds (165 kg).

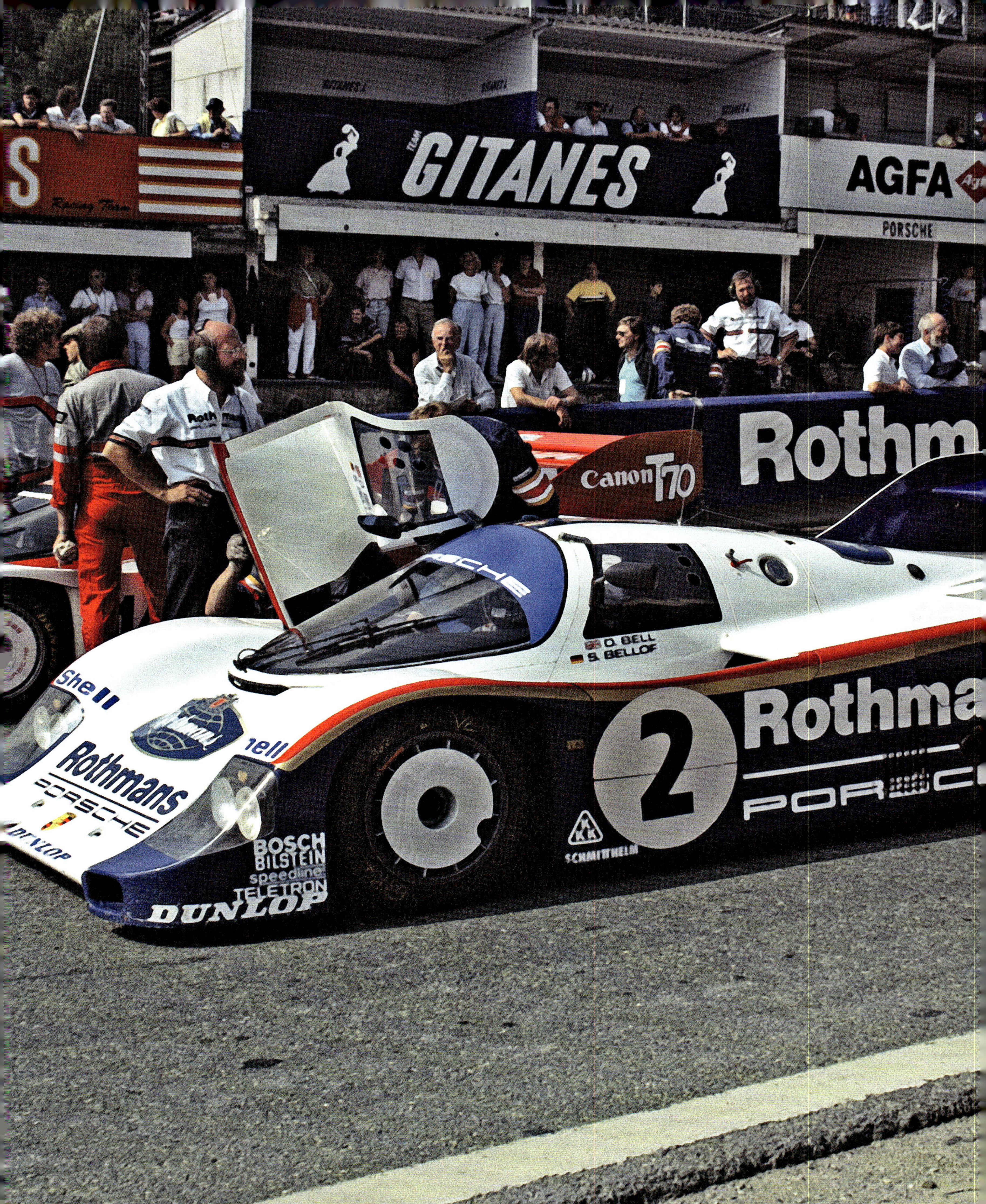

Racing Team
GITANES
AGFA
PORSCHE
Canon T70
D. BELL
S. BELLOF
2
Rothmans
PORSCHE
BOSCH
BILSTEIN
speedline
TELETRON
DUNLOP
SCHMITTHELM

1983–1995

Leaving Racing to Customers

Typ 956, 962

Norbert Singer and Valentin Schäffer upgraded the 956's spark-ignition/fuel-injection control system with Bosch's new Motronic. It gave Works cars trouble at the opening round of the WEC at Monza, but several private teams already had their own Typ 956s, and the best of them also did their own testing and upgrades. As a result, Reinhold Joest, who owned Joest Racing, won Monza in his 956, and his backup car placed third behind the second-place Works car. Under WEC regulations, a Porsche win—whether Works or privateer—awarded points to the marque.

The Works team earned victories at Silverstone, the Nürburgring, Le Mans, Spa, Fuji, Mugello, and Kyalami, nailing down the WEC championship by a large margin over second-place Lancia: 140 total points to 32.

Through 1983, Singer, Horst Reitter, and Eugen Kolb developed a 956 Group C car suitable for IMSA's GTP series, generating a new Typ designation, 962. The fuel tank was a rigid element in the center of the structure. Its forward wall was the driver's seat back, and its rear bulkhead was the engine firewall. Moving the front axle required a new nose and so much of a new body that Singer spent hundreds more hours in wind tunnels perfecting what had been nearly perfect.

1984 TYP 956-83 at Spa Derek Bell and Stefan Bellof qualified second fastest for the 1000-kilometer race at Spa-Francorchamps. Nearly six hours after the start, the two racers crossed the finish line first overall, averaging 105.6 miles per hour (169.95 kilometers per hour), on this notoriously fast circuit.

(Top) 1984 Typ 956-83 at Sandown Park One of the unique charms of the season-ending 1,000-kilometer race at Sandown Park near central Melbourne, Australia, was that Porsche's mechanics ferried the three Works entries to the circuit using city streets. Bell and Bellof, in No. 2, qualified on the pole and finished the race first overall, three laps ahead of teammates Ickx/Mass. Porsche invited Australian Alan Jones, former Formula One World Champion, to join fellow Aussie Vern Schuppan in No. 3 and they placed eighth.

(Above) 1984 Typ 956 C1 at Nürburgring The new 2.82-mile (4.54-kilometer), Grand Prix circuit at Nürburgring debuted with the fourth round of the 1984 WEC. Team owner Reinhold Joest received a request to make a place for a third driver. When he asked what the driver was paying him, Joest learned *he* had to pay. Formula One star Ayrton Senna needed to learn the new circuit for a Formula One race later in the season. He joined Henri Pescarolo and Stefan Bellof in No. 7 and they finished eighth overall.

Porsche debuted the Typ 962 at the 24 Hours of Daytona in February 1984. Singer seated American legend Mario Andretti and his son Michael in 962-001 for the race, a decision that upset several team owners who believed Porsche had promised *them* 001 for Daytona. No matter; the Andrettis did not finish. IMSA regulations allowed the 962 to run with Porsche's 3,211cc engine, the power plant from the 1978 Moby Dick, and most did through the season. The Daytona victory went to a South African team driving a Porsche-engined March 83G. A 935 placed second and another took fourth—boxing in a potent newcomer, the Jaguar XJR-5, at third.

Daytona had invited FISA president Jean-Marie Balestre to watch Americans run a 24-hour race. IMSA imposed no fuel restrictions, and the race was exciting and competitive. Balestre returned to France ebullient over the way Americans raced; unexpectedly, he canceled a FISA regulation he had championed that imposed another 15 percent fuel use reduction for 1984, and he completely eliminated them in the future. Singer and Schäffer had struggled to meet these now-canceled regulations, which had required far more than simply twisting a screwdriver one turn tighter.

At the 1984 WEC opening round, Porsche Works entered a pair of 956/83s, finishing first and second ahead of a Lancia and three private 956s. At Silverstone, the template for the year emerged: the Works won, and six of the top ten finishers were customer 956s; then came a pair of Lancia LC2-84s, and tenth place went to the second Works 956/83.

Frustration with FISA continued, and to protest its inconsistency, Porsche withdrew from Le Mans. The private teams, however, responded as Porsche hoped: Joest Racing won, Preston Henn took second, and John Fitzpatrick was third, all in new 956 Bs.

Porsche took nine of the top ten finishing spots at the Nürburgring; eight of ten at Brands Hatch; first, second, and fourth at Mosport in Canada; the top eight at Spa and Imola; six of ten at Fuji; and nine of ten at Sandown Park in Australia, with wins at each. Porsche again beat

(Top) 1985 Typ 962 C at Spa Derek Bell and Hans-Joachim Stuck, No. 2, started second on the grid beside the Lancia LC2-85 No. 4 with Patrese, Nannini, and Baldi driving. At the other end of the 1,000-kilometer seventh round of the WEC, Bell and Stuck finished second, two minutes behind the Lancia team's other car, No.5, with Mauro Baldi, Bob Wollek, and Riccardo Patrese taking the overall victory.

(Above) 1985 Typ 962 C at Norisring Manfred Winkelhock drove the Kremer brothers' Liqui Moly Racing Porsche to fifth place overall in the Deutsche Rennwagen Meisterschaft at the Norisring.

(Top) 1986 Typ 962 at Daytona Team owner Al Holbert co-drove with Porsche Works driver Derek Bell and Indy champion Al Unser Jr. to capture first overall in the 1986 WEC season opener at Daytona. At the end of 24 hours, the three drivers had completed 712 laps and driven 2,532.72 miles (4,079.23 km), beating the second place Typ 962 of A.J. Foyt by 1 minute 49.15 seconds.

(Above) 1986 Typ 962 IMSA at Sebring Team owner Jim Busby raced his B.F. Goodrich-sponsored Typ 962 IMSA to second place overall in the 12 Hours of Sebring. Darin Brassfield and John Morton co-drove the 279 laps of the 4.86-mile (7.82-km), classic airport circuit in central Florida. They finished eight laps behind winner Bob Akin in his Porsche Typ 962 IMSA.

Lancia, 120 manufacturer points to 57, and its drivers won the top four places in the 1984 Drivers' Championship.

Starting with 1985, Porsche concentrated on supporting its privateers through Jürgen Barth's efficiently run *Kundensport* (customer racing) program. Customers' 962s won Daytona, Sebring (both IMSA events), Mugello, Monza, Le Mans, Hockenheim, Mosport, Brands Hatch, and the season closer at Malaysia. Two races went to Lancias. The WEC title and top four driver's points again belonged to Porsche. Ironically, by this time, Porsche's private teams had begun to spread their wings and stretch their creativity. The ever-inventive Kremer brothers developed a new version of the 956/962 they designated the CK5. They were successful enough to earn second in WEC standings, behind Porsche but ahead of Lancia!

Porsche's 962s were one-two-three at Daytona and again at Sebring to start the 1986 season. Monza opened the WEC calendar, and while Porsche won with its 962 C, a Lancia LC2-85 was second. Then a Jaguar XJR-6 won Silverstone. Porsche won Le Mans with a Works 962 C, and a mix of Porsche models claimed nine of the top ten places. One of those was a unique all-wheel-drive car, the Typ 961, which placed seventh and won the GTX (GT Experimental) class. Joest Racing beat two Jaguars at the Nuremberg "Supersprint," a new shorter race series FISA introduced for lucrative television broadcasts. Porsche privateers won Brands Hatch, Jerez in Spain, Spa, and Fuji but lost the long race at the Nürburgring to a Sauber Mercedes-Benz. Porsche teams ranked first through third in the World Sports Prototype Championship (WSPC), which replaced the WEC. Porsche racers still dominated the Drivers' Championship.

In 1987, Porsche's 962s triumphed, sweeping the top six places at Daytona as well as the top four at Sebring. But it lost to Jaguar at the opening WSPC race at Jarama, Spain, and then at Monza and Silverstone. Porsche Works won the 24 Hours of Le Mans with private teams in second and fourth. Privateers were one-two-three-four at the Norisring in Nuremberg, but they followed Jaguars at Brands Hatch, the Nürburgring, and Spa, earning Jaguar its first season championship since the mid-1950s.

A troubled economy in 1988 forced Porsche to pull back further. At Daytona, a Jaguar won and a Porsche 962 came second. A Sauber Mercedes C9-88 won Sebring with a Jaguar second and a Porsche 962 third. Jaguar took the Jarama Supersprint. A new pattern emerged: Porsche won, occasionally, but Jaguar and Mercedes-Benz waged a two-prong assault on the venerable—vulnerable—five-year-old 962s. At Sebring, Porsche's 962s finished first through fifth overall. But at Monza, the fourth race of the season but the third for championship points, Jaguar won, as they did at Siverstone, Le Mans, and Brands Hatch. Mercedes won in Czechoslovakia, Nürburgring, Spain, and in Australia at Sandown Park. The season finale, a Supersprint-type race at Tampa, Florida, emphasized the changing of the guard when a Nissan GTP ZX-Turbo won ahead of a pair of 962 Cs. The team championship went to Jaguar, second place to Mercedes-Benz, and third to Joest Racing's Porsche operation.

For 1989, the FIA and FISA stirred up the regulations again. The premier series, Formula One, announced engine regulations that banned turbochargers and enlarged maximum displacement to 3.5 liters, hinting at the sports cars' future. For Group C, FISA required every team to commit to the entire season, with heavy fines for skipped races, hoping to encourage Japanese teams to race more than Le Mans each year. In another appeal to television, it reset race lengths everywhere except Le Mans to 279.6 miles (480 km), for 1989. The Supersprint series had been popular, but it seemed FISA misunderstood trends. Le Mans, at its full 24 hours, and America's Indy 500 remained television's biggest draws. When FISA and the ACO could only disagree on

(Top) 1986 Typ 962 Short Tail at Norisring Supercup Hans-Joachim Stuck won the inaugural Supercup championship race at Nürnberg's Norisring in April 1986. Stuck won the 39-lap contest around the tight city circuit in 1 hour 22.5 seconds at an average speed of 109.38 miles per hour (176.04 kilometers per hour).

(Above) 1986 Typ 962 C at Le Mans Eventual 24-hour-race winners Derek Bell, Al Hobert, and Hans-Joachim Stuck, No. 1, right front, started alongside Works teammates Jochen Mass, Vern Schuppan, and Bob Wollek. At the end, Bell/Holbert/Stuck had completed 368 laps, driving 3,089.92 miles (4,972.73 km), and finished eight laps ahead of a privateer 962 team. The Works No. 2 car retired following an accident on its 180th lap.

television rights, the ACO simply withdrew the Le Mans race from the WSPC for 1989 (and 1990, as it turned out).

The IMSA series in the US did somewhat better; founder John Bishop sold his enterprise, and the new owner promoted Mark Raffauf, IMSA's former FIA liaison, to Bishop. Raffauf instigated regulations that eventually eliminated turbocharging, paralleling the FIA's moves in F1.

For 1989, Nissan and Toyota engaged fully in the international series, and Mazda returned. While Daytona, Sebring, and Le Mans remained outside the WSPC, the Daytona and Sebring grids looked familiar. Victory went to a Porsche 962. Nissan won Sebring with its GTP ZX-Turbo. Suzuka, Japan, opened the WSPC season, and a Sauber Mercedes was first. In France at Dijon, it was Joest Racing's 962 C. Mercedes won Le Mans. Victories mostly eluded the Porsches. At Jarama, Spain, Walter Brun's Porsche was third behind a Mercedes and a Jaguar. Joest claimed second at Brands Hatch behind a Mercedes; at the Nürburgring, Porsche's best was third. In the United Kingdom at the classic Donington Park venue, Porsche 962 Cs only reached fourth. Joest Racing took second at Spa. Mercedes won the season finale in Mexico. The championship results reflected reality: Sauber Mercedes sat on top, Joest was second, Brun third, Jaguar fourth, and Nissan fifth.

For 1990, the ACO and FISA continued sparring. The ACO *was* Le Mans, and it had never needed FIA or FISA approval to fill grids. But the dispute became a childish sandbox fight when FISA threatened to the revoke competition licenses of anyone who raced Le Mans. This only served to illuminate the path toward the WSPC's demise in 1992. Its races drew ever fewer entries, discouraging crowds, and repelling sponsors as if some scandal had occurred. Porsche's thinning support of the cars further reduced entry fields. Teams such as Joest or Kremer, Brun or Obermaier, weren't going to other makes—just to other series. (Touring-car racing was steadily growing in popularity.) Or they retired. Of forty-four cars registered for the full season, only seventeen were Porsches. It was only a slightly smaller proportion in the United States with IMSA.

The 1990 Daytona went to Jaguar one-two with Porsche 962s at three-four; Sebring went Nissan, Nissan, Jaguar, Porsche; Suzuka, the WSPC season opener, saw Mercedes, Mercedes, Nissan, and Toyota finish in front of a squad of seven Porsche 962s. Joest made Porsche's best finish at Monza, albeit fifth. At Spa, it was the same place for Walter Brun's 962.

Le Mans had often brought out the best in Porsche cars, drivers, engineers, and teams, but others had gotten better while the 962s had aged. In 1990, Jaguar won; Porsche was second. Mercedes won Dijon as the 962s raced toward their "use-by" date. Joest was sixth at the Nürburgring, Brun placed eighth, and a less-known independent, Jochen Dauer, finished eleventh as Mercedes once again swept first and second. At Donington Park for the WSPC seventh round, Porsche's

(Top) 1986 Typ 961 and 962C at Le Mans This aerial photo shows the middle of the starting grid for the 24-hour race at Le Mans. Just at the word "CLUB" on the pit wall, Porsche's unique four-wheel-drive racing Typ 961 waited for the race to start. With no official category for four-wheel-drive, the organizers entered it as in the IMSA GTX class. Drivers René Metge (who also won the Paris-Dakar Rally earlier in the year) and Claude Ballot-Léna drove the 961 to seventh overall, completing 321 laps and winning its class.

(Above) 1988 Typ 962 Fabcar The Fabcar-bodied 962s were distinctive with their exaggerated rooftop air intake. And the Hotchkis Racing Wynn's No. 10 became even more so when drivers John Hotchkis, Sr., or Jr., or Jim Adams cranked up the boost and left a tail of flames when they lifted off the accelerator. They finished fifth overall.

1994 Dauer Porsche 962 LM Long after the Le Mans organizers believed they've seen the last of the Porsche 962s, privateer Jochen Dauer, who had previously raced a pair of them, retired them to street-use GTs. Norbert Singer saw an ACO rules loophole and plugged Dauer's car in to the new GT-1 category in which they qualified fifth and seventh.

heroes took seventh through seventeenth—but they were shut out of the first six by Mercedes, Jaguar, Spice, and Nissan. The Montreal race, shortened to half length by several crashes, went to Mercedes, which took the championship again with 67.5 points; Jaguar, Nissan, and Spice followed, with Joest doing the best of the Porsche teams at fifth, but with just 9.5 points.

Joest Racing won the 1991 Daytona 24 Hours, and Jochen Dauer placed fifth with Mario Andretti, son Michael, and nephew John driving. There were just six 962s entered—two from Dauer, one of which did not finish, and the same with Joest. Joest kept his two Porsches in the United States for Sebring, where he finished third and fourth behind a pair of Nissans. The remainder of the 1991 season was painfully similar to 1990: Joest Racing carried on nobly, sometimes with assistance from Walter Brun or Kremer. At Le Mans, Mazda won. The Kremers ranked sixth in season standings, and Brun sat at ninth.

FISA's new management—attorney Max Mosley as president and Formula One Constructors' Association founder and F1 team owner Bernie Ecclestone as FISA's VP of promotions—attempted to kill the sports-car series soon after their election in November 1991. They intended to eliminate any competition for F1 for television and sponsorship revenues. But Peugeot, Toyota, and Mazda pleaded for one more season. They succeeded, but 1992 was a pathetic ending. Just thirty cars signed on for the season, and not a single Porsche was among them. The WSC ran just six races, which Peugeot claimed by 114 points to Toyota's 74.

FISA had killed the WSC once and for all in the hopes teams either entered Formula One or reverted to Grand Touring events. Ironically, no organizer had stepped forward with a GT series proposal. Racing historian János Wimpffen refers to 1993 as the Lost Year. Le Mans bestowed a one-more-year extension to the "old" Group C cars, now primarily running 3.5-liter natural engines or the smaller "turbocharged" C2 class cars. Le Mans encouraged GTs, and Porsche responded with a series of 911-based specials from Jürgen Barth's customer sports department.

While both Joest Racing and the Kremers entered their Porsche 962 Cs and Hans Obermaier sent his, the GT class swelled with innumerable Porsche 911 Carreras and a unique 911 S-LM as a Works entry. Peugeot won the race, sweeping first, second, and third. Obermaier was Porsche's best finisher in seventh, and privateer Jack Leconte won the GT class in his Porsche 911 Carrera RSR. Unexpectedly, the resurrection of GT racing reset

Porsche to the top of the Manufacturers' Championship for 1993.

Racing year 1994 saw GT racing achieve new legitimacy. Three individuals lent their names and expertise to forming a series. Porsche's Jürgen Barth, Parisian vintage race promoter Patrick Peter, and Venturi sports-car maker Stéphane Ratel organized the Global Endurance Series, always better known as BPR—a combination of their initials, ideas, and influence. FISA's Group A, B, C, and so on became BPR's GT1, GT2, and GT3, based on similar criteria.

Porsche racers were immediately interested, as were Ferrari, Corvette, Dodge Viper, and other teams from various national series. But it also inspired an unexpected entrant.

German racer Jochen Dauer, with nowhere to race his now-obsolete Typ 962 Cs, converted them for street use, naming them Dauer 962 GTs. He did little beyond modifying the nose and tail panels to mount a license plate. When he read about Le Mans's regulations for road-going GT cars, he approached Norbert Singer and Porsche for help in getting his cars homologated as a street legal. Singer's boss, Horst Marchart, was cool to the idea, but he also knew Gordon Murray at McLaren was designing a GT car. When he finally saw Murray's McLaren F1, he visited Dauer to make it clear Porsche was not doing what Jochen wanted, and instead he must do what they wanted. Dauer happily agreed. Le Mans had outlawed underbody tunnels and narrowed tire width from 16 to 14 inches (406 to 356 mm). It also required a windshield defroster and specified a minimum weight of 2,205 pounds (1,000 kg), 220 pounds (100 kg) more than Group C. As a GT, however, the 962 was allowed a 31.7-gallon (120-liter), tank instead of the Group C's 26.4-gallon (100-liter), capacity.

Singer's *Rennabteilung* prepared Dauer's two cars, now designated Dauer 962 GT-LM. At scrutineering, Le Mans's technical director was not happy. "A GT car should be derived from a road car," Alain Bertaut lectured Singer. "This is a racing car which has already won Le Mans many times!" When Singer reminded Bertaut his own rules did not prohibit it, the ACO reluctantly accepted the Dauers, Singer explained in an interview in 2016.

The cars qualified fifth and seventh, with team driver Hans-Joachim Stuck reaching 203.8 miles per hour (328 kilometers per hour), through the timing traps along Mulsanne. Because their larger fuel tanks gave them greater range, they pitted twice for every three stops the other teams made. But there were some problems through the race. On both cars, lubricating grease leaked from the rubber seals on the driveshafts. Singer worried about them for 18 hours, then relaxed and let the worry go. When the leading Toyota broke its gear linkage 90 minutes before the finish, the second-place Dauer passed the Toyota as it limped to the pits, giving Works drivers Hurley Haywood, Yannick Dalmas, and Mauro Baldi the lead and victory. The other Toyota placed second, and Dauer's second GT-LM was third.

Alain Bertaut convened the ACO Technical Committee. New regulations appeared that drove a precisely worded golden spike through the heart of Porsche's 962.

1994 Dauer Porsche 962 LM Through the night, the two Dauers suffered problems with broken drive shafts but at the end of 24 hours, co-drivers Mauro Baldi, Yannick Dalmas, and Hurley Haywood brought the No. 36 Porsche 962 one final overall victory. They completed 345 laps, finishing one lap ahead of second place Toyota. Thierry Boutsen, Danny Sullivan, and Porsche Works driver Hans-Joachim Stuck came home third in the Dauer No. 35, also with 344 laps complete.

Rothmans
BB-PW 306
Shell
Rothmans
DUNLOP
BILSTEIN

1985–1989

22

What's a Supercar?

Typ 953, 959, 961, 964 Carrera 4

Norbert Singer, Horst Reitter, and Eugen Kolb had just started on Porsche's new Group C contender, the Typ 956. Within days, another trio came to see Weissach director Helmuth Bott. Peter Falk, Jürgen Barth, and Roland Kussmaul were the company's rally loyalists, and they proposed a car for the new Group B. This class combined Group 4 significantly modified production-based cars with barely modified Group 3 cars the FIA accepted for its rally series.

Falk, Barth, and Kussmaul recommended installing the 2.1-liter turbocharged engine in a reinforced 916 coupe fitted with a low shovel nose and a high, hooplike rear wing. Bott respected the three but declined. No manufacturers he knew of had committed to a new formula requiring 200 cars. What was more, he didn't like this specific approach.

"We do so many mid-engine cars; we cannot learn anything,'" he recalled in 1991. "*If* we *DO* a Group B car, let's look at what's the future of the 911?" He had monitored Audi's progress developing four-wheel-drive variations of its front-engine, front-wheel-drive cars. To him, everything about Audi's Model 80 was backward—its engine overhung the front

1986 Typ 959 Paris-Dakar Development engineers Roland Kussmaul (driving) and Kendrick Unger slice effortlessly through the soft sand. The 2.85-liter flat-sixes developed 400 horsepower with lowered compression for low-octane African fuels. The engine had dual overhead camshafts and four valves per cylinder.

axle! But in the late 1970s, he heard from an Audi engineer who had achieved extraordinary traction and handling improvements when he brought power to the rear axle. Audi introduced this as the Quattro for 1980. Now, a year later, after he and CEO Peter Schutz had saved the 911 from extinction, Bott had ideas.

"There is really a very big love from our customers for this 911," he said. "So let's take a very powerful engine to see the limits of the chassis and road holding and the four-wheel drive. It was a goal, a task much greater than to build a race car. In my mind, I could take *this* car into the future!"

Bott authorized a prototype, "911 4 A," using modified Quattro pieces. He sent Falk, Herbert Linge, fellow engineer Manfred Bantle, and rally driver Walter Röhrl to the Austrian Alps in February 1982 for evaluation. Their tests answered dozens of questions and clarified Porsche's concept.

"We decided against adopting any system from another manufacturer," Bott said. "These systems typically restrict traction to one axle most of the time the car is moving, but they automatically switch to four-wheel-drive when the information management system indicates it is necessary. Our view is the Porsche driver needs to know exactly what kind of handling characteristics to expect in any circumstance. That meant we develop a permanent four-wheel drive with adjustable torque split between front and rear axles to take account of the variations of road and weather conditions. Unfortunately, human beings tend to make mistakes, so it is better to relieve them of the responsibility for making decisions."

Following the Alpine tests, Bott's race shops assembled a four-wheel-drive 911 prototype—designated C-20—as his everyday-use "company car." The more he used it, the more convinced he became of its benefit.

1985 Typ 953s 4×4's line up for the start at the Porte de Versailles Nearly a year of work got these Porsche 953 4×4s to the start line of the 1984 Paris-Dakar. The racers was based on the 3.2 Carrera platform but with four-wheel drive. The engine produced 225 hp in a 2,668-pound (1,120.2 kg) car.

1983 Gruppe B Studie Porsche unveiled the Gruppe B Studie at the Frankfurt Auto Show in September 1981 Porsche stylist Richard Soderbergh designed the car body's wind-cheating forms.

Then, early in 1983, Jacky Ickx visited him in Weissach. Ickx had just won the Paris-Dakar rally, more than half of which crossed desert terrain. "I thought at the time it could be possible to do it with a 911," Ickx recalled in an interview with the author in 2014. "And the reason was I saw in the museum already a 911 from the East Africa Safari in 1978." Ickx asked Bott to prepare an all-wheel-drive 911 for him to race to Dakar in 1984. Significantly, he offered his services as test, development, and competition driver—and, crucially, sponsorship from Texaco. When Schutz agreed, Bott summoned Falk and Kussmaul into his office. Both men remembered the moment.

"Mr. Bott asked if it would be possible to field a car at the 1984 Dakar," Falk said in an interview in 2012. "We answered, 'Yes, if we can have your company car immediately for our tests!' That was a little cheeky, but he gave us his car and we began adapting it and then took it for testing."

Volkswagen's factory grounds in Wolfsburg incorporated not only a high-speed oval but also an "off-road" area used to test tanks. Because army tanks tested nearly every day, Porsche got access only during weekends. Falk, Kussmaul, other engineers and a handful of mechanics converted the C-20 into a desert race car; meanwhile, Bott took the matter to his fellow engineers, Falk, Bantle Hans Mezger, and production engine chief Paul Hensler. Bott assigned Bantle to shepherd the Typ 953, Porsche's 911 four-wheel-drive development project, to completion.

"The driving [at Wolfsburg] was very risky. Trees lined every trail," Falk recalled. "We drove as fast as possible around the clock until something broke or we needed to add fuel or change drivers or tires." When the sun rose Monday morning, they had added 935 miles to Bott's bright red C-20. Over the weekend, it turned brown from thrown dirt. Kussmaul's memories were equally vivid: "Every day parts broke. A lot of parts broke—front

Engineers Peter Falk, Roland Kussmaul, and others put Helmuth Bott's "Company car," a prototype known as C20, through rigorous testing on Volkswagen's military vehicle development trails.

suspension, rear suspension. And we had no special tires."

Bott already had a car in mind for Ickx: a four-wheel-drive 911 running a 2.8-liter twin-turbocharged flat six using water-cooled four-valve cylinder heads. The FIA rated this as 4.0-liter displacement and set a 2,425-pound (1,100-kg) minimum weight. Bott wanted 450 to 550 horsepower for competition, which suggested 400 to 450 horsepower for the 200 "production" cars for homologation. By the end of a three-day meeting, this car also had a number: 959. While the FIA offered no category for four-wheel drive, there was Ickx's desert.

On New Year's Eve 1983, 310 trucks and SUVs, 114 motorcycles, and three sports cars queued up in the parc fermé constructed within Paris's largest square, the Place de la Concorde. Jacky Ickx Racing entered three Porsche four-wheel drive Typ 953s, dressed out in Rothmans colors, to contest the sixth Rallye Paris-Algiers-Dakar.

"And when we arrived there, it's full with SUVs and off-road cars," Ickx remembered. "They were all smiling at us. And we knew they were saying, 'Look at them, going to Dakar in a sports car. We will tow them out!'"

The route spanned 7,456 miles (12,000 km), and organizers allowed twenty days (with no rest day) for the entrants to reach Dakar, Senegal. A crowd of some 30,000 spectators watched the entrants begin, more than a few scratching their heads in wonderment. "Was that really a Porsche? A 911? Wait, two of them? What? Three!" In addition to the 953s, the team had a massive support truck—also competing, as the rules demanded.

The 953s looked unusual. Kussmaul had settled on a 10.6-inch (270-mm), ride height, riding on heavy-treaded truck tires; the cars used front double-wishbone

Part of the development process required driving hard until things broke to determine where the weaknesses were. Engineers broke parts repeatedly as they developed the four-wheel-drive 911.

suspensions with two shock absorbers in front and plastic-wrapped 930 Turbo semitrailing arms to protect against rock impacts at the rear. There were oil coolers front and rear, and two spare tires and wheels mounted inside above the midmounted 39.6-gallon (150-liter), fuel tank (with another 31.7-gallon (120-liter), tank in the front trunk). The naturally aspirated engines developed 225 horsepower. A five-speed gearbox and transfer cases distributed the power to four wheels. Kussmaul provided comprehensive spares and emergency kits for each car and carried more of the same burdening in the car he shared with fellow engineer Erich Lerner. Ickx raced with longtime friend Claude Brasseur, and rally veteran René Metge drove with Dominique Lemoyne. When the dust settled—and it was voluminous—Metge had reached Dakar before anyone else, finishing as overall winner. Ickx arrived sixth, and Kussmaul placed twenty-sixth, regularly sacrificing superior placement when the two engineers repaired the other cars.

"In the beginning, a lot of the people didn't like us," Kussmaul said in an interview in 2012. "Guys came to us in the evening and said, 'Come on, you don't belong here! Go home! But after three, four, five days, that feeling was gone. Because everybody had broken something. And they learned if you have trouble, if you need something, go to the Porsche guys and—if we can—we help you."

Porsche returned to Dakar in 1985, using 953 four-wheel-drive normally aspirated running gear inside 959 bodies for the now 8,700 mile (14,000 km) trek. The route originated this time at Paris's Porte de Versailles. As before, Jacky Ickx drove with Claude Brasseur and René Metge with Dominique Lemoyne; 956 racer Jochen Mass drove with engineer Ekkehard Kiefer. Kussmaul ran a Mercedes-Benz G 280 Geländewagen packed with extra fuel and spares. In addition, Porsche entered two four-axle, eight-wheel-drive service trucks.

But success eluded the team. Mass/Kiefer crashed in Algeria; Ickx/Brasseur had small problems until the big one, when a boulder just below the sand's surface ripped off a front wheel with the suspension and bodywork. They were done. Then, two stages before from the finish, an oil line split and the Metge/Lemoyne engine seized. Kussmaul, who was still running, withdrew.

The run in 1986 made up for all that. The cars were true Typ 959s with the 400-horsepower, 2.8-liter twin turbos and new six-speed transaxles, one each for Ickx/Brasseur, Metge/Lemoyne, and Kussmaul with Kendrick Unger. Porsche styling chief Tony Lapine had assigned the 959 body design to Richard Söderberg. His concept from the 1981 Frankfurt Show Gruppe B design study moved through with few changes to the desert with Rothmans colors for the 1986 start.

The 9,320-mile (15,000-km) journey departed Versailles on New Year's Day, stopped on January 13 for rest, and finished in Dakar on January 22. Metge and Lemoyne again arrived first; Ickx and Brasseur finished second, and Kussmaul and Unger placed sixth.

However, Bott had not finished his experiments. The Flacht race shops had assembled a pavement-racing version, the Typ 961; they dropped ride height by 10 millimeters and made suspension alterations

Nighttime work was routine, whether repairs or preventative maintenance. René Metge's car (middle) used only five quarts of oil in 7,000 miles (11265 km) of high-speed desert running, and mechanics saw no need to change it during the entire run. *Courtesy Porsche Corporate Archiv*

for endurance racing. The engine developed 640 horsepower, and Porsche used the car to race the 1986 24 Hours of Le Mans. With virtually no troubles, it finished seventh overall. A return in 1987 was less satisfactory; a driver's error destroyed the car.

All of this established the legend of the 959 indelibly. It was the most technologically complex vehicle of any on the Dakar in 1986, and yet the three cars ran nearly flawlessly. The 959 became, as Bott had hoped, the 911 for the future. Porsche assembled 234 of them, including development prototypes, delivered to a carefully curated list of customers from 1987 through 1988 in a Touring version with all-leather interior or a Sport version with cloth and a full roll cage. The price was $284,100 (DM 500,000). Porsche declined to sell it in the United States.

Unfortunately, the car reached the luxury market during a cyclical downturn in worldwide exchange rates for which certain board members blamed chairman Peter Schutz. Its excessive costs damaged its legacy internally, even as the outside world idolized the car on covers of enthusiast magazines and many business and general publications, featuring its engineering lavishly. But there were human costs. Not long after the board retired Helmuth Bott early for his failure to manage development costs, it accepted Schutz's offer to end his own contract a year early.

Auto historians assess the 959 as the world's first

Cynics at the start line in Paris predicted the 911s were "never going to see Dakar." Here Metge and Lemoine have an almost unobstructed view arriving first into town. The 911 4×4s defied all expectations.

(Left) The 959 road cars had their own production facility. In all, Porsche assembled 234 including the prototypes necessary to prove each of the complex first-of-its-kind systems and a few customs.

(Below) After winning Paris-Dakar, Porsche prepared a road-course version, Typ 961, for Le Mans. The same engine, retuned, produced 640 hp and pushed the 2,535-pound (1,200 kg) car to 249 mph. In 1986, this one finished seventh overall.

(Opposite) Following a disappointing effort in 1985, the team returned in 1986 driving actual 959s. A computer-assisted traction-and-drive system delivered 100 percent of engine output to the rear axle or split it in a selection of front-to-rear biases with a simple in-car adjustment.

supercar, a 200-mile-per-hour vehicle (317 kilometers per hour, 197 miles per hour, according to Porsche) that average, albeit well-connected, auto enthusiasts could acquire. It provided brakes and safety features equal to its capabilities. In an unexpected move that Schutz and Bott had initiated before leaving, Porsche then offered the car to the masses.

Engineers derived the 959 from the 911 G-series 3.2 Carrera platform. Its replacement, the Typ 964 Carrera 4, appeared in the fall of 1989 as a 1990 model. Porsche unexpectedly spun the supercar definition around 180 degrees and, with the 911 Carrera 4, gave any customer anywhere a 155-mile-per-hour (250-kilometer-per-hour), version of the supercar at one-quarter the price. The 964 Carrera 4's price on introduction was $69,500.

Boxster
S GO 1040

1997–Present

Taking the Middle

Typ 986 Boxster, 987 Cayman

At Porsche, development costs for new models, especially in the late twentieth century, represented substantial expenses shared over few automobiles, if any at all. But what if there were a way to avoid much of that cost for at least one new model?

By 1989, Horst Marchart had risen through Porsche's engineering ranks to take charge overall of new-car development. He inherited a Porsche strategy from Ferry Porsche, established by Ferdinand Porsche, that the company always made more than one use from any research and development program. Marchart wondered whether entire car lines could be designed in the same way. Porsche had done that with VW projects, envisioning a new VW sedan and a 911 replacement from the same engineering.

The front of any new car was its most expensive part. It required crash testing and contained front-impact safety, steering, airbags, instruments, driving controls, heating, air-conditioning, entertainment, navigation, door frames—not to mention the doors themselves. With this idea barely a concept, October 1991 served as a pivotal time for Porsche. Marchart was invited to join the company's board, giving him more authority to undertake projects or investigate ideas.

2006 Typ 986 Boxster Roadster Engine output increased nearly every year with the Boxster and Boxster S versions. For 2006, the base model had climbed from 225 to 240 horsepower and the S advanced from 258 to 280 horsepower. From the start, both versions enjoyed precise steering and exemplary roadholding.

Two weeks later, design chief Harm Lagaay traveled to the Tokyo Motor Show with recently named chairman Arno Bohn. Bohn, decidedly not a car guy, came from the computer world, and what he saw surprised him. The two prowled the show halls with several board members and a group of Lagaay's designers. Bohn wondered why other carmakers showed futuristic concepts, but Porsche did not. Lagaay replied, "You just have to ask!" So Bohn did. Lagaay phoned Weissach and asked his designers to flood him with concept sketches. The hotel installed a fax in his room, and he awoke in the morning to find a long roll of ideas. He took his choice to Bohn at breakfast. Bohn approved it immediately.

At the same time, Marchart's idea of making two cars with the same front engine had coalesced into a plan he could move forward. His fellow board members had approved a 911 replacement and adding a second two-seat sports car underneath the 911.

Then things got very frantic. In the space of two weeks, Lagaay suddenly had to put together three different proposals for the two new cars and start Bohn's future show car. He set up three pairs of designers in adjoining studios—his interpretation of Marchart's ideas was that both cars shared not only mechanicals and structure but also front-end appearance. This guaranteed three pairs of egos, three pairs of styles and tastes, having to accommodate their partner. Lagaay likened it to being part marriage counselor, part referee, part divorce lawyer. Complicating things, one of his six new car designers, Grant Larson, had won the contest for the show car. Complicating that, the winning design for the two new cars—Typ 986 and Type 996—came from Larson and teammate Pinky Lai. Complicating everything was a world economy that had hit Porsche hard. Rumors of a Mercedes—or General Motors or Toyota—takeover were in all the trade magazines.

2001 Typ 986 Boxster Roadster Porsche introduced its Boxster as a show car at the 1993 Detroit Motor Show. The car was a huge hit so CEO Wendelin Wiedeking decided within days to put the car into production. It arrived as a 204-horsepower 1997 mid-engine two-seater that sold for $43,966 (DM 76,500), at the factory. By 2001, the base Boxster had 220 horsepower and a new S version gave customers 252 horsepower.

"It didn't work in terms of design," Lagaay admitted in an interview with the author a decade later. "It wasn't good enough because what we had in our heads was so difficult to put under one hat that we were in trouble. Because, in the meanwhile, in the background, we had this fairy tale, this futuristic concept car, going on at the same time. And it was different from what the teams were doing, what we had selected of Grant and Pinky."

Porsche's design department finished Larson's concept in time for the Detroit Auto Show. Based on Porsche's sales in the United States, the show organizers allocated them the smallest, darkest corner. Lagaay recalled, "Detroit didn't want us. They ignored us. The night before the show, the Porsche execs who had come to Detroit met to consider worst case situations for the next day.

"We wrote down all the difficult questions we anticipated would come from the journalists the next day. What will Porsche do when it goes bankrupt? What happens to American customers when you are finished and gone?'"

The next day, their press conference was packed. Every journalist wanted to witness what might be Porsche's

(Top) 2006 Typ 987 Cayman S Coupe Soon after Wiedeking approved Grant Larson's 1993 show car for production, design chief Harm Lagaay asked Larson to consider how a Boxster Coupe might look. An eventual design competition led Lagaay and Wiedeking to select the design from Pinky Lai. Atypically, when Porsche introduced the coupe, named Cayman, the 291-horsepower S version preceded the base 245-horsepower model in 2007.

(Above) 2007 Typ 987 Cayman Coupe Porsche provided two different mid-mounted engines for the Cayman, as it did the Boxster. This base Cayman used a 2.7-liter six-cylinder engine while the S ran with a 3.4-liter six. A five-speed manual gearbox was standard in the base model while a six-speed transmission was optional in the base and standard equipment in the S. Porsche also offered its optional five-speed Tiptronic for either model.

last auto show as an independent company or as an automaker at all. By this time, Arno Bohn had left Porsche, never a perfect fit. The Supervisory Board promoted production engineer Wendelin Wiedeking to corporate chairman in 1993.

"There were hundreds of journalists," Lagaay continued. "All our people had prepared their answers to all these terrible questions." When they finished their prepared remarks, Porsche's US CEO, Fred Schwab, asked for questions.

An American journalist went straight to the most important issue: "What's under the cover?'" Wiedeking, relieved, waved to Lagaay to pull off the silver cloth.

The Boxster—a name designer Steve Murkett had come up with in a marathon brainstorming session, combining Boxer, the nickname for the flat-six engine, with "Speedster"—was an instant and huge hit. Journalists loved it. Newspapers, magazines, and television featured it. Through the week, Detroit-area dealers manned the stand and recorded deposits from people who demanded they be first on the waiting list even though no one could promise them the car would even reach production.

Lagaay phoned the Weissach studio. The car had renewed interest in Porsche. The company was not dead; Porsche had this great Boxster. Though Larson was thrilled, it didn't lessen the challenge he and Lai faced back home: they could not get their styling themes to work. Worse, the Boxster concept was a tiny car, while the 986 was midsized and the 996 was a full-size 911. What was more, the Boxster looked nothing like the Larson-Lai 986/996 concepts. And therein lay the revelation and solution. Lagaay suggested that they take the Boxster design, enlarge all the proportions 20 percent to make the new 986, and share the front-end treatment with the 996.

If styling was a challenge, engine and chassis questions were nightmares. Standards for noise and noxious emissions were tightening, competing directly

(Above) 2008 Typ 987 Cayman RS 60 Spyder From the start, Porsche's 1958-1960 Typ 718 RS 60 race cars had inspired Larson as he designed the Boxster. To honor that heritage, Porsche introduced a 50-year commemorative with a specially tuned 3.4-liter opposed six-cylinder 303-horsepower engine. It was capable of 170 miles per hour (275 kilometers per hour).

(Left) 2014 Typ 981 Cayman (left) and Cayman S (right) Coupes A new platform with new engines generated a new Typ number for Porsche's third generation Cayman. The wheelbase grew by 2.7 inches (60 mm), to 97.4 inches (2,474 mm). Modifications and upgrades gave the 2.7-liter engine 260 horsepower and the 3.4 liter delivered 310 horsepower. Buyers had a choice of six-speed manual transmission or optional seven-speed PDK.

with customer demand for stronger, faster, and more fuel-efficient engines. There were some who believed that no more improvement was possible for the 911 engine. Every option they considered led them to the same conclusion: water cooling was essential, crucial, the only answer. It allowed four-valve technology, enabling more power and better efficiency. It quieted combustion noise. Engine chief Jürgen Kapfer and his team created one of Porsche's most innovative engines ever, featuring an integrated dry-sump lubrication, with truly interchangeable heads—not mirror images but inverted pairs with four valves, single spark plugs, overhead camshafts, and cam drive chains at one end. There were challenges to cooling the 986 Boxster's mid-engine placement just as there were problems to controlling rear-end lift on 996. But the public and media reaction to the Boxster show car had lowered the collective blood pressure on Porsche's board, and scarce funds materialized to resolve problems.

(Top) 2016 Typ 981 Cayman GTS Coupe Porsche introduced the Cayman GTS in 2014. It used the 3.4-liter opposed six, tuned to develop 335 horsepower. This provided acceleration from 0 to 62 miles per hour (0 to 100 kilometers per hour) in 4.5 seconds with the PDK and on to a top speed of 176 miles per hour (283 kilometers per hour).

(Above) 2015 Typ 781 Boxster Spyder This was Porsche's open-car variation of its Cayman GT4. The Spyder used a 370-horsepower 3.8-liter opposed six-cylinder engine in a car weighing 2,899 pounds (1,315 kg). This combination moved the car from 0 to 62 miles per hour (0 to 100 kilometers per hour), in 4.5 seconds. Top speed was 180 miles per hour (290 kilometers per hour).

S KY 718
GTS 4.0

Both cars shared a controversial headlight design, a large one-piece module containing every front light function. "Having the module was a typical Porsche decision," Lagaay explained. "They needed to mount the headlamp in twenty seconds. Push it in, fix it in place. Twenty seconds. So we came up with these five functions in one piece: main beam, dipped beam, fog lamp, turn signal, light washer. It was a typical business decision."

Porsche took a big gamble with its Boxster and 996. Giving the two cars front-end styling so nearly identical validated Horst Marchart's engineering, design, and financial estimates. Yet the timing of introductions confused enthusiasts and journalists. The 996, introduced as a 1998 model in Europe, was the company flagship, yet it appeared too much like the entry-level Boxster, introduced as a 1997 model.

The differences truly were beneath the skin. The two-seat Boxster was a roadster with a cloth top, introduced with a transverse-mounted 2,480cc opposed six that developed 200 horsepower and provided acceleration from 0 to 62 miles per hour (0 to 100 kilometers per hour) in 6.9 seconds and a top speed of 149 miles per hour (240 kilometers per hour). The 996 was the new 911, a 2+2 introduced as coupe and cabriolet a year later, with a 3,387cc opposed six developing 300 horsepower for 0-to-62-mile-per-hour acceleration (0-to-100-kilometer-per-hour), in 5.2 seconds and a top speed of 174 miles per hour (280 kilometers per hour).

By model year 2000, Porsche had assembled 55,705 Boxsters. For 2000, base engine displacement grew from 2,480cc to 2,687cc. With 220 horsepower, the car reached 62 miles per hour (100 kilometers per hour,) in 6.6 seconds and made a top speed of 155 miles per hour (250 kilometers per hour). Porsche introduced a Boxster S version whose 3,179cc opposed-six delivered 252 horsepower, shot the car to 100 kilometers per hour, 62

2020 Typ 718 Boxster GTS 4.0 Spyder Designations changed again, and Porsche's most potent Boxster gained a 4.0-liter engine somehow squeezed into the middle of the car. This developed 414 horsepower at 7,600 revolutions per minute. With optional PDK transmission and Sport Chrono packages, acceleration from 0 to 62 miles per hour (0 to 100 kilometers per hour), took 3.7 seconds and top speed was 186 miles per hour (300 kilometers per hour).

2022 Typ 718 Cayman GT4 RS Coupe Porsche described this coupe as "a razor-sharp track tool." Its 4.0-liter engine developed 493 horsepower. Acceleration from a standstill to 62 miles per hour (100 kilometers per hour), took 3.2 seconds. Top speed was listed as 196 miles per hour (315 kilometers per hour). It price started at $141,700 in the United States.

miles per hour in 5.9 seconds, and on to 162 miles per hour (260 kilometers per hour). The S version came with a tighter suspension mounted on 17-inch (432 mm) wheels.

A year later, 2001, technology took another leap with electronic throttle linkages. "Fly by wire throttle linkage," Jürgen Kapfer explained in an interview with the author in 2012, "offers no friction, and they don't break. All signals go directly to the motor management system which instantly calculates timing, fuel flow, and all other factors."

For 2003, Porsche Styling gave the Boxster line a face-lift with a new nose, new tail, and reconfigured side air inlets. New engine management from the Motronic ME 7.8 system boosted output for the base model to 228 horsepower and the S up to 266. Porsche offered a 50th-anniversary Boxster, acknowledging the 1953 550 RS Spyder, with production limited to 1,953 copies.

The Typ 987 second-generation Boxster debuted at the 2004 Paris Auto Salon. The base 2,687cc engine delivered 236 horsepower, and the S's 3,179cc produced 276 horsepower. New round headlights simplified the nose. Engineers increased displacement of the S to 3.4 liters and incorporated Porsche's innovative VarioCam Plus system into the Typ 987 engines. This complicated intake-valve mechanism provided two-stage valve lift on the intake side by electro-hydraulically operated tappets, two for each cylinder, which continually alter valve timing and profile depending on driving conditions and engine loads. . A long-awaited 295-horsepower Boxster coupe, named the Cayman, appeared as a 2005 model in S trim and Pinky Lai's handsome fastback body. In a kind of reverse procedure, Porsche followed the S with a 2.7-liter base model in July 2006. As with its sibling Boxster, the base Cayman used a five-speed manual or five-speed Tiptronic automatic transmission, and the S was delivered with a six-speed gearbox.

Boxsters received face-lifts again for 2008: base engine displacement grew to 2.9 liters, and the S engines incorporated direct fuel injection. The cars introduced new front and rear lights, and the back end incorporated twin diffusers. Six-speed manual gearboxes accompanied the new seven-speed Porsche Doppelkupplungsgetriebe (PDK) for each car. The Cayman base and S followed suit for 2009.

New design director Michael Mauer gave the third-generation Boxster (Typ 981) and Cayman (Typ 982) a more sculpted appearance, aided by a wheelbase stretched by 1.57 inches (40 mm). Both cars debuted at the Geneva Motor Show in spring 2012; Boxsters were available that summer, and Cayman models appeared in early 2013 as 2014 models. Thanks to rigorous engineering, the Typ 981 Boxster weighed 77 pounds (35 kg), less than the Typ 987 despite its slightly greater dimensions. Porsche also introduced 911-type options to the two cars, including Porsche Torque Vectoring (which enabled crisper turning) and Sport Chrono Plus (an electronics system that improved performance on PDK-equipped models). For 2014, it introduced the Cayman GTS with either six-speed manual or seven-speed PDK and an additional 15 horsepower over the standard 3.4-liter engine. Finally, it introduced the Cayman GT4 with a 3.8-liter, naturally aspirated opposed six-cylinder engine delivering 385 horsepower. By 2016, this evolved to the six-cylinder 4.0-liter engine in the compact car; this car also introduced a Cayman Cup racing series, and the road-going GT4s guaranteed the necessary homologation "proof of production." It sported an aggressive nose and prominent elevated rear wing, which rendered it instantly recognizable. The road-going model delivered 414 horsepower.

As part of Porsche's new strategy to improved power and performance with lower emissions and fuel consumption, Porsche developed an entirely new line of Boxsters and Cayman coupes designated Typ 718, an homage to the company's very successful 718 spyder and coupe racers in the late 1950s and early 1960s. The base engine was a turbocharged 2.0-liter opposed four-cylinder, and the S used a 2.5-liter turbo four. The turbo on the S was similar to Porsche's 911 Turbos, incorporating variable turbine geometry (VTG) vanes; the exhaust-driven turbine featured adjustable blades that spun up to boost speeds much quicker. The fourth-generation 718s arrived mid-2017, and GTS variants of the Boxster and Cayman with 385 horsepower soon followed. Then, in 2020, Porsche introduced its updated GTS 4.0, incorporating a slightly detuned 4.0-liter opposed six (394 horsepower) in Boxster and Cayman body styles. For 2022, the GT4 carried over its 4.0-liter, 414 horsepower engine, which accelerated from 0 to 60 miles per hour (0 to 96.6 kilometers per hour), in 4.2 seconds and reached 189 miles per hour (305 kilometers per hour). Porsche offered the Spyder 4.0, also with 414 horsepower, matching acceleration and a 87-mile-per-hour top speed (300 kilometers per hour). One of its most outstanding design features incorporates twin aero-type fairings trailing off from the headrests, also in the style of Porsche's 718 spyders of 1960–1962.

Mobil
IBM
BILSTEIN
Mobil
IBM
BILSTEIN

Going for Overall Victory. Again.

911 GT1

Porsche had long produced cars that won races for its clients. Their unique 1994 911 S-LM evolved into the 911 GT2 to race within BPR rules, which required twenty-five identical cars each year. Customer sport sold forty-five GT2s before introduction, forty-three in 1995, and fourteen in 1996. Flacht converted twenty-one of these for road use.

The 2,447-pound (1,110-kg), cars gave racers 480 horsepower; road customers got a 2,850-pound (1,293-kg), version with 430 horsepower. Customers could order airbags, electric windows, and air-conditioning, but GT2s were strictly rear-wheel drive for homologation.

As its name implied, GT2 was not BPR's premier category. In that group, GT1, Porsche found daunting challenges from former F1 ally McLaren—designer Gordon Murray's carbon-fiber F1 GTR won Le Mans in June 1995. Perpetual competitor Ferrari had its new V-12-engined 333SP prototypes.

Rules for BPR's GT1 category required that manufactures offer road versions for sale. To Norbert Singer, it appeared that one single car was enough. Singer knew the 911 GT2 needed better aerodynamics, greater downforce, and more horsepower to compete for

1998 Typ 911 GT1 No. 26 and No. 25 at Le Mans The two new Works GT1s stretched out their lead. The heavily revised 3.2-liter opposed six-cylinder engine developed 550 horsepower and Porsche used updated six-speed sequential gearboxes. Allan McNish, Stephane Ortelli, and Laurent Aiello were overall winners in No. 26, completing 352 laps and finishing one lap ahead of teammates Jörg Mueller, Uwe Alzen, and Bob Wollek in the No. 25 GT1 at second.

1996 Typ 911 GT1 at Le Mans Thierry Boutsen, Hans-Joachim Stuck, and Bob Wollek shared driving duties in the Works 911 GT1, bringing the car to the finish in second place overall and first in the new LM GT1 class. They completed 353 laps and finished one lap behind the overall winners driving Reinhold Joest's TWR-Joest Porsche WSC95. The second Works GT1 placed third overall and was second in the new category.

overall wins. GT1 cars had to have a flat bottom from the nose to the rear axle; from there back, rules permitted the undercarriage to rise and form one or more venturi to help hold the car down. Singer and Porsche Motorsport manager Herbert Ampferer believed this could work if they mounted the engine backward, ahead of the rear axle. Singer stretched the GT2 wheelbase from 89.4 to 98.4 inches (2,271 to 2,499 mm) for the GT1.

The supervisory board provisionally okayed this, but one condition for final approval was clear: the car had to be "identifiable as a 911 at first glance." So chassis designer Horst Reitter incorporated the production car's front end; it had passed both US and German crash tests, essential for the single road car's homologation. This allowed him to use the 993 instrument panel as well. These considerations drew stylist Tony Hatter into the project. He had designed the series 993, and, unexpectedly, Porsche Styling had the company's most powerful computers.

"Initially, my job was to keep the cars looking like Nine-Eleven Porsches," Tony Hatter recalled in an interview with the author in 2012. "Norbert Singer soon found out we worked with the newest technology in the automotive world which the racing department didn't have. We could build cars digitally. He was very skeptical at first. He's a man with a lot of hands-on experience, and he couldn't touch anything. He'd walk away. I'd do something on the screen while he was gone."

Hatter lengthened the 993 and widened it to accommodate racing tires. Computer aided systems accomplished this faster and more easily than Singer's collaboration with Dick Söderberg on the 1978 935/78 Moby Dick, or Reitter and body designer Eugen Kolb converting the 956 to the 962. The board gave the go-ahead in late July 1995.

Between then and January 1996, work progressed feverishly. To mount a production nose over a racing suspension forced Reitter to modify his concept. Ampferer revised the engines that had propelled the 962 coupes to victories throughout 1994. He retained the 3,164cc displacement but water-cooled the entire engine. Porsche completed a road-going version for homologation requirements with a tame 3.3-liter Carrera engine tuned to develop 300 horsepower. Barth drove the race car prototype on March 14. Through the rest of the month, the pace turned downright frantic.

In Singer's typical manner, he and his staff tested the new car exhaustively, running more than 1,200 miles (1,930 km) in one five-day test alone. When chassis 001 and 002 reached Le Mans in June, they were ready. At the checkered flag, chassis 002, with Bob Wollek, Thierry Boutsen, and Hans-Joachim Stuck driving, finished second overall and first in the GT1 class, behind Joest Racing in their Porsche-engined open sports racer.

"Less than 48 hours after Le Mans," Jürgen Barth recalled, "we got ten calls, orders for street cars. By Friday, we had close to 40 orders and they only

(Above) 1996 Typ 911 GT1 Strassen Looking like something that just landed from somewhere else, the 911 GT1 Street Version was required by BPR regulations. Just like the racing version, the car was 184.4 inches (4,683 mm) long, 76.6 inches (1,946 mm) wide, and 46.2 inches (1,173 mm) tall. It weighs about 2,206 pounds (1,000 kg).

(Below) 1996 Typ 911 GT1s at Zhuhai 4 Hours, China The BPR wrapped up its first season with its 11th and final race at a new circuit in Zhuhai, China. Porsche, with an eye to future vehicle sales in Asia, was the only Works team supporting the inaugural event. Emmanuel Collard and Ralf Kelleners in No. 36 lead teammates Yannick Dalmas and Bob Wollek in No. 35. Kelleners and Collard were overall winners, completing 149 laps and winning by two lap ahead of a private entry Ferrari F40 GT-E.

(Top) 1997 Typ 911 GT1 and 911 GT2 There's a resemblance there, if you look closely. The Works GT1, No. 7, entered the pits during the Nürburgring 4 Hours in June 1997. Yannick Dalmas and Bob Wollek drove to twenty-fifth overall, suffering fuel feed problems throughout the race. No. 71 is the 911 GT2 of Luigino Pagotto and Luca Drodi, which placed thirty-first.

(Above) 1997 Typ 911 GT1 Evo Strassen For the second season, Porsche produced an evolution of the GT1 and again had to assemble a street version for homologation requirements. The Evo boasted new skin, new front suspension, a new six-speed sequential gearbox, and new headlights, mandatory due to the 1997 introduction of the new series Typ 996.

slowed down when we told them they got a car with 300-horsepower, not the Le Mans engine!"

Weighing just 2,328 pounds (1,056 kg), and running with 600 brake horsepower, the race car's performance was astonishing. From a standstill it reached 130 miles per hour (210 kilometers per hour), in 9.8 seconds; using longer gearing for Le Mans allowed top speeds near 235 miles per hour (380 kilometers per hour).

At the last three BPR events—at Brands Hatch, Spa, Zhuhai, China—one or the other car won outright. By year end, Weissach began filling nearly thirty orders for road and racing versions of the car known as GT1/96. Road cars ultimately got 544-brake-horsepower engines, not the Carrera engines. They sold for about $930,000 (DM 1.4 million) .

In the rarified stratosphere in which Porsche GT1 road cars and racers operated, the company found itself in an unexpected crossfire. McLaren had improved its F1 GTR as well as its own million-dollar three-seater road car. Now, however, neighboring Mercedes-Benz set Porsche's GT1s as its target for 1997, announcing plans to compete in the GT series that the FIA had annexed from BPR as an eleven-race series. Mercedes unveiled its V-12 6.0-liter CLK GTR. Whatever had been Wendelin Wiedeking's earlier plans for the GT1 prior to Mercedes's announcement, now he supported Singer and Weissach boss Horst Marchart. Singer sought to develop a competitive evolution; he and Tony Hatter made enough changes that they had to create a new road car as well. This picked up styling cues from the new production Typ 996 nearing completion in the design department. Porsche committed to the full eleven-race FIA series.

The GT1s did not distinguish themselves through 1997 against the Mercedes-Benz. Singer knew Porsche needed a new carbon-fiber monocoque chassis, the sure way for the car to shed the 200-pound (90-kg), disadvantage it carried against Mercedes and McLaren. Wiedeking, after becoming CEO in 1993, instituted cost-saving efforts that had coalesced successfully, trimming losses and production time. This benefited the final run of series-production 993s that captured customers' imagination. The company and its chief executive now were in a position to renew Porsche's commitment to customer racers. With support from Porsche's highest officials, Singer, Reitter, Hatter, Ampferer, and dozens of other engineers and mechanics had a new assignment: GT1/98.

"I got lost in the racing department with various hybrids based on the 993," Tony Hatter recalled. "First, this was based on the 993, and then, still based on the 993, but with the new headlights. And in the end, of course, we made one car without anything to do with a 911, and we still stuck the new headlights on it. Strange when you think about it."

The *Formsprache*, or form language, that Pinky Lai and modeler Eberhard Brose created for the 996 made adaptation easier for Hatter as he designed a successor. He had to fit a 26.4-gallon (100-liter) fuel bladder behind the cockpit. This forced him, Singer, and Reitter to lengthen the wheelbase from 98.4 inches (2,500 mm), to 113 inches (2,870 mm). At that point it *was* a new car.

(Top) 1997 Typ 911 GT1 EVO at 1998 Daytona 24 Hours Private team owner Dave Maraj acquired one of the 600-horsepower, 2,314-pound (1,050-kg), customer cars. Overheating shortened his race debut at the season opener at Daytona. Drivers Thierry Boutsen, Ralf Kelleners, and Andy Pilgrim retired after 614 laps.

(Above) 1998 Typ 911 GT1 Strassen Version This was the most sinister looking of the GT1s homologation models for the street, and one of the most radical 911s ever to exist. Following a disappointing 1997 season, Porsche returned to the starting point and created an all new car for 1998. It built its first carbon-fibre monocoque which reduced overall weight to 2,094 pounds (950 kg).

Hatter and the racing engineers started from scratch. They developed the body and carbon-fiber tub entirely on computer screens; Hatter's computer design reflected work he and racing engineers did with scale models in the wind tunnel. They shifted the driver to the right side. Hatter enlarged the new 996 headlamps to accommodate extra bulbs. A family resemblance preserved Porsche's form language, but this definitely was a race car. Revisions to the engine left it with 3,198cc total displacement. It developed 550 brake horsepower.

1998 Typ 911 GT1-98 at Le Mans Porsche waited until Le Mans to introduce its third generation GT1. Here, No. 26, the eventual overall winner, streaks from the pits after a routine Saturday evening stop. Engineers lengthened the wheelbase to 106.3 inches (2,700 mm), to relocate the fuel tank amidships. The car measured 192.5 inches (4,890 mm) in length, .

The 1998 season, however, was frustrating for Porsche as its latest GT1 perpetually finished behind new 1998 Mercedes-Benz CLKs except at Le Mans.

Toyota, Nissan, Ferrari, McLaren, and of course Mercedes-Benz each supported teams and presented new cars to challenge Porsche's three GT1/98s in France. When the 24-hour race ended on Sunday, June 7, Porsche was first and second. Then, on Monday, motorsports and customer sports learned of a new project at Porsche, but it was one that left them out.

Wendelin Wiedeking announced a Porsche-Volkswagen collaboration. Porsche's $1.05 billion (€1 billion) commitment expanded the company's product line in a direction few immediately understood; it added a new factory and fueled a firestorm of criticism that took years to extinguish. The size of this investment on a new type of Porsche vehicle left no money for motorsports beyond ongoing commitment for 911-based racers.

GT1 had ended anyway—the FIA discontinued the category for 2000. Two new Le Mans Prototype (LMP) categories replaced it. Porsche began to develop an open spyder, the LMP1/98, for Le Mans in 1999. Months after Wiedeking's Le Mans decision, Porsche announced plans to wait for another year, until 2000. As the rules changed for 2000, this decision made sense. Wiedeking had authorized the engineers to develop the new racer. Original plans for the car, known as LMP2000, used a turbocharged flat six. However, Herbert Ampferer had developed a normally aspirated 3.5-liter V-12 and then a similar 3.5-liter V-10 for the Footwork Arrows Formula One effort. This Typ 3512 engine had been a frustrating project, and Footwork and Porsche ended their relationship during 1991. Porsche shelved the V-10. As Le Mans rules dictated, a normally aspirated engine fit the bill, and engineers increased its displacement to 5.5 liters. It developed 680 horsepower.

1998 Typ 911 GT1 at Suzuka, Japan Porsche sent a single GT1 to Japan for the FIA GT 6th round. Allan McNish, Yannick Dalmas, and Stephane Ortelli finished third overall in the 623-mile (1,000 km), race, completing 168 laps. A pair of Mercedes-Benz CLK LMs were first and second.

Lola Composites of Britain fabricated a carbon-fiber tub in the summer of 1999. Singer upgraded the LMP1 suspension and finished its carbon-fiber body in the wind tunnel. Soon after Porsche and Lola completed the first chassis, Singer's engineers completed assembly and ran a two-day test on the car at Weissach in late November 1999. Within days, Porsche announced it was abandoning the project. Kussmaul retired the car to storage. He and Le Mans winners Allan McNish and Bob Wollek drove the car. Kussmaul recalled, "It set a new lap record at Weissach."

Porsche's press department issued a release at the time announcing that ending the project was a business decision. This enabled it to concentrate engineering resources on the development of new products. People assumed that meant the coming sport utility vehicle.

S PR 128

1998–Present

Water-Cool the 911? Heresy!

Typ 996, 997, 991, 992

Unexpected? For enthusiasts outside Weissach's gates, water-cooling the 911 engine was a big change few anticipated. There had been hints. Hans Mezger developed water-cooled cylinder heads for Norbert Singer's 935/78, Moby Dick; then had come the 936s and, more recently, the 956 and 962 racers.

Weissach engineers had considered water cooling for the Typ 993. But budget and time forced Porsche to postpone it. There was no chance to put it off again, however—emissions standards in several of Porsche' key markets were tightening. Several countries were tightening noise standards as well, and putting water-cooling jackets around cylinders and heads contained engine combustion sound.

This came at a difficult time in Porsche's history. Germany revalued its mark, and exchange rates between it and other currencies shifted adversely when stock markets tumbled in 1987. When sales fell, Porsche released its two great 911 enthusiasts—Peter Schutz and Helmuth Bott—from their contracts early. Rumors spread that Daimler-Benz, Toyota, General Motors, and even diminutive Lotus Cars of England were in talks to take over. Revenue tumbled to $15 million for 1988. Word leaked out that the 911 was again in

1998 Typ 996 Cabriolet Porsche introduced the Typ 996 in late 1997 as a 1998 model. Both coupe and cabriolet models introduced a water-cooled 3,387 cubic centimeter displacement opposed six-cylinder engine that developed 300 horsepower. Typical Porsche attention to detail pulled 110 pounds (50 kg), from the car.

peril. Porsche promoted comptroller Heinrich Branitzki to head the company and brought in Ulrich Bez from BMW Technik to replace Bott.

The economy regained stability, and Porsche's efforts calmed nervous customers, suppliers, and financiers; profit for 1989 more than doubled to $32.3 million. Imprudently, Bez followed in Bott's footsteps, pushing costly projects that either stumbled badly or never left development but nonetheless had counted for millions in unrecoverable costs. A rear-axle assembly from an ill-fated four-door sedan appeared on the Typ 993. Branitzki retired, Bez was asked to leave, and the board promoted longtime Weissach engineer Horst Marchart to replace Bez. Arno Bohn spent a brief two years from 1990 to 1992 as CEO before Porsche rehired and then promoted Wendelin Wiedeking to CEO. Wiedeking rigorously streamlined every operation inside Porsche. Sales figures reinforced Schutz's conclusion: the 911 was too profitable and popular to end. Instead, Wiedeking canceled the front-engine water-cooled models.

As previously written, designers Grant Larson and Pinky Lai were slaving away on a pair of new cars that shared entire front ends, saving tens of millions of marks in development costs. But budgets were so tight that Lai was not even allowed to incorporate the clever elevating rear spoiler Porsche had introduced two generations earlier on the 964 and carried through the current 993.

One of Bohn's final acts was to authorize a show car for the international auto show circuit. The result was the Boxster, a car that reversed the world's view of Porsche's future. The board fed styling and engineering a bit more funding.

The result was Porsche's first water-cooled 911, the Typ 996. The company introduced the Carrera Coupe and Cabriolet in April 1998 as 1999 models. A new 300-horsepower 3,387cc engine used dual overhead

1998 Typ 996 Coupe Comfortable cruising was a goal of the new water-cooled models. Porsche targeted owners of BMW 6-series coupes and Mercedes-Benz 380 and 450 SLs with a plush interior and milder road manners. The car still handled, capable of 1.0G lateral acceleration and acceleration from 0 to 62 miles per hour (0 to 100 kilometers per hour) in 5.2 seconds, and to a top speed of 174 miles per hour (280 kilometers per hour).

camshafts (DOHC) to operate four valves per cylinder. The car accelerated from 0 to 62 miles per hour (0 to 100 kilometers per hour) in 5.2 seconds and to a top speed of 174 miles per hour (280 kilometers per hour). Several months later, the all-wheel-drive Carrera 4 (C4) variations arrived, followed by an FIA-inspired GT3. This introduced a 360-horsepower 3,600cc water-cooled DOHC four-valve engine, a power plant eventually known as "the Mezger Engine" for designer Hans Mezger. The GT3 proved again that when Porsche assembled vehicles such as the 1973 911 RS Carrera 2.7, customers lined up to purchase one. Between 1999 and 2001, it assembled 31,135 Carrera coupes, 23,598 cabriolets, 12,643 C4 coupes, 9,411 C4 cabriolets, and 1,868 GT3s.

Porsche attributed the new water-cooled coupes' success to several factors. The 993 had emphasized nimble sportiness, whereas the 996 shifted toward luxury grand touring. The car was quieter and more comfortable, and Porsche targeted owners of Mercedes-Benz SL two-seaters, BMW two-door coupes, and Chevrolet Corvettes. For air-cooled enthusiasts, this

(Top) 2003 Porsche Carrera Cup The company had introduced the Carrera Cup for 911s in 1990, staring with Typ 964 Carrera 2 models. This third generation gave racers water cooling and the most power yet, 370 in 1999. It climbed to 390 for 2003. The car, without fuel, weighed 2,557 pounds (1,160 kg). Racing was always extremely close.

(Above) 2002 Typ 996 Targa Porsche had innovated the sliding glass roof variation on its classic Targa concept with the Typ 993. For the 996, with an all-new car body, the sliding glass area enlarged and the rear hatch opened. For 2002 as well, Porsche enlarged the engine to 3.6 liters. This delivered 320 horsepower.

(Top) 2005 Typ 997 at Shanghai, China Porsche introduced the Typ 997 in August 2004 as a 2005 model. Subtle styling changes characterized the body, including a return to traditional round headlights. The base 997 carried over the 3.6-liter 996 engine but with a gain of 5 horsepower to 325 while the new S introduced a 3.8-liter engine with 355 horsepower.

(Above) 2006 Typ 997 GT3 Porsche had launched a racing-derived GT3 in the 996 series in 1999 using a 3.6-liter engine Hans Mezger had designed with 360 horsepower. The 997 version offered owners 415 horsepower. Porsche Active Suspension Management (PASM) was standard with the car, as was an electronic limited slip differential and a variable traction control that let talented drivers turn it off.

was something near heresy: nimbleness *and* noise were gone. Coupled with a longer wheelbase 92.5 inches (2,350 mm), for the 996 versus 89.4 inches (2,271 mm) for the 993, despite a slight 100-pound (45-kg) weight loss for the new model, its softer forms and gentler manners provoked consternation among purists.

One of its most controversial—and unexpected—features was its headlights, which were one-piece pods resembling those in the companion Boxster. To the uninitiated, it was hard to discern the Boxster from the new 911. For the "face-lift" that arrived with the 2001 turbo and 2002 model-year normally aspirated cars, Porsche redesigned the fixture.

For these second-generation 996s, engine displacement grew to 3,596cc, increasing output to 320 horsepower. The turbo used the Mezger 3,600cc engine as in the GT3s. The turbo provided owners 420 horsepower and incorporated VarioCam Plus, first introduced on 968s.

Similar to the naturally aspirated GT3's racing links, production-based racing series for turbocharged cars ran in GT2 class, and Porsche's 996 GT2 debuted for 2001 with 462 horsepower, boasting a top speed of 196 miles per hour (315 kilometers per hour). Model year 2002 brought Carrera and Carrera 4 cabriolets, a new Targa with an innovative sliding glass roof, and a Turbo-body Carrera 4S coupe.

Second-generation GT2 and GT3 models appeared in early 2003, the GT3 with 381 horsepower, the GT2 with 472 horsepower and a top speed inching up to 198 miles per hour (320 kilometers per hour). The same year saw a C4S cabriolet, followed in 2004 by a 420-horsepower turbo cabriolet. Porsche produced a 911 GT3 RS coupe for 2004 and 2005. This 381-horsepower coupe was actually slightly quicker to 62 miles per hour (100 kilometers per hour) (4.2 versus 4.3 seconds) but slower at the top end (190 versus 198 miles per hour [305 versus 320 kilometers per hour]) due to its functional aerodynamic rear wing.

Assessing the legacy of the 996 (and its sibling Boxster Typ 986) was simple: the two cars saved the company from either absorption or extinction. With replenished coffers, Wiedeking authorized a successor, the Typ 997; approved racing programs at the highest levels; and launched other projects guaranteed to take Porsche in more completely unexpected directions.

From the earliest days planning the 901 in the late 1950s and early 1960s, Ferry Porsche had intended to offer a cabriolet version. It eventually appeared in 1982 as the SC Cabriolet. Since then, engineers had created successive 911 cabriolets from coupes whose roofs were removed. This process forced engineers and stylists back into the car's structure to strengthen and reinforce it to meet Porsche safety and handling standards. Weissach unexpectedly flipped that sequence on its head as it began the 997. Here, the "lead car" was the cabriolet, and once it was finished, they added a roof to an already rigid platform.

2007 Typ 997 GT2 Porsche had offered GT2s since the air-cooled 993 days, as homologation vehicles for the BPR series. GT2 class allowed turbochargers and the 997 version was the fastest street-legal Porsche to date: top speed was 204 miles per hour (328 kilometers per hour). The twin-turbo, twin-intercooler 530-horsepower engine accelerated the 3,175-pound (1,440-kg) coupe from 0 to 62 miles per hour (0 to 100 kilometers per hour) in 3.7 seconds.

(Above) 2010 Typ 997.2 Turbo S Coupe The company introduced second-generation 997s starting in 2009. Engineering and drivability upgrades included direct fuel injection for the engines and the long-awaited PDK seven-speed transmission. The seventh-generation Turbo and Turbo S appeared in 2010. The S utilized Variable Turbine Geometry in its two turbos which boosted pressure more rapidly. The 3.8-liter Turbo S delivered 530 horsepower.

(Below) 2011 Typ 997.2 GT3 RS (left) and GT3 RSR (right) The 997 second generation GT3 RS redefined GT driving with 450 horsepower, a shorter-ratio six-speed manual transmission, a more aggressive PASM configuration, massive 19-inch (483-mm) 35-series at front and 30s at the rear. The large carbon fiber rear wing reduced maximum speed but enhanced stability. The RSR was a pure racing machine sold only to qualified customers. Its 4.0-liter engine developed 493 horsepower in the 2,998-pound (1,360-kg) racer.

The Typ 997 appeared as a 2005-model coupe, some 80 percent changed from the 996. The 996 used 18-inch (457-mm) wheels and tires; the 997 used 19s, which necessitated shorter final gears to best use engine torque and horsepower. Their additional grip and cornering power dictated new electronic spring and damper suspension systems. This allowed engineers to introduce the Porsche Stability Management (PSM) system, first seen in the 959.

Marchart insisted they carry over the most expensive elements: the roof panel, the interior rear seats and structure, and the water-cooled 3,596cc engine block, crankshaft, and pistons, now producing 325 horsepower. Porsche reintroduced the S, and this used a 355-horsepower water-cooled 3,824cc engine. Owners acknowledged the 996 interior was the best in user comfort and friendliness of any Porsche model to date; the 997 interior was nearly all new while continuing to respect its new clients. Four seating choices cradled and supported occupants of all sizes and shapes.

2013 Typ 991 50th Anniversary Edition Coupe The longer wheelbase and new body styling reduced aerodynamic lift to near zero at front and rear. Buyers chose between the seven-speed PDK or a new seven-forward-gear manual transmission. This commemorative edition used the Carrera 4 wide-body and platform and the interior resurrected the 1963 "Pepita" houndstooth-style upholstery. Production stopped after 1,963 cars.

Porsche phased in new 997 models through model year 2005 and wound down assembly of 996 Turbo S coupes and cabriolets while Weissach engineers put final touches on their replacements. Typ 997 cabriolets reached dealers worldwide in April 2005. Carrera 4 and 4S versions arrived midsummer. Then glass retracting-roof Targas (now strictly on all-wheel-drive platforms), 480-horsepower turbos (in coupe and then cabrio body styles), 415-horsepower GT3 and 530-horsepower GT2 models, and other variants followed into 2006, 2007, and 2008.

Porsche introduced engineering updates with 997 Gen II for 2009. A new 345-horsepower base 3,614cc engine relied on direct fuel injection, a system that blasted a fuel-air mix into the most critically effective area inside the cylinder for more efficient combustion, higher output, and reduced carbon emissions. The DFI 3,800cc S engine produced 385 horsepower. For the first time, acceleration times were slower with the standard six-speed manual transmission than the long-awaited seven-speed Porsche Doppelkupplungsgetriebe (PDK) gearbox.

The new Typ 991 base Carrera model arrived as a 2012 model with 3,436cc displacement developed 345 horsepower; the Carrera S ran with a 3,800cc opposed-six producing 395 horsepower. Porsche unveiled the cars at the 2011 Geneva Motor Show. Eight months later, at the Los Angeles show, Porsche announced cabriolet versions of the two rear-wheel-drive versions. In September 2012, the company presented the all-wheel-drive Carrera 4 and 4S coupe and cabriolet bodies. The GT3 arrived at the 2013 Geneva show, boasting 469 horsepower from a 3,799cc revised Mezger engine. The GT3s introduced Porsche's electronic active rear-wheel steering for sharper handling and increased maneuverability.

The new car suffered an unexpected setback when

2015 Typ 991.2 Targa Porsche stunned audiences with its revised Targa. Designer Grant Larson returned to Butzi Porsche's original stainless-steel roll bar. But Larson's new version also displayed an intricate ballet with a retracting central roof panel that stowed beneath an opening rear window. As with the original, this blended the best elements of open top motoring with a coupe's wind protection and security.

some customer-owned cars caught fire; the automaker ultimately recalled 785 cars before resuming assembly in March 2014 with a new intake system.

Porsche introduced the track-enthusiast-oriented GT3 RS in Geneva in 2015. Initially it used the same 3.8-liter, 469-horsepower engine, but then Porsche revealed what it earlier had called impossible—a 4.0-liter flat six. This model, the 911 GT3 RS 4.0, offered customers 493 horsepower, rear-wheel steering, and another innovation, Porsche Torque Vectoring Plus, which employed electronic differential management to slow the inside rear wheel in a turn. The RS sported a rear wing, side graphics, and an interior roll cage; in these, it differed from a new 2016 model, the 911 R, reminding customers of ultralightweight 911s from 1967 and 1968. By eliminating the roll cage, rear wing, and other bodywork, the new R weighed 110 pounds (50 kg) less than the GT3 RS but still used the 4.0 engine. Production was limited to 991 units.

Turbos remained the 991 flagships. The "base" Turbo provided buyers with 513 horsepower, with comfort and sophistication. The Turbo S appealed to those who could never have too much power, giving them 552 horsepower. Turbo buyers chose either a seven-speed manual or a PDK gearbox; Turbo S owners got the PDK. This gave it a 0-to-62-mile-per-hour (0-to-100-kilometer-per-hour) time of 2.9 seconds on its way to its 198-mile-

2013 Typ 991 Carrera 4 Cabriolet Since the earliest days of Porsche's 356s, the company has argued its rear-engine placement made its cars more sure-footed in snow than cars with front engines. When Porsche introduced its Carrera 4 in 1990, that became especially true. Porsche's 991 lengthened its wheelbase 100 millimeters, 3.9 inches beyond the 997. Base 3.4-liter engines developed 350 horsepower while the S offered 400.

per-hour (320-kilometer-per-hour), top speed. (Only the 911 R had a higher terminal velocity; its lighter weight and aerodynamically cleaner body got it to 201 miles per hour [323 kilometers per hour]).

Just when enthusiasts suspected Porsche had reached the limits of its performance, it took another unexpected turn and turbocharged every 911 model, these designated 991.2. This reduced engine displacements to 2,981cc for Carrera, Carrera S, and GTS models (providing 365, 414, and 444 horsepower, respectively). Only the GT3, the GT3 RS, and a new Speedster model remained naturally aspirated (GT3 is a naturally aspirated racing class). With their Mezger 3,966cc engines, the GT3 offered 493 horsepower, the Speedster delivered 503 horsepower, and the GT3 RS produced 513 horsepower. Then, somewhat reminiscent of the understated bodywork of the recent 911 R, Porsche introduced a wingless, cageless, manual-transmission 911 GT3 Touring.

Turbos again—those using Porsche's more sophisticated variable turbine geometry technology rather than fixed turbine vanes in regular models—reached extraordinary new output levels. The "base" Turbo (now PDK only) delivered 533 horsepower, the Turbo S was good for 577, and a Turbo S Exclusive Series boasted 599 horsepower. Porsche retuned its GT2 lineup: The GT2 RS, and the RS Clubsport offered drivers 690 horsepower. Performance matched expectations: 0 to 62 miles per hour (0 to 100 kilometers per hour), in 2.7 seconds with a top speed of 211 miles per hour (340 kilometers per hour).

During the sixth Porsche Rennsport Reunion in Monterey, California, in 2018, Porsche unveiled its evocative designation 935, displaying a prototype club racer that resembled Norbert Singer's Moby Dick, complete with Martini racing livery. With its extended nose and long tail, the 3,042-pound (1,380 kg), car stretched just shy of 16-feet (4.9-m), long. Its 3,800cc engine, derived from the GT2 RS, developed 700 horsepower. Everything about its specifications spoke to racing purposes, and Porsche priced it appropriately, at $739,740 (€701,948), with the first delivery scheduled for June 2019. It limited production to a run of seventy-seven cars.

The final production vehicle in the 991.2 run was a 2020 Speedster, assembled December 20, 2019. Porsche already had unveiled its next generation, the Typ 992, which debuted at the just-opened Porsche Experience Center south of LA International Airport, on November 27, 2018.

The 992s introduced a new 911 styling language, sharp lines and edges—a first in 54 years—and the cars grew in all dimensions once again. Safety features,

2021 Typ 992 Turbo Cabriolet
There are two schools of thought about Turbos. One is "You can never have enough horsepower." The other is, "Hmm, 572 in a cabriolet might be just fine." With 3,790 pounds (1,719 kilograms), the car was full of creature comforts while providing startling performance. One online review called it a time machine, pointing out that this convertible with its standard all-wheel drive had twice the horsepower and twice the number of drive wheels as the first 930 coupe in 1975.

mechanical and electronic innovations, and ever taller and wider tires accompanied the changes. Model designations carried over: Carrera and Carrera S, Carrera 4 and 4S, Targa 4 and 4S, GTS and 4 GTS, GT3, and GT3 Touring. Horsepower output rose slightly; the base Carrera offered 380 horsepower, the Carrera S delivered 444 horsepower, and the GTS offered 473 horsepower, all from the 2,981cc twin-turbocharged DOHC, four-valve, water-cooled opposed six-cylinder engine. Buyers had the choice of seven-speed manual or new eight-speed PDK.

The flagship Turbos held their post as fast, luxurious cruisers: the 3,745cc engine gave the base Turbo 572 horsepower, while the Turbo S offered buyers 641 horsepower. And for the purists, the 992 GT3 and GT3 Touring delivered a naturally aspirated 503 horsepower from the 4,000cc six, with a choice of either six-speed manual gearbox or seven-speed PDK. As Porsche follows its now-decades-old practice, its GT cars group planned a GT3 RS as well as a GT2 or GT2 RS. And it seems safe to expect that latter vehicle will slide past the 700-horsepower benchmark.

(Top) 2022 Typ 992 Targa Porsche Design 50th Commemorative Edition Under a pale blue sky, the black Porsche Design commemorative Targa honored 50 years of product design Butzi Porsche's design firm in Zell am See, Austria, brought the world. It started with his original black-face Chronograph, hence the color options for this Targa: Black or Jet Black Metallic. Porsche assembled the car on its 992 Carrera 4 GTS platform, and limited production to 750 examples.

(Above) 2022 Typ 992 Carrera 4 GTS In contrast to the limited-run Porsche Design commemorative Targa, the company was happy to produce as many C4 GTS coupes as there was demand. Porsche first used the GTS designation on an ultra-rare 1969 racing model but then pulled it out again in 2010 for the most GT-like of the 997 variations. With the 992, the GTS offers 473 horsepower on either rear or all-wheel-drive chassis.

10
SIGMA
S TS 2601
HELLA
HELLA
HELLA
HELLA
Transsyberia 2007

2002–Present

26

Porsche's Building an SUV? Heresy!

Cayenne

Despite immense challenges, Horst Marchart's Typ 986 and 996 "two cars, one face" project began to coalesce. CEO Wendelin Wiedeking believed if these were successful, they would save the company. But he wanted more: to get the company growing and then thriving. Growth in which direction was the question the supervisory board asked in exchange for conditional approval. The group agreed to fund research, and then, on condition that the discoveries and conclusions made sense, funding to proceed with design and development.

Wiedeking saw potential for vehicle markets in areas of the world whose infrastructure was expanding in response to its citizens' increasing resources. He asked Marchart to develop a list and then select the suitable vehicle Porsche should pursue. Marchart grabbed Klaus-Gerhard Wolpert to assemble a team to investigate Porsche's options. Wolpert, like Marchart, had worked at Weissach for decades, mostly for outside clients—automakers Audi, Chrysler, Daimler-Benz, Ford, and VW, for whom he did all-wheel-drive prototypes of Passat and Golf models. He worked on antilock brakes, four-wheel steering, air suspension, and electronically controlled chassis systems.

2007 Typ E2 Cayenne Transsyberia Rallye This was car wash, Siberia-style. This two-week rally began in Moscow and headed east for 4,100 miles (6,600 km), to Ulaanbaatar, the capital of Mongolia. Armin Schwarz, driving No. 10, and co-driver Oliver Hilger led the first nine days but retired after a high-speed rollover.

(Top) 2003 Typ 9PA Cayenne Prototype CEO Wendelin Wiedeking asked his engineers to create a machine that was "the Porsche of sport utility vehicles." To project manager Klaus-Gerhard Wolpert, this meant an SUV that matched capabilities with the legendary Land Rover off road and had impeccable manners on a highway or road course. The resulting Cayenne will climb or descend 45-degree slopes.

(Above) 2005 Cayenne S Not only up hills and down, but it will travel along them. The Cayenne is capable of a 45-degree side lean; one section of Porsche's Leipzig demonstration circuit leans them at 42 degrees. Instructors always enjoyed new owners' reactions to what their SUV can manage.

He and his group worked nearly a year off-campus, examining everything from small sports cars to sport utility vehicles.

"We did a lot of consumer tests, marketing tests, and in the end, we decided to invest into the SUV segment," Wolpert explained in an interview in 2011. "The SUV segment is, worldwide, still the area with the most growth. In the early 1990s, especially in the exclusive upper end, there was no real competition."

Porsche needed a partner for such a project. When Wolpert learned Daimler-Benz already had planned its own SUV, both sides were interesting in collaborating. But Daimler asked impossible concessions, and Wiedeking refused. Wiedeking, Marchart, and Wolpert approached VW, who already produced some extremely utilitarian four-wheel-drive vehicles—not only a Passat and a Golf Combi but also an all-wheel-drive VW van, the Syncro, and a commercial version of that. They agreed: Porsche will produce a Cayenne and VW will offer the similar Touareg.

Designer Steve Murkett was part of Wolpert's team from the earliest days. On slow days, he busied himself sketching, creating, and inventing, and he had won two international design competitions, one with a six-passenger hybrid, the other with a smart-sized urban vehicle. He designed the production 959 and 964. He conceived a Porsche "school bus," a self-assigned project that was essentially a minivan with a Porsche cabin out front on the chassis. His colleagues in the studio warned him to hide. "It'll be a career killer," he recalled in an interview in 2012, them warning him when he said he wanted to show it to Ulrich Bez.

Instead, it inspired Bez and Harm Lagaay to have Murkett create something unexpected for the 1989 Frankfurt Motor Show to show off Porsche's new all-wheel-drive 964 platform. Murkett's roadster sat up on big tires and resembled a stylized dune buggy. His Panamericana was one of Porsche's most controversial concepts even though it introduced forms and shapes that defined later models from the 993 on. Now Wolpert told Murkett to shift his efforts toward an SUV.

"The Cayenne was a very controversial car to work on back then," he said. "The step from a Nine-Eleven to a Cayenne was a big step."

Defining that big step, delineating its boundaries, was Wolpert's job. "From the technical . . . the product point of view, we wanted to make a sporty SUV for daily use as every Porsche is," he explained. "That was a target for this new vehicle. It had to be a sporty vehicle, not a car for over a rocky mountain."

Wolpert told Wiedeking that he needed for all his project managers to sample all the competitors in daily use. "It's different to drive a car for an hour," he said, "You get feedback. But if you drive a car [for weeks] in every situation, winter, summer, to the opera or carrying kids . . . you know it. We bought them all. Jeep Grand Cherokee, Range Rover, ML, later the BMW. We exchanged the cars every three to four months.

"If you drive it and use it, you can see a lot of small details. Seating position, seat comfort, how you fold the seat. How you use a switch, what is the position of the switch? After three, six months, you have a good overview of what is best in this category. Then you can think about what you can do better than your competitors or what you can make different? What is *not* Porsche? Questions such as this made it clear that VW's definitions were different from Porsche's, and it became essential to let each go their own way."

Porsche routinely established targets in performance and among its competitors. Acceleration times, top

(Top) 2011 Cayenne Turbo (left) and Cayenne S Hybrid (right) The second-generation Cayenne Turbo gave customers 500 horsepower from its 4.8-liter turbocharged, intercooled V-8 engine. Engineering efficiencies decreased bodyshell weight by 221 pounds (110 kg), and cut 132 pounds (60 kg), from the chassis. The S-Hybrid combined a 333-horsepower supercharged V-6 with a 47-horsepower electric motor. Porsche targeted the hybrid mainly to US customers, having settled on diesel power for European buyers.

(Above) 2015 Macan Turbo Porsche's compact SUV arrived as a Turbo model which operated with a 3,600 cubic centimeter displacement, 400-horsepower V-6. The companion Macan S also was turbocharged but that fact was downplayed. The compact SUV rode on a 2,807-millimeter wheelbase and weighed 4,565-pounds (2,070-kg). Acceleration to 62 miles per hour (100 kilometers per hour), took 4.2 seconds.

2015 Macan S The Macan S was the companion model to the Turbo. It relied on a 3.0-liter V-6 with two turbochargers and intercoolers to produce 340 horsepower in a 4,351-pound (1,974-kg), five-door vehicle. The run from standstill up to 62 miles per hour (100 kilometers per hour), required 4.6 seconds.

2015 Macan Turbo interior The interiors of the Macan lineup reflected the approach Style Porsche took to the interiors of each of its vehicles. Large center-island consoles were ubiquitous throughout the company and have touch screens in the middle of the instrument panel. The Macans, reflecting their compact form, offer only three gauges in the instrument pod while Porsche's other products get five.

speeds, fuel economy, and CO2 emissions got attention. Dr. Heinz-Jakob Neusser directed the engine project; he started with a normally aspirated V-8 and the same engine with a turbocharger. Eighteen months into the development process, they added a V-6.

"We started with the V-Eight in a competitive area where nearly none of the other cars had this performance level," he explained in an interview in 2012. "But the Turbo was outstanding. There was nothing to compare to that. When we found that we already were at a high enough performance level that it made sense to have something below this. There were some customers interested in driving a Cayenne off road. The V-Six just positioned into this starting segment."

Porsche introduced the Typ 955 SUV in autumn 2002 as the 2003 normally aspirated Cayenne S and Turbo. The shapely vehicle had undergone extreme testing, the most rigorous of any Porsche vehicle ever because once the Cayenne excelled at its on-road capabilities, the engineers felt challenged to make it an excellent off-roader.

"We had one test," Neusser explained, "our testers drove into a small river. They shut off the engine, waited two minutes, then restarted the engine and drove out. People drive into water and panic and do the wrong thing."

They drove more than 940,000 miles (1,512,800 km), in testing. "We did tests for road driving then go onto a race track for two thousand kilometers, then back on the road, then the track, then the road."

The first-generation Cayenne, Typ 9PA, Chassis E1, shared common parts below the cockpit with Volkswagen's Touareg and Audi's Q7, including the heating box and air-conditioning, the seat structure (but only structure), some of the suspension body controllers, and some of the engine controllers. But the cars had different B and C pillars (the center and rear pillars), different roofs, and different cockpits. The gearboxes were the same, but the Cayenne used different software from the Touareg—there is a Porsche drivetrain.

The first-generation 4.5-liter V-8s developed 340 horsepower in the S and 450 horsepower from the Turbo. The S accelerated from 0 to 62 miles per hour (0 to 100 kilometers per hour), in 6.9 seconds and reached 150 miles per hour (240 kilometers per hour); the Turbo reached 0 to 62 miles per hour (0 to 100 kilometers per hour), in 5.6 seconds and topped out at 165 miles per hour (265 kilometers per hour). Permanent all-wheel drive split traction 62 percent to the rear and 38 percent up front. The six-speed Tiptronic transmission coupled to an electronically controlled locking differential, a low-range gearbox, and an automatic braking differential (ABD). Porsche Stability Management (PSM) controlled vehicle stability. Optional air suspension offered six ride heights, from as low as 6.2 inches (160 mm), for loading to as much as 10.7 inches (270 mm), for off-road. An entry-level naturally aspirated six-cylinder appeared in 2004, using a 24-valve 3,289cc engine of 247 horsepower. Later that model year, Porsche offered the S model with a six-speed manual transmission (though not in the United States) and offered the manual gearbox worldwide in a 399-horsepower 4,806cc V-8 GTS version. In an effort to appeal to broader markets, Porsche followed with a 237-horsepower 2,967cc V-6 diesel.

The success of the Cayenne surprised critics. It sold well in the United States and did better its second year, in 2004. Porsche's original plan was to assemble 20,000 each year. Unexpectedly, in 2005, its third year, Cayenne became Porsche's largest-selling car line, with 42,000 vehicles manufactured compared to 40,000 Boxsters

(Above) 2015 Cayenne GTS Porsche underwent a "Smart-Sizing" project with all its engines, reducing overall displacement and replacing it with turbos. The 2015 Cayenne drove with a new 3.6-liter twin-turbo V-6 compared to 2014's GTS with its 4.8-liter V-8. However, engineers coaxed 440 horsepower out of the V-6 compared to 420 from the V-8. The GTS sat slightly lower than base and S model Cayennes and accelerated from 0 to 62 miles per hour (0 to 100 kilometers per hour), in 5.2 seconds and on to a top speed of 155 miles per hour (250 kilometers per hour).

(Below) 2015 Macan GTS The GTS designation had become as plentiful as turbochargers throughout Porsche's product line up. This Macan ran with a twin-turbo 3.0-liter V-6 producing 360 horsepower. It reached 62 miles per hour (100 kilometers per hour), in 5.2 seconds and topped out at 159 miles per hour (255 kilometers per hour).

(Top) 2018 Cayenne The first generation Cayennes underwent hundreds of thousands of kilometers of testing in deserts, snow, and on a number of racetracks. Porsche continued that diligent—and lengthy—development work including weeks of sub-zero (Fahrenheit) driving on snow and ice across a variety of Canada terrain.

2017 Macan Turbo Exclusive The Exclusive department did not only interiors and exteriors but also running gear upgrades. Such was the case with this 440-horsepower, 3.6-liter twin-turbo V-6. Its 21-inch (533-mm) Turbo wheels filled the wheel wells while red brake calipers and a Carmine Red trimline low on the bodyside set off the exterior appearance. The black leather and Alcantara interior incorporated red trim elements to reiterate the exterior trim.

and 911s combined. Its popularity and sales in China, Russia, and the Mid-East outpaced US enthusiasm.

Cayenne's second edition, the Typ 958, debuted at the 2010 Geneva Motor show as 2011 models. The Cayenne had grown in dimensions, yet it weighed 551 pounds (250 kg), less owing to deleting the low-range transfer case. Engines included the 296-horsepower, 3.6-liter V-6; the 400-horsepower, 4.8-liter V-8 in the S; 493 horsepower from the twin-turbo; and a new hybrid S that mated a 328-horsepower V-6 from VW with a 46-horsepower motor powered by a metal-hydride battery. The maker introduced Porsche Dynamic Chassis Control (PDCC) electronic suspension, part of its stability management system that limited body roll in corners by strengthening outside electronic dampers while softening those inside in a turn. Then, in July 2014, Porsche restyled the Cayenne lineup, its subtle updates masking driveline changes that included a new plug-in E-Hybrid option and, in keeping with Porsche's history of improving performance through downsizing, reducing the Cayenne S engine from a 4.8-liter V-8 to a 3.6-liter turbocharged V-6.

2022 Cayenne Coupe Turbo GT Porsche stretched a body style definition, "coupe," traditionally a two-door automobile, to encompass their new five-door fastback, hatchback Cayenne GT. They weren't first to adopt the designation; both BMW and Mercedes-Benz have similar fastback SUVs. Porsche's 4.0-liter twin-turbo V-8 with 631 horsepower accelerates to 60 miles per hour (97 kilometers per hour), in 3.1 seconds.

2022 Cayenne E-Hybrid At the other end of the Cayenne spectrum from the Coupe Turbo GT is the base E-Hybrid. This plug-in hybrid delivers a combined 455 horsepower from its 355-horsepower 3.0-liter turbocharged V-6 and its 134-horsepower electric motor. Full acceleration synced both and provided 60 miles per hour (98 kilometers per hour), in 4.7 seconds.

The third-generation Cayenne Typ 9Y0 appeared online first and revealed substantial body redesign on a new shared VW chassis, the MLB platform. The base Cayenne used a 2,995cc V-6 with 335 horsepower; the Cayenne E-Hybrid ran a 2,995cc turbocharged V-6 and electric power for a total output of 456 horsepower; the Cayenne S ran with a new 2,894cc twin-turbo V-6 providing 434 horsepower. The GTS and the entire Cayenne Turbo line used Porsche's 3,996cc twin-turbo V-8: the GTS offered 454 horsepower, the Turbo delivered 542, and the Turbo S provided 690. A Turbo S E-Hybrid may have been a kind of contradiction in terms, with 671 horsepower and a nearly 30-mile range on its plug-in-hybrid 136-horsepower motor.

In 2019, Porsche joined a trend among other SUV manufacturers with a fastback four-door model bearing the designation GT "coupe," a body type traditionally using only two doors. The Cayenne Turbo GT and the Turbo GT with Performance Kit provided drivers with 631 horsepower for the GT and an astonishing 764 horsepower from the performance upgrade. Porsche quoted acceleration from 0 to 62 miles per hour (0 to 100 kilometers per hour), for the performance-kit version at 2.73 seconds. The GTs were available late in 2021 for the 2022 model year.

2022 Macan S Porsche did some engine shuffling for its 2022 model year and promoted the 375-horspower 2021 Macan GTS engine into the mid-range Macan S model. The S also provided the Porsche Adaptive Stability Management system (PASM) along with Porsche's seven-speed PDK transmission. Acceleration from 0 to 60 miles per hour (0 to 98 kilometers per hour), needed only 3.9 seconds.

2004–2005

27

Another Supercar? About Time!

Carrera GT

The story goes back to the earliest days of Wiedeking's second coming. By 1993, Porsche was reckoning with its unsuccessful 80-degree Typ 3512 3.5-liter V-12 Formula One engine for the Arrows team. The engine threw Weissach into a period of self-doubt, despite F1 successful effort with McLaren. Horst Marchart challenged engineer/racing director Herbert Ampferer to determine whether Porsche still had the engineering talent and capabilities to develop such an engine successfully. With a small budget and crew, Ampferer succeeded. While his new V-12 achieved reliability, it still was too big for an F1 car, and too heavy. Encouraged to start again, Ampferer's group had a new engine by late 1994.

"This was a V-Ten engine," Ampferer explained during an interview in 2016, "with pneumatic valve systems, with variable intake valves, variable exhaust valves, with variable trumpets. All our variables were on that engine." The cylinder heads underwent a 20-hour durability test in 1994 at 20,000 rpm. This represented ten Formula One races in one day of testing. "I tell you, it was a lot of fun from an engineer's point of view. Then we had the entire engine on the dyno and ran it for two hours supplying seven

2004 Typ 980 Carrera GT Porsche Works racing and rally driver Walter Röhrl adopted new duties when the Typ 980 Carrera GT came into being. After development and testing, he became a photographers' model, driving the striking spyder in the Arizona desert and through rainy-rush hour traffic in Paris on the night of its world debut.

2004 Carrera GT Concept While working on the series production 997 in Porsche's California design satellite studio in 1999, Grant Larson got a call to interrupt that and give management ideas for a new supercar. His love of Porsche's racing history inspired several elements of the concept, including the flat fan from the 1970s Typ 917s.

hundred sixty horsepower with pump fuel." Marchart was convinced Weissach had engineers capable of anything. Ampferer used this accomplishment to push ahead with the GT1 for Le Mans in 1996, 1997, and 1998.

"And what do we do with that V-10 engine?" Ampferer asked. "Nothing. We put it into storage." Then right after Le Mans 1998, he talked to Wiedeking. "What's now?" the chairman asked. Ampferer knew that seven months between July and Le Mans the following April was not enough to produce a new racer.

"'I said, 'But 2000, that would be something. New car, new engine.'" Wiedeking authorized design and testing, but he planned to decide later about the race.

"So what was the logical step in terms of engine? The V-Ten Formula One? The carbon chassis from Ninety-Eight?" He took that new V-10. But 3.5 liters was not enough for Le Mans. An engine designed for 2 or 3 hours was not good for 24. He needed something different.

Ampferer's engineers redesigned their V-10, enlarging displacement from 3.5 to 5.0 liters. They replaced pneumatic valves with standard spring valves. However, the 65-degree V angle of the Ampferer engine, the torsional vibration of the crankshaft, of cam drive, gearing systems of cam drive, the cams themselves remained unchanged. He believed that if it worked for an F1 engine at 15,000 rpm for 2 hours, it should serve as well for Le Mans, where engines ran at 8,000. It went into a unique prototype, designated LMP2000, with a Horst Reitter carbon monocoque, a Eugen Kolb carbon body, and Norbert Singer project management.

Wiedeking came to Weissach for the first tests of the LMP2000. After some two dozen laps with its two development drivers, Wiedeking told Singer and Ampferer to put it away; it was not going to race. Days later, he questioned Ampferer: Did it matter to anyone whether Porsche, which had won Le Mans sixteen times, got a seventeenth? He asked Ampferer, "Are we *the* sports car manufacturer in the world?'"

2004 Typ 980 Carbon Fiber Monocoque The new supercar was an outgrowth of a couple of discontinued projects, a V-10 engine and a planned Le Mans Spyder for year 2000. CEO Wiedeking called on his engineers to apply all that technology to a new super sports car for Porsche's road-going customers.

By early 1999, the supercar genre that Porsche's 959 invented had fathered challengers. Ferrari announced an Enzo. McLaren and Mercedes leaked hints about an SLR. Bugatti had resurfaced. "'So we need a sports car like that,' Wiedeking told me, 'Doesn't it make more sense than to go once again to Le Mans?'" Ampferer formed a team to define a new car.

Grant Larson, who had designed the Boxster, got the assignment to sketch a mid-engine supercar. At that time, he was designing the next 911, the Typ 997, in Porsche's satellite design studio in Huntington Beach, California. By May 1999, Marchart approved one of his concepts, and Grant divided his time between the 997 and the new supercar. He spent seven months on tuning the latter design. Near the end, Wiedeking and Harm Lagaay commuted to California every other week to review Larson's model. In early 2000, Wiedeking gave Marchart approval to move forward—and unexpectedly, asked for two!

Walter Röhrl was to drive one for a video and live presentation at the Paris show. The second was strictly a "push-around" for occasions when two shows overlapped, such as Los Angeles and Detroit around New Year's 2001. A year later in Detroit, on January 8, 2002, Wiedeking announced Porsche's intentions to produce the car called the Carrera GT.

Porsche show cars were rooted in reality. They had to be manufacturable and—under Wiedeking, especially—return a profit in production. But a direct translation from the auto-show turntable to the street was not always realistic.

"When you see these two cars, you think they are the same car," Tony Hatter explained. Hatter, who had designed the 993, came in to make a production car out of Larson's show car. "Every single millimeter was completely new and different from the show car to the production model. We had to change everything whether it was safety or packaging or snow chain clearances or cooling the engine which was a major thing. And the thing had to have a roof which our boys hadn't exactly thought about.

"When we started to make a production car out of it, we made a digital model of the exterior and interior. We milled it. That was the basis for the wind tunnel tests.

(Top) 2004 Typ M80 engine for Carrera GT Engineers developed a 5,733 cubic centimeter displacement naturally aspirated V-10 engine for the new super car. It developed 612 horsepower at 8,000 revolutions per minute. Very much in Porsche's race car tradition, the engine sat amidship and drove rear wheels through a six-gear trans-axle.

(Above) 2005 Typ 980 Carrera GT Assembly at Leipzig Porsche specially trained 110 of its assemblers to master a variety of tasks needed for a team approach to assembling the Carrera GT. Production took place at the Leipzig Works where, at the time, Porsche also assembled the Cayenne. Production ended at 1,270 examples.

But at the same time, because of the shortened period of work, they took this data set that we made here in the studio and made the first series of prototypes. They assembled ten or twelve running cars from data made here on our little computer screens.

"What came out of the wind tunnel was horrible," Hatter said of the earliest tests with Norbert Singer. "Air blowing down the side of the car does not automatically turn ninety degrees and go into air scoops. To get the car to cool, those openings at the back had to be so big that the car looked nothing like the show car. Cooling went to the

(Top) 2004 Typ 980 Carrera GT Through miracles of photographic technique, Walter Rohrl appeared to be racing through the Arizona desert when in fact he was barely traveling 40 miles per hour (65 kilometers per hour). The hand-assembled prototype was too fragile to risk running faster.

(Above) 2004 Typ 980 Carrera GT The racecar-derived Carrera GT rode on a 107.5-inch (2,730-mm), wheelbase. It measured 181.6 inches (4,613 mm) long, was 75.6 inches (1,921 mm) wide, and sat 45.9 inches (1,166 mm) tall. It weighed 3,605 pounds (1,380 kg).

(Right) 2004 Typ 980 Carrera GT Design director Harm Lagaay recognized much of the appeal of this supercar was its exotic engine. Designers Grant Larson and Tony Hatter worked with engineers to make the mechanicals visually attractive. Lagaay devised the screened cover, which he called the negligée.

front." This 200-mile-per-hour (320-kilometer-per-hour), Autobahn supercar also had to crawl through city traffic.

Engine compartments baked. Carbon fiber typically did not survive more than 266 degrees Fahrenheit, or about, 130 degrees Celsius, the temperature at which most of it was created. The fibers were okay, but resins failed, and the part collapsed. The challenge was to create something that resisted 356 degrees Fahrenheit, about, 180 degrees Celsius, by using different resin. To help, they isolated exhaust pipes and mounted temperature-controlled fans in the compartment to cool the engine, gearbox oil, and air-conditioner condenser.

The car was mostly carbon fiber, but not its front crash structure. Porsche had vast experience with crash structures in steel, and their suppliers developed a new high-energy-absorption stainless steel that saved some weight. But the steel structure offered another benefit to buyers. "It was made on a simple bending machine," overall project manager Michael Hölscher explained during an interview in 2012. "It was bolted through the carbon fiber structure. It could be replaced easily if the customers had a crash."

Herbert Ampferer had warned the development team, "If we want to do a super sports car, you need a modern racing engine in that," Ampferer recalled. "A high-revving V-Ten with this typical sound, WooWooWoo, we needed something like that.

"Our engine in this car was a real race engine," Hölscher added. "It was designed for this Le Mans car and the most important point in the design of a race car engine was to have a low center of gravity." Race cars ran 4-inch (100-mm) diameter carbon fiber clutches, and teams threw them away after one or two races. Porsche could not ask customers to change clutches as often as motor oil.

Hölscher and Ampferer remembered Porsche's success with carbon-reinforced ceramic brakes. They tested prototype composite clutches. At high revs, they burst. Sachs fabricated composite ceramic clutch discs. The V-10's rev limit was 8,400 rpm; Porsche typically demanded its clutches survive nearly double that speed for safety reasons. The new ceramic clutches withstood 20,000 rpm tests. Exceptional wear resistance and a working diameter of 6.3 inches (160 mm), let Porsche mount the engine so low it set a world record for crankshaft height above the pavement of 4 inches (100 mm), at its lowest rotating point. This left room to incorporate aerodynamic tunnels beneath the car. At top speed, the car underbody generated nearly 880 pounds (400 kg), of downforce.

The 3,043-pound (1,380 kg) car delivered racing-world performance: top speed was 205 miles per hour (330 kilometers per hour), 62.5 miles per hour (100 kilometers per hour) acceleration to took 3.9 seconds. The final 5.7-liter version of the V-10 developed 612 horsepower. It sold for $444,400, or about €390,000. But none of this would have satisfied Wiedeking had no other considerations been met. First, the car had to be usable. Just like Porsche's SUV, this had to be *the Porsche* among the supercars. Second, the car had to have a Porsche feeling and a Porsche look.

Usability was a huge challenge. The engine's tiny clutch provided one-tenth the inertia of a big flywheel. Lifting off the throttle dropped revs instantly. The Bosch engine-management system sensed this, and when rpms plummeted, electronics increased injection fuel volume, enabling smoother gear changes.

Usability also meant operating the car in all conditions. "It had to have a top that stayed on at two hundred miles per hour," Tony Hatter said. "We had to have wind-up windows and the top of the windows at the B-Pillar had to meet the roof. We created two removable panels. The packaging guys stacked them on top of each other in different directions." There was a leather overnight bag that fit in the boot with a small space below for a bit of luggage.

Production began as a 2004 model. Advanced orders suggested Porsche might sell as many as 1,500. A small crew of 110 workers completed three cars a day at the new factory in Leipzig. Porsche invited custom exterior and interior colors, though these weren't run until the end of 2005. Ultimately, Porsche assembled 1,270 of its unexpected Carrera GT.

86
S VM 1219

And Now a Sedan? Heresy!

Panamera

The Panamera was more evidence of Wendelin Wiedeking's far-sighted vision and thorough investigation of possibilities for Porsche. To too many outsiders, this represented looking further away from what had been essential Porsche. With the Cayenne SUV and now the Panamera sedan, Wiedeking had dispatched his engineers, designers, and researchers to search seemingly unrelated markets and then invent vehicles for them that diluted Porsche's essence. Or was identifying markets in which Porsche's interpretation of a suitable vehicle might meet such success something that might provide a cushion for the company so it could advance its traditional sports cars and even introduce the occasional supercar? That perspective, in hindsight, reflects what actually happened.

Consider that Porsche chose to unveil this large, heavy, four-door, four-seat, luxurious, high-performance sedan not in the United States, a market with a known appetite for such vehicles, nor at home in Germany, where at least two other companies already manufactured such cars. Porsche first revealed the Panamera at the Paris International Salon de l'Automobile, the birthplace and showplace for decades of the *grands routiers*,

2011 Typ 970 Panamera 4S in Finland Porsche has long insisted its cars are easily manageable in snow, and to prove it to European drivers, it developed winter driving courses at its testing and training facility in Rovaniemi, Finland, opening for customers in 1999. Here a Panamera 4S driver enjoys a full drift as part of the Porsche Ice Experience.

the great road cars from Bugatti, Delahaye, Delage, and Voisin—and, since the war ended, those of Citroën. That made one statement about the car's purpose, but its most significant introduction to the world took place during the April 2009 Shanghai International Automobile Show. Well-heeled potential customers saw it the Sunday before at a reception/introduction on the 94th-floor observation deck of the 101-story Shanghai World Financial Center (after Porsche engineers tugged it vertically, nose up, through the freight-elevator shaft on a specially designed mount). By then, Porsche was so well known in China—for the Cayenne, its other large, heavy, five-door, five-seat, luxurious, high-performance SUV—that when marketing also displayed a Typ 997 coupe on the show stand, visitors approached Porsche representatives and exclaimed their excitement: "Oh! So Porsche has started to make a sports car, too?"

Porsche and Wiedeking had a history of unexpected products by this time. There was the startling and then startlingly successful Cayenne SUV in 2002. Then the stunning and successful Carrera GT supercar in 2004. The totally updated and successful Typ 997 followed in 2006. Then the world economy crashed and burned in 2007, sucking in nation after nation in 2008 and 2009. Millions of individuals lost jobs and homes. Families shattered. Businesses shuttered their doors. As real money losses climbed toward trillions of dollars, euros, and British pounds—not to mention rubles and renminbi—the world's governments tightened their belts, or loosened them, as their economists recommended and their politicians allowed. Inside the government of Porsche, the new product was too far along to shelve; by 2007, Weissach had running prototypes turning lap after lap on its track and in remote locales in road tests.

Porsche project manager Gernot Döllner started work on the Typ 970 sedan almost from the minute the company introduced the Cayenne. Porsche launched the Panamera as a 2010 model in three versions, the rear-drive normally aspirated S, the all-wheel-drive 4S, and the all-wheel-drive Turbo. The direct-fuel-injection engine, a 4.8-liter V-8, offered S and 4S owners 400 horsepower at 6,500 rpm while the Turbo delivered 500 at 6,000 rpm. The only transmission available initially was the seven-speed PDK twin-clutch gearbox.

While the Panamera took the concept of the diminutive 989 sedan of the 1980s and upgraded it with countless creature comforts and safety and performance features, the car grew in size. And many first-time observers were moved to silent observation on first seeing its back end, described by one as "elephantine

2009 Typ 970 Panamera Turbo Porsche introduced its five-door sedan as a 2009 model in rear drive S, or all-wheel drive 4S and Turbo versions. All used a new Porsche 4.8-liter V-8 developing 395 horsepower in the naturally aspirated S and 4S, and 493 horsepower in the twin-turbo model. It was conceived as a high-speed luxury four-door hatchback and the Turbo was capable of 188 miles per hour (303 kilometers per hour).

2009 Typ 970 Panamera in Shanghai Based on the enthusiastic reception Chinese customers had shown Porsche's Cayenne, the company chose to stage the world debut at the Shanghai auto show in April 2009. The night before the show opened, the company hosted a private reception on the 94th floor of the Shanghai World Financial Center. Porsche engineers fabricated a platform and raised the car 1,397 feet (425 m), on the roof of a freight elevator.

2012 Typ 970 Panamera Turbo The message was intentional: the Panamera is the vehicle of private jet owners; aspire to it if you dare. The resemblance to the 911 coupe was intentional too, emphasizing the family ties and sporting heritage. The first-generation sedan, modeled to accommodate the 3 foot (1 m). Porsche CEO who wished to work in the back seat, entered the market with a slightly ungainly roof line.

hatchback wagon styling." As one member of the design team explained it, "the car would have looked quite different if we didn't have a big tall CEO who wanted to be able to work in the backseat." In fact, other standards influenced its dimensions: it had to carry four 95th-percentile males (that is, 6 feet 1 inch tall [1 m 85 cm], and weighing 216 pounds [98 kg]) and one suitcase each.

Models proliferated, as Porsches do. Panamera and Panamera L models also appeared during 2010, each using a 3,605cc V-6—essentially the V-8 block with two cylinders lopped off one end. The normally aspirated V-6 produced 300 horsepower at 6,200 rpm, and for various markets in Europe, Porsche provided a six-speed manual gearbox as standard with the PDK as an option. A 250-horsepower diesel version of the V-6 (using the Audi-derived 2,967cc engine shared with the Cayenne diesel) arrived in model year 2011, along with a 4,806cc Turbo S (with 550 horsepower at 6,000 rpm), a 430-horsepower normally aspirated V-8 GTS, and the S E-Hybrid, using a supercharged 2,995cc V-6 for gasoline power. Both the diesel and the S E-Hybrid operated with the eight-speed Tiptronic S transmission. Each of these powertrains shared exhaustive development and widespread use with the Cayenne.

During the 2013 Shanghai show, Porsche showed the updated, "face-lifted" Panamera with minor exterior changes but significant engine improvements. Among them, the Panamera S and 4S appeared with a new twin-turbo 2,967cc V-6, delivering 414 horsepower at 6,000 rpm. The gasoline engine of the new plug-in S E-hybrid, a supercharged 2,995cc V-6, provided a total of 416 horsepower, incorporating its 95-horsepower electric motor. (The S E-Hybrid was capable of speeds up to 84 miles per hour (135 kilometers per hour), strictly on electric mode.) Porsche also announced a longer-wheelbase version of the 4S, Turbo, and Turbo S models, adding 5.91 inches (150 mm), between the wheels for much greater rear leg room, for certain left-hand-

2016 Typ 971 Panamera Turbo S at Goodwood American racer and actor Patrick Dempsey got the assignment to provide crowds an early view of the potential of the 550-horsepower second generation Turbo S Panamera on the 1.1-mile (1.8-km), hillclimb run during the Goodwood Festival of speed, June 25, 2016. The second generation significantly reshaped the roofline.

drive markets. The Turbo S provided 542 horsepower at 6,000 rpm from its twin-turbocharged 4,806cc V-8. This executive-class *grand routier*—though perhaps the German term *Autobahn Kreuzer* is more appropriate—hurtled its driver and passengers along at as much as 305 kilometers per hour, 190 miles per hour.

In late June 2016, Porsche introduced the restyled Typ 971 G2 second-generation Panamera. The new car grew 1.38 inches (35 mm), in overall length to 198.8 inches (5,050 mm) and 0.19 inches (5 mm), in width and height to 76.3 inches (1,938 mm), and 56.0 inches (1,422 mm), respecively. It arrived on a 1.18-inch (30-mm), longer wheelbase (now at 116.1 inches [2,950 mm]), all on the Volkswagen Group MSB platform. While Harm Lagaay supervised the G1's appearance using input from designers Benjamin Dimson, Steve Murkett, and Grant Larson, current design chief Michael Mauer's team not only gracefully reshaped the roofline but also redesigned the interior, including the instrument panel, replacing previous buttons with touch-sensitive surfaces. While Porsche refers to the sedan as the Gran Turismo, it introduced a station wagon designated the Sport Turismo in mid-2017, along with Executive editions on 5.9-inch (150-mm)-longer wheelbases.

2015 Typ 971 Panamera "Edition" This "special" edition upgraded a catalog full of interior, comfort, and exterior appearance options intended to understate elegance. Porsche offered the Edition only on its V-6 platforms but available to customers worldwide.

The Panamera presented one of Porsche's growing family of faces (from 911 through Boxster, Cayman, Cayenne, and the sedan) to the public. However, it debuted a couple of months after the company's most durable face opened to the public. The 277,710 square foot (25,600 square meter) Porsche Museum was another Wiedeking big idea, initiated ahead of the Great Recession but completed during it. The supervisory board approved the idea in July 2004, and 170 architects from throughout the world submitted concepts. Porsche selected Delugan Meissl Associated Architects from Vienna to complete the project, and construction commenced in October 2005. When the museum opened on January 31, 2009—three months before the

(Top) 2021 Typ 971 Panamera Sport Turismo GTS From its original, nearly invisible use, the GTS designation has proliferated through Porsche's product lineup, infecting each designate with lower ride height, tighter handling, better road holding, and improved performance. Black trim reminded Porsche enthusiasts of the sporty 911 Carreras and Turbos from 1974 through the 1980s when design chief Tony Lapine steadily de-chromed the 911 lineup.

Panamera debut—visitors saw eighty cars (and usually as many as 200 smaller objects) displayed in dramatic and soaring spaces measuring some 60,280 square feet (5,600 square meters). The facility incorporates museum offices, Porsche's historic archive, mechanical shops for servicing and maintaining the museum and the traveling vehicles, a lobby coffee bar, a ground-floor restaurant (the Boxenstopp, or Pit Stop), and a third-floor fine-dining steakhouse, Christophorus.

Panamera production continues to this day, manufactured in the company's ever-expanding assembly facility in Leipzig. Porsche introduced another face-lift in 2021 for the 2022 model year, and the entire Panamera line now included twenty-four variations, starting with the 325-horsepower Panamera and including the Platinum Edition, all-wheel-drive Panamera 4, 4 Platinum, 4 Executive (on the extended wheelbase), and 4 Sport Turismo. The S versions offered buyers 443 horsepower over the same range of body styles; a Panamera 4 E-Hybrid provided owners with 455 horsepower in the sedan, Platinum, Executive, and Sport Turismo body styles. The sportier GTS sedan and Sport Turismo delivered 473 horsepower; the 4S E-Hybrid boasted 552 horsepower as a sedan, stretched Executive, and Sport Turismo; and the flagships remained the 620-horsepower Turbo S sedan and Sport Turismo, and the all-conquering Turbo S E-Hybrid with combined output of 690 horsepower in sedan, Executive, or Sport Turismo configurations. Rear-wheel steering was standard equipment on the 2022 4S Executive and S E-Hybrid Executive as well as both Turbo models. Porsche offered it optionally on the rest of the line along with its Adaptive Air Suspension and Dynamic Chassis Control to further improve handling.

(Above) 2020 Porsche Panamera Turbo S Executive Porsche added 150 millimeters, 5.9 inches, to the wheelbase of the Executive model, inserting the addition as rear-seat leg room. In the Turbo S configuration, the Executive was a kind of land-based bizjet with 620 horsepower, acceleration from 0 to 60 miles per hour (0 to 97 kilometers per hour), in 3.0 seconds, and a 196-mile-per-hour (315-kilometer-per-hour) top speed. For the Executive on expense account, its $190,200 price was a mere above-the-line perquisite of the job.

LUBE
Mobil 1
RACING
PORSCHE
DHL
RS Spyder
MICHELIN
7
COMPUWARE
6

2004–2019

29

Returning to Battle, the Racing Becomes Electric

Typ RS Spyder, 918, and 919

Porsche Cars North America and its competition arm, Porsche Motorsport North America, commissioned the RS Spyder (Typ 9R6) as a customer car for teams planning to compete in the American Le Mans Series (ALMS). Roger Penske took the first. Flacht engineers developed the car following rules for the Le Mans Prototype 2 category, originating with the Automobile Club de l 'Ouest (ACO). Racing in LMP2 guaranteed the 9R6 competition, but at somewhat lower costs than the premier LMP1 class. LMP2 was eligible for ALMS, the European Le Mans Series (ELMS), and the 24-hour race.

The 9R6 was Porsche's first endurance racer seen publicly following the 1998 Le Mans victory with the 911 GT1. Engineers had developed the little-known LMP2000 racing Spyder, and technology from that project went into the Carrera GT and carried on into this new car. The RS Spyder body spent hours in the wind tunnel to improve the rear wing and diffuser, providing teams with aerodynamic adjustments for each venue. Engineers redesigned intake and outflow air ducts for the radiators as well. The 9R6 used a light, stiff carbon-fiber monocoque chassis and double-wishbone suspension

2008 Typ 9R6 RS Spyder at Long Beach Grand Prix Competition was fierce during this third round of the American Le Mans Series (ALMS) in April during the Long Beach Grand Prix. Some twenty-seven cars started and seventy-one laps later, at the finish, nine cars were on the leading lap. The LMP2-class Penske Racing DHL RS Spyder No. 7 of Timo Bernhard and Roland Dumas placed fourth, just 3.8 seconds after the winner in an LMP1 class Audi. Porsche No. 6, coming into the turn, placed fifth, 5.4 seconds back from the Audi.

all around, with adjustable front and rear antisway bars and horizontally mounted dampers for handling and roadholding. The car weighed 1,653 pounds (750 kg), as limited by regulations.

It raced with a 3,400cc 90-degree V-8 developed for endurance events, with four valves per cylinder, dry-sump lubrication, and single-cylinder throttle valves in the intake manifold. ACO regulations fitted an air-intake restrictor that limited engine output to 480 horsepower. The six-speed sequential constant mesh gearbox served as chassis structure and mounting points for the rear suspension. Brakes were inner-vented carbon-fiber disks.

Penske debuted his RS Spyder in the final two ALMS races in 2005; it won its class at Laguna Seca. Penske retained exclusive use in the 2006 season (running two cars), and his Spyders took first and second overall at Mid-Ohio, beating LMP1 contenders as well as the LMP2 field. At Le Mans, the car won the LMP2 class. For 2006, Penske Racing took Drivers', Team, and Manufacturers' Championships.

(Above) 2006 Typ 9R6 RS Spyder at Mid-Ohio Sports Car Course Sascha Maasen and Lucas Luhr drove their Penske Racing Porsche RS Spyder No. 6 to second overall in the 119-lap third round of the 2006 inaugural ALMS season. Teammates Bernhard and Dumas were overall winners, finishing just 0.45 seconds ahead of Maasen and Luhr. The RS Spyders raced with Porsche's 3,397 cubic centimeter displacement V-8. For the first season, the engine developed 475 horsepower.

(Below) 2009 Typ 9R6 RS Spyder at Le Mans The Team Essex RS Spyder No. 10 finished first in LMP2 class at the end of the 24 hours, completing 357 laps. They placed tenth overall, trailing nine LMP1 cars including the winning Peugeot 908. RS Spyders in the Le Mans Series (LMS) used different smaller intake restrictors and so the cars raced with 503 horsepower at 10,000 revolutions per minute.

For 2007, Penske raced the RS Spyder Evo. Regulations slightly increased weight to 1,709 pounds (775 kg), but also increased engine output to 503 horsepower. Dyson Racing also fielded RS Spyders during the ALMS season.

The cars proved indomitable, as many Porsche endurance racers have been. RS Spyders won the ALMS championship for LMP2 again in 2007 and 2008. Penske won the 12 Hours of Sebring outright in 2008 and won the class at Le Mans in 2008 and 2009. In Europe in 2008, a Danish team, a Dutch team, and a Swiss team all ran RS Spyders in the LMS series. A Spyder won its class in every event, earning European drivers' and team championships as well. Rules for 2009 restricted engine output to 440 horsepower and narrowed the rear wing, reducing downforce. Penske and Dyson withdrew; a US team, CytoSport, acquired the ex-Dyson team car and ran four events. In 2010, CytoSport won its class at Sebring and won overall at Lime Rock, Connecticut, and at Mosport, near Toronto. The team competed against Highcroft HPD in the RS Spyder. ACO regulations for 2011 rendered the RS Spyders obsolete and the history of the 9R6 was

(Top) 2011 Typ 918 Hybrid Spyder Prototype Porsche revealed its 918 Hybrid concept at the Geneva Motor Show in March 2010, intended as the next-generation successor to the Carrera GT but full of new technology. The car used a 3.4-liter V-8 from the the RS Spyder to give the show car 500 horsepower through a revised Carrera GT transmission and two electric motors generating a total of 282 additional horsepower, all delivered to the rear wheels.

(Above) 2010-2011 Typ 911 GT3 Hybrid This was one of Porsche's more complicated race cars, relying not only on its 4.0-liter 500-horsepower rear internal combustion engine, but a complex flywheel Kinetic Energy Recovery System, KERS, to supply electric energy to two electric motors jointly contributing another 219 horsepower through the front wheels. Porsche developed the car as a test bench for future racing and road-going technologies. It won outright in May 2011, racing in the Nürburgring Endurance Series with Marco Holzer, Richard Lietz, and Patrick Long in the four-hour race.

(Top) 2013 Typ 918 Hybrid "Weissach Package" Record Run Marc Lieb jumped the 918 Hybrid on part of the Nürburgring's Nordschleife on his way to setting a new lap record at the legendary circuit of 6:57.00, making an average speed of 115.5 miles per hour (179.5 kilometers per hour).

(Above) 2014 Typ 918 Hybrid The 3,602.4-pound (1,634 kg) 918 Hybrid Spyder rode on a 107.5 inches (2,730 mm) wheelbase. It measured 76.4 inches (1,940 mm) wide, and stood 45.9 inches (1,167 mm) high. Not long after introduction, Porsche recorded 2,000 "declarations of interest," and the board approved production of 918 units.

done. Done except for its influence on two projects on the drawing boards, the 918 Spyder and the 919 LMP1 Hybrid.

By this time, it had been nearly a century since Ferdinand Porsche arrived in Vienna, Austria, from the small town of his birth in Bohemia. In 1898, when he was just twenty-three, Vienna was home to the Austro-Hungarian Empire; the Habsburg royalty attracted Europe's brightest minds, finest artists, biggest talents, and cleverest innovators. Ferdinand, young, ambitious, and inventive, found the electricity in the air inspiring, and it gave rise to a series of electric-powered automobiles. This burst of creativity culminated in vehicles combining internal combustion engines (ICE) to run generators to power batteries to drive wheels. The hybrid automobile was born in Vienna at the end of the nineteenth century, and Ferdinand Porsche was a proud parent.

More than one hundred years later, Porsche gave birth to a child of this technology: the Typ 918 Spyder, offered from late 2013 through mid-2015.

Numbers alone were impressive. One V-8 ICE, two

2015 Typ 919 Hybrid LMP1 at Le Mans Its brake rotors glowed hot in the night. Porsche's Typ 919 Hybrid LMP1 raced towards Porsche's first overall victory since 1998. Nico Bamberger, Eric Bamber, and Nick Tandy completed 395 laps of the circuit. They finished one lap ahead of teammates Timo Bernhard, Mark Webber, and Brendon Hartley who took second in the Works 919 No. 17.

electric motors, a combined output of 887 horsepower, all-wheel drive, acceleration from 0 to 62 miles per hour (0 to 100 kilometers per hour), in 2.6 seconds, a top speed of 214 miles per hour (345 kilometers per hour), a range of 18.6 miles (30 kilometers), on battery power, and average fuel economy of 78.4 miles per gallon (3.0 liters per 100 kilometers)! But Weissach's engineering director at the time characterized it best: "What I like most is how it can speed like a bat out of hell."

This bat was born in September 2009 from the depths of the Great Recession. Project XG10 was a supercar conceived to reassure customers, shareholders, and the automotive and financial worlds that Porsche remained the leader in sportscar technology—and still manufactured cars. This clarification became necessary after a discrete three-year operation launched soon after starting the XG10 project.

CEO Wendelin Wiedeking attempted to take control of Volkswagen. Financial manipulations drove up VW's stock price, benefiting Porsche, which was edging toward 75 percent ownership. In 2008, Zuffenhausen earned greater profit from financial dealings than from selling cars. European financial journals described Porsche as a hedge fund disguised as a carmaker. When banks, reeling from the world economic situation they had helped create, began calling loans that Wiedeking had used to finance VW stock purchases, Porsche's ownership fell into VW as its tenth subsidiary. Wiedeking and his collaborators left the company. Ferdinand Piëch took over. Automotive journalists felt comforted: *Motor Trend* magazine wrote "With car guy Ferdinand Piëch back in charge, the future of Porsche will differ dramatically from Wiedeking's profit-above-all-else vision. The focus will be to burnish Porsche's reputation as the world's leading sports car manufacturer."

The XG10 fit that task precisely. Frank-Steffen

2014 Typ 918 Hybrid Performance was astonishing. The 918 accelerated from 0 to 62 miles per hour (0 to 100 kilometers per hour), in 2.5 seconds; it reached 124 miles per hour (200 kilometers per hour) in 7.0 seconds; and it topped 186 miles per hour (300 kilometers per hour), in 19.1 seconds. It topped out at 214 miles per hour (334 kilometers per hour).

Walliser headed Porsche's projects for hybrid drives. A friend, Gernot Döllner, directed vehicle concepts at Weissach. Initial efforts were so secret that Walliser did not know what Döllner was doing. And when Döllner received board approval weeks after the VW debacle, his assignment was to deliver a show car for the Geneva Motor Show, starting March 1, 2010—five months later.

Engineers installed the complex internal combustion/electric hybrid running gear into a body that evolved from the Carrera GT far enough to provoke the question "Is that still a Porsche?" A 3.4-liter V-8 from the RS Spyder delivered 500 horsepower through a revised Carrera GT transmission. Electric running gear came from the Panamera hybrid, and engineers adopted the front axle from the 2011 prototype racing GT3-H hybrid, fitted with two electric motors. An Italian company, Vercarmodel Saro near Turin, created the body shell and interior, completing the project during the 2009 Christmas holiday. The completed show car, officially designated the 918 Spyder, left Turin after midnight, bound directly to Geneva for its unveiling opening hours later.

Following a predawn, preshow run-through, engineers recharged the show car's batteries. But this caused a total electronics malfunction and locked the heavy prototype in place. Calls waking up Weissach engineers at home got a crew racing to the airport for a charter flight. As they lifted off, engineers in Geneva cracked the code, and, just two hours before the unveiling, "The 918 awoke as if from a coma," as one observer put it.

The rest is history, as they say. The 918 performed its debut flawlessly. More than a thousand orders arrived within days, and in late July, Porsche's board approved production. Project manager Walliser set product launch for September 18, 2013. Engineers reconfigured the internal-combustion 4.6-liter V-8 to develop 608 horsepower—for a total of 887 horsepower with its two electric motors—creating a world-first vehicle with three independent, individually controlled propulsion sources.

2015 Typ 919 Hybrid LMP1 The 919 combined razor-sharp angles and pure-Porsche organic curves. It was carefully determined and refined through countless hours in wind tunnels and computer simulations for every racing condition imaginable at Le Mans.

The 3,693-pound (1,675-kg) "production" version incorporated rear axle steering.

Lap times around Nurbürgring's Nordschleife have become the benchmark by which performance cars are measured. From the concept days, Döllner and Walliser had a target in mind: less than 7 minutes. In early September 2013, test driver Marc Lieb turned a 6:57 laps, averaging 115.53 miles per hour (179.51 kilometers per hour). Porsche limited production to 918 examples and ended assembly in June 2015.

By this time, the latest version of World Endurance Championship (WEC) was nearly two years old, having begun in 2013. The FIA approved an open-engine formula permitting gasoline or diesel engines with various energy-recovery and storage systems. Regulations limited how much "energy" a sports car could store but did not define how a manufacturer achieved that goal. The FIA calculated energy for each car, and its regulation appendix stipulated in which hybrid energy category the car raced, how much fuel it carried, and how fast the fuel was consumed.

Audi, for example, raced a 4.0-liter V-6 diesel with one kinetic energy recovery system (KERS) from the front axle, storing energy in a lightweight electromagnetic flywheel system. Toyota had a 3.7-liter V-6 gasoline engine and recovered energy from the front and rear brakes in a fast-charge/discharge supercapacitor. Porsche chose a small 2.0-liter gasoline V-4 so it could operate two separate energy recovery systems. Its front-axle KERS was similar to Audi's, but, as racing historian Michael Cotton explained, "Porsche was the only manufacturer to perfect the MGU-H [Motor Generator Unit—Heat], a heat energy recovery system that worked with the exhaust gasses." The V-4 engine's second turbo spun a generator, recharging the batteries.

For 2014, Porsche raced in the 6-megajoule (6MJ) category; 1 joule is the amount of energy required to accelerate a 2.20-pound mass at 1 meter per second (squared) over a distance of 1 meter. A megajoule is 1 million of them. Porsche's system meant that, at Le

rience Center Le Mans
AUTOMOBILE CLUB DE L'OUEST
MOTUL
1
2

2016 Typ 919 Hybrid LMP1 at Le Mans Neel Jani had qualified the No. 2 car on the pole, which proved a great advantage when the race started at 3:00 pm in rain. All the cars followed a safety car for 53 minutes, saving fuel but cursing the weather before the circuit went green and Jani led his teammates away from the spray. After another 23 hours, Jani and his co-drivers Marc Lieb and Romain Dumas were overall winners, completing 384 laps. Car No. 1 placed thirteenth.

Mans, it could release 6 megajoules of energy back to the wheels over the course of the 8.5-mile (13.6-km) track. The WEC adjusted figures for each circuit. Porsche went to the 8MJ category for 2015 and 2016.

This affected fuel consumption as well; 8MJ was the strictest limit, allowing 1.17 gallons per lap (4.43 liters per lap), or about 7.19 miles per gallon (32.7 liters per 100 kilometers). The most generous, 0MJ, still restricted entrants to 1.31 gallons (4.96 liters), so roughly 6.42 miles per gallon or 36.64 liters per 100 kilometers. There were trade-offs: 0MJ cars had to weigh at least 1,874 pounds (846 kg), while the 2MJ, 4MJ, 6MJ, and 8MJ cars shared a minimum weight of 1,918 (870 kg). The 919 Hybrid carried only 18 gallons (68 liters) of fuel.

Porsche's program was ambitious, but it used 2013 for extensive testing. This proved crucial; an engine vibration problem threatened to damage the car since its design used the engine as a structural element. Despite the six-month scramble to deliver a new engine, Porsche ran the full 2014 season, including Le Mans, with two cars. It took its first victory at São Paulo, Brazil, in November, the season's final contest.

Hybrid development that had started on Porsche's 918 road car under Dr. Frank-Steffen Walliser continued in the 919 race car, which grew so rapidly and with such complexity that when racing journalist Glen Smale asked Walliser what the two cars shared, he smiled and admitted that "the engineers shared the same canteen" where they ate lunch.

Porsche debuted the 919 in March 2014 at the Geneva Motor Show, where forty-five years earlier it had unveiled the innovative Typ 917 just before the April trials at Le Mans. In its "Mission 2014: Our Return" program, Porsche arrived at Le Mans in June 2014 with new cars and a seasoned team. They qualified second and fourth behind a Toyota on the pole and another at third. Audis filled in fifth, sixth, and seventh for the start. Porsche's choices for power management made its cars among the lightest and most innovative in the race. A fuel-flow hiccup sent car No. 14 to the pits just 30 minutes into the race; even though it took just 9 minutes to remedy, it had fallen to fifty-first place. But by 8:30 p.m., No. 14 it climbed back to sixth. During this time, a tire puncture sent the other car, No. 20, to the pits. Putting in a grueling quadruple stint, co-driver Mark Webber steadily climbed back up the standings. Then, just into the twelfth hour, co-driver Brendon Hartley bumped a competitor and pitted to check car 20. For the next 10 hours, the car steadily moved up and held second place through the late morning and early afternoon. Meanwhile, car No. 14 fought fuel-feed problems through the night and finally parked in the garage while in fourth; the team had decided to resume the race in the final 15 minutes to "finish" the race while running. They completed 348 laps but were listed as "not classified." That was not an option for No. 20. Having held second overall for several hours, Webber slowed to a halt out on circuit. He crawled straight back to the garages on only electric power and retired. The

car having completed 346 laps, the ACO also listed it as "not classified."

"I think we never expected to be in such a great position toward the end of the race," he recalled in an interview in Los Angeles in 2021. "Few people understand how hard it is to get a car to this point in the race. There's never a good retirement from Le Mans, but that day was maybe one of the best because we ran so far and learned so much."

The Audi team won—its thirteenth Le Mans victory—and when the checkered flag waved, Webber and his other co-driver, Timo Bernhard, headed to the Audi garages. They were planning to congratulate the team, but instead, as they walked into the garages, the entire Audi organization gave the two Porsche drivers a standing ovation.

Porsche returned to Le Mans in 2015 with three cars, No. 17 in red, 18 in black, and 19 in white. No. 18 broke the lap record and got the pole. On Sunday afternoon, June 14, the third-fastest qualifier, No. 19, took the checkered flag in first overall, followed one lap later by the second-fastest qualifier, Typ 919 Hybrid No. 17. The pole sitter, No. 18, finished fifth.

For its "Return to Le Mans (Winner's Circle)" campaign for 2016, Porsche's two team Typ 919 Hybrids qualified first and second fastest, and the pole sitter won Porsche's

2017 Typ 919 Hybrid LMP1 at Le Mans Celebrating the "hat trick," three victories in a row, Brendon Harley, on top of the car, left, and Earl Bamber, right, shared a ride with Timo Bernhard in his helmet in open door, to the winner's podium.

second in a row.

The team returned to Le Mans for 2017 with a two-car effort in which they qualified third (No. 1) and fourth (No. 2) sandwiched in a five-car Toyota effort. Electric drive problems appeared again, sidelining No. 2 for a full hour and seemingly costing it any chance of a reasonable finish. But the Toyotas suffered worse problems, and by 2:00 a.m., Porsche No. 1 held a commanding lead. Through all this time, No. 2, masters at catching up with Bernhard and Hartley, veterans of a similar effort the year before, had climbed back to tenth. Webber had finished his Porsche contract and retired from racing after winning the WEC with the team, and, in 2017, the ACO honored his career by naming him grand marshal for the race. In his place, Earl Bamber joined the scramblers in No. 2.

The scramblers persevered, and with six hours remaining, car 2 was in seventh, chasing their teammates and a fleet of second-tier LMP2 cars. Then at noon, No. 1 retired after 318 laps, leaving a sea of LMP2s surrounding Porsche No. 2. By 1:00, Hartley moved into fourth, on the same lap as the leading LMP2 car. If there were no further incidents, Porsche could win. And it did! No. 2 completed 367 laps and gave Porsche the "hat trick," three Le Mans wins in a row, each year with enough drama to fill several seasons. Bernard, Hartley, and Bamber also brought Porsche the WEC title again.

At the season end, Porsche retired, only to unveil a special, the Typ 919 Evo. Without the restrictions the ACO and WEC imposed, the car collected one-lap track records; Bernhard set a stunning benchmark at 5:19.55 around the Nürburgring, completely shattering the long-standing 1986 record by Stefan Bellof of 6:11.13 in a Porsche 956.

2015–Tomorrow

30

Porsche Goes Silent

Formula E, Mission E, Taycan, Mission R, Macan

Porsche unveiled the all-electric Mission E at the 2015 Frankfurt Motor Show alongside the 991/Gen II turbocharged Carrera and Carrera S models. While technical advances with the new Carreras were impressive, the Mission E stole the show from all Porsche's competitors. It has continued to do that as the production Taycan, launched in 2020.

With striking styling simultaneously embracing Porsche's heritage and advancing it a decade, this car's statistics and capabilities also aligned with the company's existing performance standards while challenging the potential for every all-electric car in the future.

In the early part of the 2000s, Porsche and other divisions within the parent Volkswagen Group had embraced diesel engines as the fuel and power source of the future; in Porsche's case, this applied to the Cayenne, Panamera, and Macan models. Weissach chiefs from Wolfgang Dürheimer through Wolfgang Hatz vigorously defended the sports cars from such incursion, arguing, among other things, that diesel's sound just was not sports-car-like. With the 2015 revelations of diesel-engine failings, this ended up proving more than prudent. Veering away from emissions issues, developing full electric power proved prescient.

2020 Taycan Turbo S Is this style of driving hard to resist or hard to avoid? The all-electric Taycan Turbo S boasted as much as 750 horsepower on "Overboost control with Launch Control." But it's torque that spins those wheels, the Taycan had enough of that as well: 774 pound-feet with Launch Control. That brought 60 miles per hour (97 kilometers per hour), in 2.6 seconds on dry pavement.

2020 Taycan 4S All family resemblance was entirely intentional. It is only careful study that revealed the vertical sculpts alongside the headlights and differentiated the nose from its sibling Panamera. The 195.4-inch-long (4,963-mm) sedan sat on a 114.2 inches (2,900-mm) wheelbase.

Porsche engineers in motorsports have argued since the earliest days of the company that racing had served two purposes. One is promotion. The other is testing under fire. Such is the case with the permanent-magnet synchronous motors (PSMs) in the 919 Hybrid LMP1 racer. The 919 used a 2.0-liter V-4 internal-combustion engine and relied on PSM technology for much of its power generation, in part by capturing energy from braking, as the Taycan does.

Porsche adopted 800-volt technology to shorten charging times and reduced vehicle weight because engineers used smaller-gauge, lighter cables connecting batteries to motors and back. A retracting panel on the driver's-side front quarter revealed the 800-volt charging port; Porsche's system also allowed (somewhat slower) recharge times using 400-volt stations. In addition, owners might install an induction charging system consisting of a coil embedded in the garage floor, which allowed recharging without cables.

Body-materials lessons learned from the 991 put high-strength steel, aluminum, and carbon-fiber-reinforced polymer in the Taycan body. Engineers mounted the lithium-ion battery into the car's underbody, running longitudinally between front and rear axles. This distributed the weight evenly and lowered the center of gravity, increasing stability and improving handling. Porsche Torque Vectoring, the system of managing power separately for each tire, was integral to handling.

The interior of the Mission E was as advanced as its engineering and its exterior design. In place of a driveshaft tunnel, there was a passenger divider with user interfaces incorporating holographic imaging. The Carrera GT bridge-type center console appeared as a light, soaring structure with open space below it. The familiar five-gauge cluster carried forward but in nontraditional OLED technology (organic light-emitting diodes). An eye-tracking system using a micro camera detected which instrument the driver was observing,

2020 Taycan 4S Porsche manufactured all Taycans in a recently—and purposefully—built factory in Zuffenhausen. Still, a number of the cars end up in Leipzig for customer pickup, so owners learn the potential of the cars on the facility's test track. The Taycan stood 54.4 inches (1,382 mm) tall and, with mirrors folded in, it was 77.5 inches wide (1,969 mm).

allowing instant interface with the full menu for each gauge. According to Porsche's release material at the Frankfurt launch, this system also tracked the driver's body height and position. Leaning into a turn, for example, the 3D instrument display shifted in parallax view, eliminating instances where the steering wheel obscured critical instruments.

At the Frankfurt debut, Porsche's then CEO, chairman Matthias Müller, guarded company plans to manufacture the Mission E, but by year end 2016, construction was underway on the ahead-of-the-art assembly plant for the Taycan. The car was an immediate success; Porsche assembled more than 20,000, constituting 7.4 percent of total production.

Porsche initially offered a rear-wheel-drive, four-door sedan but soon introduced a striking Cross Turismo, an "estate," or station-wagon, variation. Power options ranged from a 402-horsepower base version to a 469-horsepower model using a "performance battery plus" and an all-wheel-drive 523-horsepower Taycan 4S (563 horsepower with the performance battery). By model year 2021, the line had added a 590-horsepower GTS Sport Turismo and perplexingly named Turbo and Turbo S model. With no internal combustion engine in the vehicle and therefore no turbocharger incorporated, Porsche simply redefined "Turbo" as a model designation. In sedan or Cross Turismo body styles, these provided buyers with either 671 horsepower or 751 horsepower in the Turbo S electric. Useful traveling range on a full charge varied from roughly 215 miles (346 km), for the base rear-and all-wheel-drive models to 202 miles (325 km), for the Turbo S Cross Turismo. The 800-volt charging system recharged the driving batteries from 5 percent to 80 percent useful in 22.5 minutes in optimal conditions. Porsche's electric future looked strong as 2022 progressed; rumors hinted that a two-door coupe and cabriolet model were on the way.

(Top) 2021 Taycan 4S The 4S models offered as much at 522 horsepower with Overboost and Launch Control. But with a cautious foot, the United States Environmental Protection Agency, US EPA, estimated range at 227 miles but up as much as 272 with the optional Performance Battery Plus.

(Above) 2022 Taycan GTS Sport Turismo Interior
Touch screens extended across the front passenger's view, providing them their own navigation, entertainment, climate control, and internet control. A central gauge reported cornering, accelerating, or braking forces. Display information also offered car condition indicators.

Although there was little crossover between engineering teams and their technologies during this same time, Porsche stepped away from ICE prototype racing beyond the existing Carrera and Cayman Cup series. But the company was far from finished with racing. It took technology the 919 had accumulated in the WEC and moved into Formula E with the 99X, devoting 2018 and 2019 to testing and development of the Porsche electric drivetrain in the Spark SRT chassis. For 2020, the 122.0-inch (3,100-mm)-wheelbase 99X measured 203.1 inches (5,160-mm) long, , 69.7 inches (1,77 mm) wide, and 41.3 inches (1,050 mm) tall. Unlike the 900-plus horsepower available in the LMP1 Hybrid, the 99X competed with 267 horsepower during a race with 335 horsepower for qualification laps. Power came from a 900-volt 54-kilowatt-hour battery lasting a full race. A Porsche one-speed gearbox moved the 99X from 0 to 62 miles per hour (0 to 100 kilometers per hour), in 2.8 seconds and on to a top speed of 174 miles per hour (280 kilometers per hour). With driver, minimum required weight was 1,984 pounds (900 kg). And unlike other FIA formulae or IndyCar, the cars of Formula E were not, strictly speaking, "open wheel"; motorcycle-type fenders surrounded the front tires, and aerodynamic bodywork enclosed more than half of the rears.

Through the 2019–2020 season, the team finished eighth in standings, with driver André Lotterer scoring a second in Saudi Arabia and again at Berlin. Through 2020–2021, the learning curve remained bumpy, and the team again finished eighth in the points standings. For 2021–2022, Formula E's eighth season, Porsche committed to the full sixteen-race schedule with Lotterer teamed with Pascal Wehrlein. Regulations allowed race power increase to 295 horsepower, up from 267. And while the FIA mandated carrying over powertrains from seasons seven to eight for economic reasons, Porsche engineers entirely remastered all the software in the 99X, necessitating another preseason round of exhaustive testing.

Throughout all this, Porsche's commitment to electric vehicles also was growing. The company confirmed plans to offer an electric Macan sport utility for the 2023 season (and phase out internal combustion in the SUV as soon as the 2024 model year). It recognized it must not attack the all-electric market with blunt force but more of a subtle, balanced program. "Different regions of the world are developing at different speeds," current CEO Oliver Blume explained recently. "We are well prepared with the product strategy—petrol engines and hybrids, and electric mobility. We make analyses every year, watching how markets are developing. And then we adjust our strategy year-by-year."

In the last days of 2021, Porsche unveiled a new racer, the Mission R, a fully electric 1,000-horsepower racing coupe that hinted at future directions for its mid-engine Cayman, especially for its popular one-make GT4 Clubsport Porsche Cup series. Unexpectedly, Porsche also revealed a partnership with Siemens Energy in a South American refinery working on a synthetic fuel, a kind of "e-fuel" that released virtually no carbon-dioxide on combustion. "This fits in our clear overall sustainability strategy," explained Michael Steiner,

(Top) 2022 Taycan Turbo S Porsche quoted the potential range of the Turbo S model at 323 kilometers, 201 miles. Charging time ranged from 10.5 hours to full 100% on alternating current (AC) to as brief as 22.5 minutes with a CCS DV fast charging station capable of 850 volts (270 kW).

(Above) 2020 Taycan Turbo S Interior It was very familiar but slightly different. Touch screens abounded and operated everything. In fact, to re-aim the fresh air vents, one found them on a screen menu and swiveled them with a finger! Front seats were Porsche's 18-way Sport Seats while the rear split 60/40 with foldable backrests.

a member of Porsche's executive board for research and development. "It means that Porsche as a whole can be net CO2 neutral as early as 2030. Fuels produced with this renewable energy can make a contribution to this. Our icon, the 911, is particularly suited to the use of efuels. But so are our much-loved historic vehicles, because around 70 percent of all Porsche Sports Cars ever built are still on the road today." The e-fuel Porsche will produce—initially in Chile—will consume more CO2 to manufacture than it will release after combustion.

At the other extreme, rumors emerged about a "three-row SUV," revealed to its American dealers as a flagship

2022 Taycan Sport Turismo "Off Road" Package In hopes that owners went to go sporting and touring, Porsche developed this option that raised ride height 1.18 inches (30 millimeters), to provide slightly better ground clearance and security over rough surfaces.

model above (and beyond) the two-row Cayenne, code-named Landjet. Educated observers have suggested it is another response to unexpectedly pervasive outside influences; just like the new fastback Cayenne GT, both BMW and Daimler-Benz offer high-performance, luxuriously turned-out, seven-seater SUVs.

Porsche will have battery electrics, plug-in-hybrids, and internal combustion engine power sources for some time. Days before the 2021 Los Angeles Auto Show revealed the Mission R and a broadening range of Taycan models, former racing director Frank-Steffen Walliser, who now manages Porsche sports-car development and production (911 and 718 lines), suggested that the 911 might continue with an internal combustion engine until 2040, earning him a round of applause from his audience of more than 120 enthusiasts.

Still, it raises a question about Porsche's long-term future. If the sound of a diesel engine was never right for a sports car, this acknowledges the "sound" Porsche makes as it drives *is* part of the car's identity. The silent electrics were so stealthy Porsche introduced a mechanical noise for these vehicles at parking lot speeds, which it fades as speed increases. The Formula E cars and the Mission R render the distinct high-pitched whine of electric motors, which hasn't yet proved it can ratchet up the pulse of Porsche enthusiasts. If a Porsche loses that internal-combustion intake and exhaust sound, is it still a Porsche? And if it sounds like everything else . . . what else will it lose?

Over the past 75 years, Porsche has occasionally swerved off course, or stumbled with product decisions or even financial ones. But each time, clever, capable, clear-eyed minds have brought the automaker back

(Left) 2022 Taycan Turbo S Sport Turismo Porsche's various Taycan models won't exactly walk on water, but they seemed happy playing around in it. On dry pavement, acceleration from 0 to 62 miles per hour (0 to 100 kilometers per hour) required 2.6 seconds and the car reached a top speed of 160 miles per hour (260 kilometers per hour).

(Below) 2022 Typ 99X Formula E Testing Pascal Wehrlein joined the Porsche Formula E team in 2022. The cars relied on 800-volt technology and this allows 220kW output for the race, roughly equal to 299 horsepower. Through regenerative braking, the 99x was able to restore its full 220kW to 250kW charge during the race. Wehrlein won his first race with Lotterer placing second in February 2022 at Mexico City.

(Right) 2021 Typ 99X Formula E at London Porsche Works E-Prix driver André Lotterer, No. 99, led a cluster of whirring Formula E racers during the London E Prix staged in the East London Royal Victoria Docks. The 1.4-mile (2.25-km), circuit included a segment through one of the warehouses because the cars emitted no exhaust fumes. Races were run in two heats and while Lotterer finished in fifth place in the first, he failed to complete the second race.

(Below) 2022 Typ Mission R Concept Porsche has published acceleration from 0 to 62 miles per hour (0 to 100 kilometers per hour) in 2.5 seconds and a top speed of more than 186 miles per hour (300 kilometers per hour). Much more significantly, it operated on 900-volt technology allowing it to recharge from 5% to 80% in 15 minutes. While Porsche had not yet announced plans to produce the R, company intentions to electrify the Boxster and Cayman were well known.

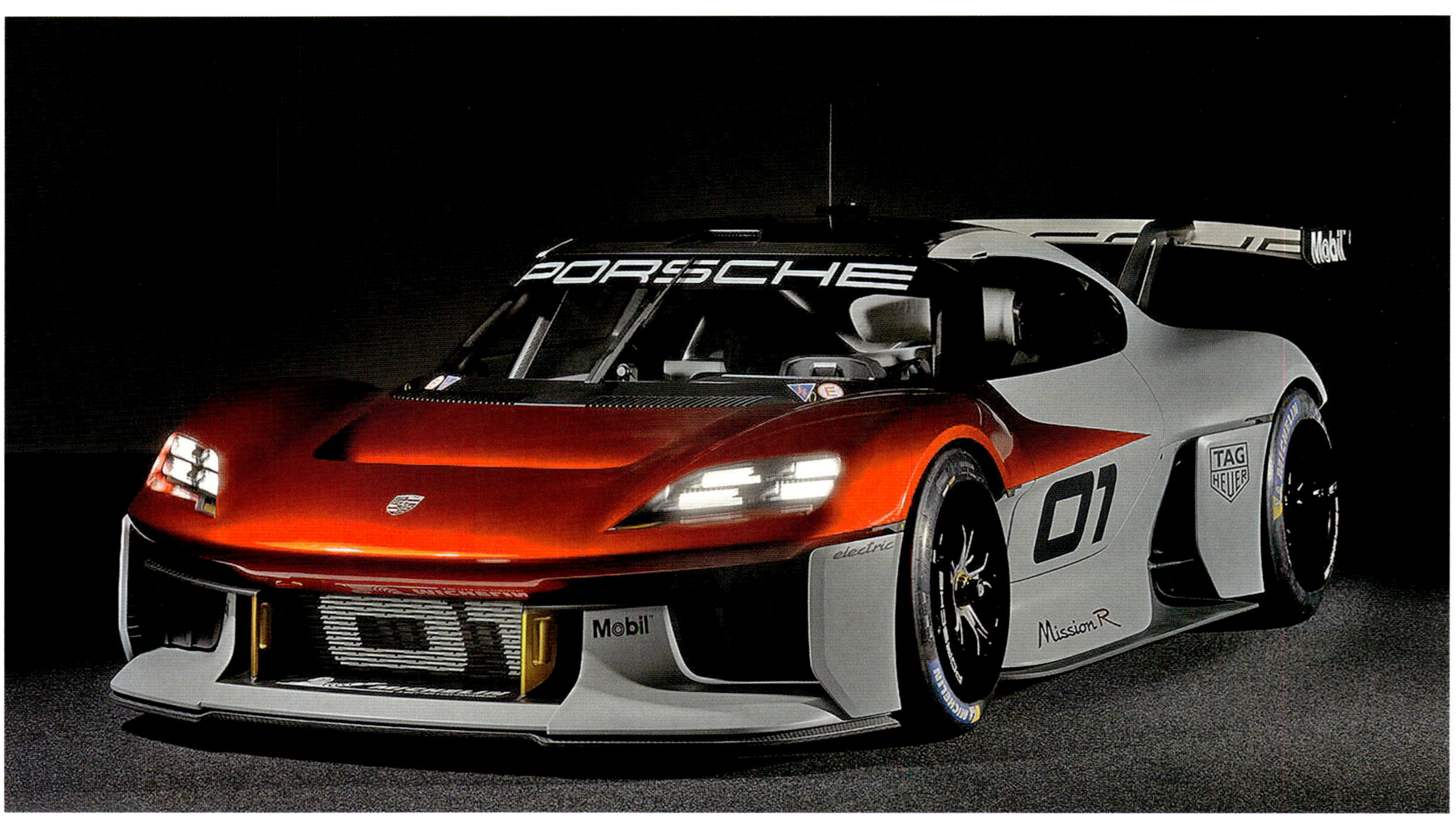

into equilibrium. Its solutions—remedies, even—have often been unexpected, as this book highlights. This is a company in which engineers and designers know when their most recent idea is turned down, they don't discard it but set it aside. They study their missteps as carefully as they reexamine their successes. Their willingness to pursue the unexpected has secured the company's position among the most profitable carmakers in the world. Even with minor dilemmas such as vehicle sound on their horizon and bigger questions of emissions and energy creation ever present, it is very safe to expect Porsche will remain independent, profitable, the target of competitors, and the goal of enthusiastic, quality-conscious drivers.

2022 Typ Mission R Concept
Porsche invented the Mission R as a way to test and develop electric technologies for customer race cars, equivalent to the 911 Carrera Cup and the Cayman Cup. The car, like most electrics, provided two output ratings, 671 horsepower in "race mode" and a startling 1,073 horsepower for qualifying.

Dedication

For Zack—

The concept for this book—and for many of the most enjoyable projects I've ever undertaken—came from my Motorbooks publisher, editor, and friend, Zack Miller. His thought for this—Porsche's unexpected ideas—sparked our imaginations immediately and the brainstorming sessions over topics and approaches were both thought-provoking and good fun. But that has been my entire career with Zack and it is for that reason that I dedicate this book, another of his great ideas, to him.

Randy Leffingwell

Acknowledgments

First of all, I am most grateful to Hurley Haywood for his Foreword to this book. Hurley brought an exceptional racing career and wonderful participation as a Porsche Driving Experience chief instructor to these pages. No one else in Porsche's vast population of accomplished individuals has this array of credentials.

I am deeply grateful to Porsche Historic Archive manager Frank Jung, Archive photo manager Jens Torner, and former manager Dieter Landenberger for their generous help and support of this project. In addition, I want to thank Yvone Knotek, Tobias Mauler, and Joerg Thilow for their many contributions.

Dozens of engineers, designers, and racers took time—over the past decades—to speak with me about their projects and experiences. I especially appreciate the information and stories from Herbert Ampferer, Jürgen Barth, Derek Bell, the late Helmuth Bott, the late Vic Elford, Peter Falk, Helmut Flegl, the late Ernst Fuhrmann, Tony Hatter, Michael Hölscher, Bernd Kahnau, Jürgen Kapfer, Eugen Kolb, Thomas Krickelberg, Roland Kussmaul, Harm Lagaay, Grant Larson, Marc Lieb, Herbert Linge, Horst Marchart, the late Hans Mezger, Erhard Mössle, Stephen Murkett, Heinz-Jakob Neusser, the late F. A. Porsche, Andy Preuninger, Valentin Schäffer, the late Gerhard Schröder, the late Peter Schutz, Norbert Singer, the late Rolf Sprenger, Frank-Steffan Walliser, Mark Webber, and Klaus-Gerhard Wolpert.

Most of the photos in the book have come from the incredible collection within the Porsche Historic Archive. One of the pleasures of doing books about Porsche is the opportunity to work alongside a longtime friend, Jens Torner, searching for images to tell these stories. I made a number of other images in the book and I wish to thank the following individuals for letting me photograph their important cars: Jerrod Bradley; the late Otis Chandler; Stephen Childs; Jacke Crumpe; Warren Eads; Frank Galogly; the late Warren Helgesen; Cameron Ingram; Dieter Landenberger; Dirk Layer; Jeff Lewis; Doug Meier; Don Meluzio; David Mills; David Mohlmann; Kent Morgan; Kerry Morse; Josh Ofstein; John Paterek; Bill Peters; Gil Ranney; George Reilly; REVS Institute; Ben Rodriguez; Chris Roman; Tony Samojen; Jon Samuels; Chuck Smith; the late Paul-Ernst Strähle; Gary Swauger; Bruce Trenery; Carl Thompson; and John Tilson.

Last but far from least I want to thank Brooke Pelletier, Editorial Project Manager, John Gettings, Group Managing Editor, Rick Landers, book designer, and my editor/publisher Zack Miller, all with the Quarto Group, for the opportunity to do this book and for their professionalism keeping me on time, and on track.

My great thanks to you all.

Randy Leffingwell
Santa Barbara, CA

Index

L

M

N

O

P

R

S

T

Quarto.com

First Published in 2022 by Motorbooks, an imprint of The Quarto Group,
100 Cummings Center, Suite 265-D, Beverly, MA 01915, USA.
T (978) 282-9590 F (978) 283-2742

EEA Representation, WTS Tax d.o.o.,
Žanova ulica 3, 4000 Kranj, Slovenia.
www.wts-tax.si

26 8 9

ISBN: 978-0-7603-7266-1

Digital edition published in 2022
eISBN: 978-0-7603-7267-8

Library of Congress Cataloging-in-Publication Data available

Book Design: Landers Miller Design
Cover Design: Landers Miller Design
Jacket photos: Michael Furman
Hardcover photos: Michael Furman
Endpapers: Porsche Archive
Photography: Historical photos courtesy of Porsche Archive unless noted otherwise.

Printed in Huizhou City, Guangdong, China TT012026

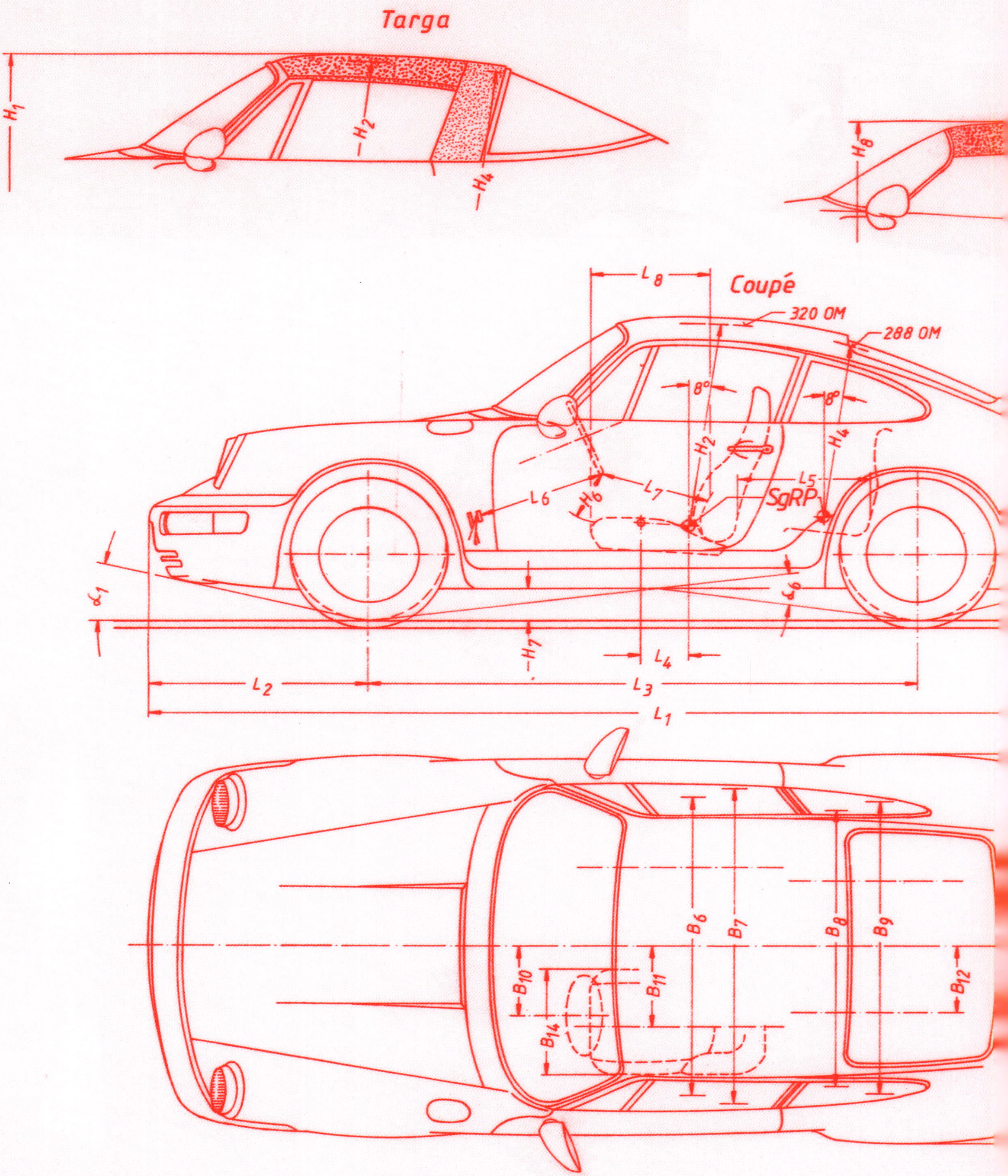

Targa

Coupé

320 OM

288 OM

Vereinfachte Darstellung

simplified representation

ZV

16.6.92	Riefle	Dr. Ing. h. c. F. Porsche Aktiengesellschaft, Stuttgart	Baumaße / vehicle

0834-01-2000-12-82